Article 2

The Right of Non-Discrimination

A Commentary on the United Nations Convention
on the Rights of the Child

Editors

André Alen, Johan Vande Lanotte, Eugeen Verhellen,
Fiona Ang, Eva Berghmans and Mieke Verheyde

Article 2
The Right of Non-Discrimination

By

Bruce Abramson

Lawyer, International Human Rights Law

MARTINUS
NIJHOFF
PUBLISHERS

LEIDEN • BOSTON
2008

This book is printed on acid-free paper.

Library of Congress Cataloging-in-Publication Data

Abramson, Bruce.
   Article 2 : the right of non-discrimination / by Bruce Abramson.
     p. cm. — (A commentary on the United Nations Convention on the Rights of the Child, ISSN 1574-8626)
   Includes bibliographical references and index.
   ISBN 978-90-04-14917-5 (pbk. : alk. paper) 1. Convention on the Rights of the Child (1989). Article 2. 2. Discrimination—Law and legislation. 3. Children—Legal status, laws, etc. 4. Children's rights. I. Title. II. Title: Article two. III. Title: Right of non-discrimination.
   K3242.A927 2008
   342.08'772—dc22

                                                                    2008023333

Cite as: B. Abramson, "Article 2. The Right of Non-Discrimination", in: A. Alen, J. Vande Lanotte, E. Verhellen, F. Ang, E. Berghmans and M. Verheyde (Eds.) *A Commentary on the United Nations Convention on the Rights of the Child* (Martinus Nijhoff Publishers, Leiden, 2008).

ISSN 1574–8626
ISBN 978–90–04–14917–5

Cover image by Nadia, 1 1/2 years old

http://www.brill.nl

PRINTED IN THE NETHERLANDS

CONTENTS

FOREWORD

Jean Zermatten
Vice Chair, Committee on the Rights of the Child
Founder and Director, *Institut International des Droits de l'Enfant*

The Convention on the Rights of the Child

All of the great international texts on human rights clearly guarantee non-discrimination. Does the CRC give broader protection? Does it give stronger protection?

Generally speaking, people understand that human rights include children. In addition, because of their particular position, children have been given special provisions; moreover, the CRC can be considered *lex specialis* with regard to the Universal Declaration of Human Rights. And at the very beginning of the CRC, in Article 2, children have *a right not to be discriminated against*.

Furthermore, Article 2 applies the right of non-discrimination to all of the other rights in the CRC, including the articles that protect children who are especially at risk of being discriminated against, such as refugee children (Article 22), children with disabilities (Article 23), and indigenous children (Article 30).

The CRC is unique because, unlike the earlier UN human rights treaties, it establishes 'disability' as a forbidden ground of discrimination. And, in light of the fact that children are usually dependent upon their parents, Article 2 also takes the child's parents into account. Indeed, it often through the parents that the child is treated in a discriminatory way.

In my opinion, Article 2 is truly a personal right: the child's right not to be treated in a discriminatory way. This, I believe, is very important because the aim is to ensure the dignity of every human being, and this includes children. The right of non-discrimination belongs to the child. The parents and guardians cannot renounce it or relinquish it; they might fail to exercise it, but they cannot do away with it.

Unfortunately, despite having legal guarantees, children are often subjected to discrimination; many of their rights are violated because of the colour of their skin, the language they speak, the nationality they possess, the religion they practice, or because the child is a girl rather than a boy. Sadly, the number of cases of discrimination worldwide is immense. Many of these children suffer a double violation of their rights: their rights are violated because they are children, and again because they are black, or migrants, Roma, disabled, girls, soldiers, and the list goes on and on.

An Important Work

Mr. Bruce Abramson, who devotes most of his writing to the Convention on the Rights of the Child, has examined Article 2 with the rigour that he is known for. By the end of a very serious legal analysis, he has given us the fruits of his reflections, with forceful examples or hypothetical situations that vividly illustrate his points. He dissects the right, and examines all the kinds of discrimination, even the most delicate, the ones that are taboo to talk about.

You have in your hands an important book, on a difficult and sensitive topic, that the author has handled in a complete and precise matter. Professionals who work in the field of children's rights, the protection of childhood, or the promotion of children as the bearers of rights, and human rights defenders in general, will find information here that is very useful. And also, most likely, material for broader reflection: the situation of children in societies that are increasingly globalized, which boast of 'differences' and 'tolerance', but which also distinguish themselves by powerful attitudes of discrimination, by reflexes of rejection, and even exclusion, based on criteria that are questionable, and that are proscribed by Article 2 of the CRC. And often, alas, children are the first victims.

LIST OF ABBREVIATIONS

Article 2	Article 2 of the Convention on the Rights of the Child
CCPR	International Covenant on Civil and Political Rights
CEDAW	Convention on the Elimination of All Forms of Discrimination Against Women
CEDAW Committee	Committee on the Elimination of Discrimination Against Women
CERD	International Convention on the Elimination of All Forms of Racial Discrimination
CERD Committee	Committee on the Elimination of Racial Discrimination
CESCR	International Covenant on Economic, Social and Cultural Rights
CESCR Committee	Committee on Economic, Social and Cultural Rights
Comm.	Committee
Concl. Obser.	Concluding Observations
CRC	Convention on the Rights of the Child
CRC Committee (or Committee)	Committee on the Rights of the Child
CRPWD	Convention on the Rights of Persons With Disabilities
ECHR	European Convention on Human Rights
ECtHR	European Court of Human Rights
GA	General Assembly of the United Nations
Gen. Com. (or Recom.)	General Comment (or Recommendation)
HRC	Human Rights Committee
NGO	non-governmental organization
UDHR	Universal Declaration of Human Rights

AUTHOR BIOGRAPHY

Bruce Abramson is a human rights lawyer practicing across a wide spectrum of issues, and, since 1992, specializing in the Convention on the Rights of the Child. He has attended every review session of the CRC Committee, and actively participated in all of the Days of Discussion, including serving, on behalf of UNAIDS, as rapporteur on the Day of Discussion on Children Living in a World with AIDS. He has authored numerous papers on the CRC, and has worked for the UN High Commission for Refugees on refugee children and adolescents, where he was a contributing author to *Refugee Children: Guidelines on Protection and Care*, and for UNAIDS, UNICEF, and children's rights NGOs. He has also actively participated in other human rights forums, including the former Commission on Human Rights, the SubCommission, and four of the UN treaty-monitoring bodies.

Mr. Abramson has been a trial and appellate lawyer in three legal aid programmes for poor people, focusing on economic and social rights, indigenous land rights, and law reform litigation. He has also held several legal posts with the State of Alaska, including District Attorney, and Assistant Attorney General for juvenile delinquency, and for child abuse-and-neglect cases.

He also served as Assistant Attorney General of the Federated States of Micronesia, and as the Attorney General of the Republic of the Marshall Islands, during those countries' transitions to independence.

Mr. Abramson is a graduate of the UCLA School of Law.

TEXT OF ARTICLE 2

ARTICLE 2

1. States Parties shall respect and ensure the rights set forth in the present Convention to each child within their jurisdiction without discrimination of any kind, irrespective of the child's or his or her parent's or legal guardian's race, colour, sex, language, religion, political or other opinion, national, ethnic or social origin, property, disability, birth or other status.

2. States Parties shall take all appropriate measures to ensure that the child is protected against all forms of discrimination or punishment on the basis of the status, activities, expressed opinions, or beliefs of the child's parents, legal guardians, or family members.

ARTICLE 2

1. Les Etats parties s'engagent à respecter les droits qui sont énoncés dans la présente Convention et à les garantir à tout enfant relevant de leur juridiction, sans distinction aucune, indépendamment de toute considération de race, de couleur, de sexe, de langue, de religion, d'opinion politique ou autre de l'enfant ou de ses parents ou représentants légaux, de leur origine nationale, ethnique ou sociale, de leur situation de fortune, de leur incapacité, de leur naissance ou de toute autre situation.

2. Les Etats parties prennent toutes les mesures appropriées pour que l'enfant soit effectivement protégé contre toutes formes de discrimination ou de sanction motivées par la situation juridique, les activités, les opinions déclarées ou les convictions de ses parents, de ses représentants légaux ou des membres de sa famille.

ARTICULO 2

1. Los Estados Partes respetarán los derechos enunciados en la presente Convención y asegurarán su aplicación a cada niño sujeto a su jurisdicción, sin distinción alguna, independientemente de la raza, el color, el sexo, el idioma, la religión, la opinión política o de otra índole, el origen nacional, étnico o social, la posición económica, los impedimentos físicos, el nacimiento o cualquier otra condición del niño, de sus padres o de sus representantes legales.

2. Los Estados Partes tomarán todas las medidas apropiadas para garantizar que el niño se vea protegido contra toda forma de discriminación o castigo por causa de la condición, las actividades, las opiniones expresadas o las creencias de sus padres, o sus tutores o de sus familiares.

СТАТЬЯ 2

1. Государства-участники уважают и обеспечивают все права, предусмотренные настоящей Конвенцией, за каждым ребенком, находящимся в пределах их юрисдикции, без какой-либо дискриминации, независимо от расы, цвета кожи, пола, языка, религии, политических или иных убеждений, национального, этнического или социального происхождения, имущественного положения, состояния здоровья и рождения ребенка, его родителей или законных опекунов или каких-либо иных обстоятельств.

2. Государства-участники принимают все необходимые меры для обеспечения защиты ребенка от всех форм дискриминации или наказания на основе статуса, деятельности, выражаемых взглядов или убеждений ребенка, родителей ребенка, законных опекунов или иных членов семьи.

第二条

1、缔约国应遵守本公约所载列的权利，并确保其管辖范围内的每一儿童均享
受此种权利，不因儿童或其父母或法定监护人的种族、肤色、性别、语言、宗教、政治或
其他见解、民族、族裔或社会出身、财产、伤残、出生或其他身份而有任何差别。

2、缔约国应采取一切适当措施确保儿童得到保护，不受基于儿童父母、法定监护人
或家庭成员的身份、活动、所表达的观点或信仰而加诸的一切形式的歧视或惩罚。

المادة 2

1. تحترم الدول الأطراف الحقوق الموضحة في هذه الاتفاقية وتضمنها لكل طفل يخضع لولايتها دون أي نوع من أنواع التمييز، بغض النظر عن عنصر الطفل أو والديه أو الوصي القانوني عليه أو لونهم أو جنسهم أو لغتهم أو دينهم أو رأيهم السياسي أو غيره أو أصلهم القومي أو الإثني أو الاجتماعي، أو ثروتهم، أو عجزهم، أو مولدهم، أو أي وضع آخر.

2. تتخذ الدول الأطراف جميع التدابير المناسبة لتكفل للطفل الحماية من جميع أشكال التمييز أو العقاب القائمة على أساس مركز والدي الطفل أو الأوصياء القانونيين عليه أو أعضاء الأسرة، أو أنشطتهم أو آرائهم المعبر عنها أو معتقداتهم.

CHAPTER ONE

INTRODUCTION*

1. '[T]here is an alarming ignorance of what the Convention [on the Rights of the Child] is and what it means.' That is the conclusion of the International Save the Children Alliance in *Children's Rights: Reality or Rhetoric?*, a review of the first ten years of the CRC's implementation. The Alliance identified two fundamental problems. First, 'it is difficult for many to accept children as right-bearers,' and second, the 'provisions of the CRC . . . have not been fully understood . . . either by government or the public.' These two problems are especially serious when it comes to Article 2 of the CRC.[1]

2. Of all the rights in international human rights law, the right of non-discrimination is probably the most misunderstood. There is a large literature on the topic of discrimination, and references to 'non-discrimination' appear with ritual-like frequency in United Nations and NGO publications, but both the rights-rhetoric and the rights-analysis tend to be 'superficial', to borrow a key word from *Reality or Rhetoric?* Ironically, people are making

* March 2008. The author would like to thank all those who have helped make this commentary possible. For commenting on earlier manuscripts that formed the basis of the present work, for discussing ideas, or for providing materials: Alexei Avtonomov, Michael Banton, Marc Bossuyt, Ralph Boyd, Thomas Buergenthal, Roger Clegg, Carl Cohen, Jaap Doek, Evelyn Ellis, Charu Garg, Tarcisio Gazzini, Steven Gilmartin, Régis de Gouttes, Yugi Hirano, Morten Kjaerum, Lothar Krappman, Christopher McCrudden, Alexandre Ovsiouk, Brent Parfitt, Linos Alexander Sicilianos, Partick Thornberry, Yogesh Varhade, Yozo Yokota, and Jean Zermatten. Their personal and professional generosity must not be mistaken for endorsement of any of the author's views, however.

For translation assistance: Sayed Abdulhay, Mounir Al-Khudri, Julia Bassam, Charles Habel, Laurence Leitenberg, Lutz Lücker, and Grace Poizat; and for computer support, Younis Ahmed. For editorial assistance: Henrietta Wilkins and David Hay-Edie; and special thanks to Mieke Verheyde and Fiona Ang, the series editors, for their attention to detail, for their probing questions that improved the text, and for their stewardship over the commentary series: without the whole, this part would not exist.

Deep appreciation also to Camille Kryspin, Documentation Centre, Defence for Children International, and to the generous librarians at the UN Palais, Geneva, who have made the research possible. And warm thanks to Mr. Werner Simon, Librarian, Legal and Political Section (retired), for his years of support and assistance on many projects, including the first stages of this one.

[1] International Save the Children Alliance, *Children's Rights: Reality or Rhetoric?* (London, International Save the Children Alliance, 2000), pp. 287, 288, and 292, respectively.

too much of the right of non-discrimination, and, at the same time, they are making too little of it. For instance, commentators will stretch the notion of discrimination to cover situations in which there is no discrimination at all, while simultaneously averting their eyes from blatant acts of discrimination perpetrated on account of race, sex, and the other forbidden grounds in international law. The result is to preserve the *rhetoric* of non-discrimination, but to empty the *right* of its contents. This simultaneous expansion-and-contraction is happening to the right of non-discrimination irrespective of whether the right-holder is an adult or a minor. However, it is particularly serious when the victims of the discrimination are children and adolescents. It is here that the failure to take young people seriously as right-holders is most poignant, since their vulnerability and relative powerlessness are not even partially offset by being accorded the status of possessing a *right* not to be deprived of important things in life because of their race, sex, religion, and other forbidden grounds.

3. This commentary is intended to be a resource for people who are working to secure the full enjoyment of human rights by all boys and girls throughout the world. It is based on two simple premises: Article 2 cannot be applied correctly unless it is correctly understood; and understanding a right requires legal analysis. To meet these needs, the commentary will provide as thorough a legal discussion of Article 2 as possible, within the space limitations of this series of commentaries on the Convention.

4. There are actually three different rights in this one provision. Article 2(1) is the right of non-discrimination, and it is essentially the same as the rights contained in the second articles of the Universal Declaration of Human Rights, the International Covenant on Civil and Political Rights, and the International Covenant on Economic, Social and Cultural Rights. For convenience, all four of these rights of non-discrimination will be referred to collectively as 'Common Articles 2'. Paragraph (2) of Article 2, on the other hand, contains two rights – a right not to be discriminated against for reasons pertaining to the actions of the youngster's parents, and a right not to be punished on account of the deeds of the parents, two rights that have no counterparts in other treaties. And finally, the phrase 'within their jurisdiction' in Article 2(1) is part of the Convention's jurisdictional statement.

5. Over the years, confusions about the right of non-discrimination have entered from numerous directions, so this commentary will concentrate on interpreting Article 2(1). The legal analysis will adhere to traditional legal

methodology: (i) the discussion will apply the established rules of legal interpretation, in particular, the Vienna Convention on the Law of Treaties; (ii) it will lay out the lines of reasoning with as much transparency as possible within the page limitations of this series, along with citations to the views of other commentators; and (iii) it will focus on key legal issues and on the most important concepts in the literature, such as '*de jure* and *de facto*' discrimination, 'direct and indirect' discrimination, 'purpose or effect', 'structural discrimination', and 'affirmative action'.

6. Two final introductory observations need to be made. First of all, a legal commentary is not an exercise in pure logic, with the rules of legal interpretation being applied to a particular legal provision to solve a specific legal question as if the rules of interpretation were a software program that mechanically runs a hard drive. Rights are social-constructs or 'tools' that society uses to promote the well-being of its members, and each right contributes to both the individual's welfare and the collective welfare in particular ways. A legal analysis must therefore take account of the functions that the rights are performing for society, and the values that are embodied in the rights.

7. Secondly, to state the meaning of Article 2 is to give an opinion, and a legal analysis is simply a structured presentation of the reasons for accepting an opinion that law should be read in a particular way. But to call something 'an opinion' is not a trivialization: all of our facts, all of our knowledge in life, boil down to beliefs, to opinions. Indeed, the extent to which the law promotes the well-being of people – the degree to which individuals are actually enjoying their rights – is the combined result of what all of the members of society believe – believe about the rule of law, about human dignity, about what they owe each other, and so forth. Beliefs determine actions, and our actions reveal our beliefs. So the amount of discrimination that adolescents and children will experience in their lives will depend in significant part upon what people believe about the rights in Article 2.

8. The aim of this commentary is to empower people to make up their own minds about the meanings of the rights recognized in Article 2, grounding their opinions in an understanding of CRC rights as *rights* under international law, rather than mere rhetoric.

CHAPTER TWO

COMPARING THE CRC'S RIGHT OF NON-DISCRIMINATION WITH OTHER PROHIBITIONS OF DISCRIMINATION

1. *Introduction*

9. All of the commentaries in this series start by comparing the CRC right in question with provisions in other international and regional agreements. Article 2(2) – the prohibition against deprivations and punishment based on the conduct of a youngster's parents – has no counterpart in other treaties, so this chapter will be concerned with the right of non-discrimination in Article 2(1).

10. But readers may be wondering, 'Why should we be interested in making comparisons? Since the topic is the right of non-discrimination in the CRC, aren't we losing our focus by shifting to other bodies of law?' Moreover, they might ask, 'How can we make comparisons before interpreting Article 2(1)? Is that not putting the cart before the horse? Or like trying to read one's email before turning on the computer?'

It is certainly true that our comparisons will be limited until we have established an authoritative understanding of Article 2(1), which is the task of the next chapter. On the other hand, while the expression 'the right of non-discrimination' is used in jurisdictions throughout the world, people give it different meanings. So before beginning the detailed legal analysis of the CRC, we should do some basic 'contrasting and comparing'.

2. *The Four Rights of Non-Discrimination in Common Articles 2*

11. The starting place of the right of non-discrimination in international human rights law is the Charter of the United Nations. The Charter defines the purposes of the UN, which include promoting 'respect for human rights and for fundamental freedoms for all without distinction as to race, sex, language, or religion'.[2] The Charter is a special kind of treaty because it

---

[2] Article 1(3) of the Charter of the United Nations, 892 UNTS 119 (1945; in force 1945); also, Articles 13(1)(b), 55(c), and 76(c).

plays a constitution-like role in the international community of States. In joining the United Nations, Member States obligate themselves to fulfil this purpose, not only with respect to their own domestic laws, but also collectively throughout the world.

12. The creation of the Universal Declaration of Human Rights, in 1948, was the first collective step in fulfilling this purpose. It not only declares rights that cover the major spheres of life, it also pronounces a right to be free from discrimination in the enjoyment of those rights (Article 2, first paragraph of the UDHR).[3] This right was then strengthened by being included in the first two human rights treaties, the International Covenant on Civil and Political Rights (Article 2(1)),[4] and the International Covenant on Economic, Social and Cultural Rights (Article 2(2)),[5] both in 1966. And it was strengthened again when it was included in the Convention on the Rights of the Child (Article 2(1)),[6] in 1989.

13. As mentioned above, these four rights of non-discrimination can be referred to collectively as Common Articles 2 since they are essentially the same. To simplify the discussion, we will look at just two of the texts, adding italics to facilitate the comparisons:
Article 2(1) of the CCPR reads:

> Each State Party to the present Covenant undertakes to respect and to ensure to all individuals within its territory and subject to its jurisdiction the rights recognized in the present Covenant, without *distinction* of any kind, such as race, *colour*, sex, language, religion, *political or other opinion, national or social origin, property, birth or other status.* (Emphasis added.)

Article 2(1) of the CRC says:

> State Parties shall respect and ensure the rights set forth in the present Convention to each child within their jurisdiction without *discrimination* of any kind, irrespective of the child's *or his or her parent's or legal guardian's* race, colour, sex, language, religion, political or other opinion, national, *ethnic* or social origin, property, *disability*, birth or other status. (Emphasis added.)

---

[3] GA Res. 217A (III) (UN Doc. A/810, 1948), p. 71. The UDHR, and the UN treaties cited in this commentary, are available at www.ohchr.org, along with the reservations, State reports, and the concluding observations and general comments of the treaty-bodies.
[4] 999 UNTS 171 (1966; in force 1976).
[5] 993 UNTS 3 (1966; in force 1976).
[6] 1577 UNTS 3 (1989; in force 1990).

14. There are seven important points to note about Common Articles 2. First, non-discrimination is not just an obligation that each State owes to the other States; it is a *human right*: the individual adolescent or child is the right-holder, and the State Party is the corresponding duty-bearer, with the regulation of those legal relationships being the subject of international law.[7]

Second, children and adolescents possess the right of non-discrimination in all four Common Articles 2; 'children's human rights' did not begin with the CRC.

Third, the right of non-discrimination works in conjunction with the other rights in the agreement of which it is a part: it is an *umbrella right* that adds protection to the *sectoral rights* (*e.g.*, Articles 6 to 40 of the CRC). All commentators recognize the interconnection, although they normally use other terminology, like 'accessory right' and 'substantive right', respectively. Unfortunately, 'accessory' suggests inferiority, and 'substantive right' is best reserved as a contrast to 'procedural right'. *Umbrella right*, on the other hand, indicates that Article 2(1) attaches to, or forms a part of, the other rights, each of which pertains to some sphere or *sector* of life, like education, health, and self-expression.[8]

Fourth, there has been an expansion of the forbidden grounds of adverse distinction: the Charter names four grounds (*race, sex, religion, language*); the two Covenants add six more (*colour, political or other opinion, national or social origin, property, birth*), plus an *or other status* clause (that we will examine later); and the CRC adds two more (*ethnic origin*, and *disability*).

---

[7] In a treaty, each State Party is a reciprocal right-holder and duty-bearer to every other Party. There is, however, considerable puzzlement as to how a treaty can make a State a duty-bearer to a right-holding private individual since neither the General Assembly nor the States Parties are a global parliament with the lawmaking powers of a national legislature. One answer, and maybe the only convincing one, is the legal notion that private individuals are 'third party beneficiaries' to the State-to-State obligations. See L. Henkin, 'Introduction', in: L. Henkin (ed.), *The International Bill of Rights: The Covenant on Civil and Political Rights* (New York, Columbia Univ. Press, 1981), pp. 1, 14–15. This commentary accepts as an axiom that individual young people hold internationally recognized rights against the State under the CRC.

[8] The word 'umbrella' was used during the drafting of the Covenants; Commission on Human Rights, *Report of the 8th Session* (UN Doc. E/2256, Supl. No. 4, 1952), p. 14; and it is occasionally used by commentators; *e.g.*, M. Nowak, *U.N. Covenant on Civil and Political Rights: CCPR Commentary* (2nd ed., Kehl/Strasbourg/Arlington, N. P. Engel Publ., 2005), p. 29. 'Sectoral' is used here in a way similar to CRC Comm., *Gen. Com. No. 5: General Measures* (2003) (UN Doc. HRI/GEN/Rev.8, 2006), para. 22; quoted in M. Rishmawi, *Article 4: The Nature of States Parties' Obligations*, in: A. Alen, J. Vande Lanotte, E. Verhellen, F. Ang, E. Berghmans and M. Verheyde (eds.), *A Commentary on the United Nations Convention on the Rights of the Child* (Leiden/Boston, Martinus Nijhoff Publ., 2006), p. 25.

Fifth, the CRC also forbids adverse distinctions on the grounds of the *parent's* or guardian's race, sex, etc.

Sixth, *distinction* is the operative word in the Charter, the UDHR, and the CCPR, while it is *discrimination* in the CESCR and the CRC. As we will be seeing, these are only stylistic variations that do not affect the meaning of the right of non-discrimination.

And seventh, the prohibition is not qualified: the General Assembly did not add any words of conditionality, like 'unreasonable' or 'unfair' discrimination.

All of these points will be elaborated on in Chapter 3.

3. *The Rights in Common Articles 2 Compared to Other Prohibitions*

15. When making comparisons about the right of non-discrimination, commentators tend to restrict themselves to comparing verbal formulations of legal texts, focusing on just two variables, the taboo grounds of differentiation, and the spheres of life to which the prohibitions pertain. While this is a helpful beginning, we need to expand our points of comparison.

For one thing, we need to take account of the fact that there are different kinds of rights. A contract right, a statutory right, a constitutional right, a right in a regional treaty, a right in a universal treaty, a moral right, and a natural right – each of these rights is different in 'nature' from the others. And for another, we must take in account that some international agreements impose an obligation on States not to discriminate but do not give rights to individuals. So we need to compare types of *rights*, and types of *legal prohibitions*.

The CRC is a universal treaty created within the United Nations' system of lawmaking, which means that we are interested in the *right* of non-discrimination in Article 2(1) as a *human right* within the body of law known as 'international human rights law'. This focus gives us four points of comparison: We need to contrast the right of non-discrimination in Common Articles 2 with: (i) prohibitions that are framed only as state obligations, rather than as an individually-held right of non-discrimination; (ii) rights contained in regional agreements; (iii) the built-in anti-discrimination clauses in certain sectoral rights; and (iv) prohibitions of discrimination that are inherently contained within provisions framed in terms of 'equality'.

3.1. *International Agreements That Do Not Create Rights*

16. Other treaties also forbid discrimination, but without making individuals the holders of a right of non-discrimination; these agreements are written so as to only impose obligations on States. The most prominent examples are the International Convention on the Elimination of All Forms of Racial Discrimination (CERD);[9] the Convention on the Elimination of All Forms of Discrimination Against Women (CEDAW);[10] the Convention Concerning Discrimination in Respect of Employment and Occupation (ILO No. 111); and UNESCO's Convention Against Discrimination in Education.

These treaties are specialized framework treaties. They obligate States Parties not to make adverse distinctions between people based on specified grounds, in relation to specified areas of life. For example, CERD pertains to adverse differentiations based on 'race, colour, descent, or national or ethnic origin', in regard to all spheres of life covered by human rights law. As framework treaties, they also contain obligations aimed at secondary objectives, and they include monitoring mechanisms, all of which contribute to the primary goal of ending the discrimination in question.

Minors are not excluded as beneficiaries of the prohibitions in these four treaties, so there is considerable overlap with Article 2(1). Readers can compare for themselves the taboo grounds and the protected areas of life in the specialized treaties to those in the CRC, as their interests and needs require; for our purposes, suffice it to say that none of these specialized treaties exceeds the scope of Article 2(1).

17. What is more important in making our comparisons is to clarify the nature of the obligations. The CRC and the Covenants are *human rights treaties*: individuals have rights that they hold against a duty-bearing State. ('States Parties shall respect and ensure the rights set forth in the present Convention...', in Article 2(1), for example). But CERD, CEDAW, ILO No. 111, and the UNESCO convention are not, strictly speaking, human rights treaties: they are *support treaties*; they help the State to fulfil its duties to the right-holders under the human rights treaties, but they do not create a right-holder/duty-bearer relation between an individual and the State. The States that created these support treaties made policy decisions not to frame them in terms of rights held by individuals; that is why they only speak the language of state duties. ('Each State undertakes to engage in no

---

[9] CERD, 660 UNTS 195 (1965; in force 1969).
[10] CEDAW, 1249 UNTS 13 (1979; in force 1981).

act or practice of racial discrimination…', for instance, in Article 2(1)(a) of the CERD.) So, for the purposes of this commentary, a human rights treaty is considered to be one that is framed in terms of individually-held rights.[11]

3.2. Regional Prohibitions and Rights That Are Not 'International Human Rights'

18. Rights of non-discrimination are also found in regional treaties and declarations, the most well-known being the European Convention on Human Rights (Article 14, and Protocol 12); the American Convention on Human Rights (Article 1); the African Charter on Human and Peoples' Rights (Article 2); and the African Charter on the Rights and Welfare of the Child (Article 3). Their verbal formulations are similar to Common Articles 2, with the State's obligations to the right-holders expressed as an umbrella prohibition against adverse distinctions on specified grounds (similar to those in Common Articles 2), with respect to the enjoyment of the other rights in the treaty.[12]

So, here too, there is considerable overlap with the right of non-discrimination in CRC Article 2(1). But two important differences need to be noted.

19. First, our comparisons must take account of the differences in the nature of the rights under discussion: regional treaties are not, in the strictest manner of speaking, 'international human rights treaties'. For one thing, the four main UN human rights agreements are global – they aim to secure 'universal respect for and observance of' the rights they contain, based on 'a common understanding' of what those rights mean,[13] while sub-global treaties are created in order to allow for regional differences. For another, people use the term *human rights* to mean different things. In the interna-

---

[11] Also of note is the Convention on the Rights of Persons With Disabilities (Ad Hoc Committee on a Comprehensive and Integral International Convention, August 2006) (not in force) (UN Doc. A/61/611, 2006). For a post-CRC treaty framed in terms of individually-held rights, see International Convention on the Protection of the Rights of All Migrant Workers and Members of Their Families (1990; in force 2003) (adding grounds of nationality, age, economic position, and marital status, in Article 7).

[12] The European Convention includes 'national minority', and Protocol 12 is an 'autonomous' prohibition of discrimination, in contrast to the umbrella (or 'accessory') Article 14; the American Convention includes 'economic status' and 'any other social condition'; and the two African Charters both contain 'ethnic group' and 'fortune'.

Also of note: European Social Charter (Revised, 1996); Framework Convention for the Protection of National Minorities; Arab Charter on Human Rights (Revised 2004; in force March 2008); Cairo Declaration on Human Rights in Islam (1990).

[13] Sixth and seventh preambular paragraphs of the UDHR; see also proclamation paragraph.

tional human rights movement, people are said to have human rights 'simply because they are human beings', but the regional agreements exclude most of humanity as right-holders, simply because of where they live.

20. The second important difference stems from the role that judges can play in the regional treaties. When a court is viewed as having the power to determine the meaning of the rights in a regional treaty, the 'right', for all practical purposes, is not what is contained in the text of the treaty article; the content of the right is determined by what is written in the decisions of the court. So there would be a difference in comparing Article 2(1) to (let us say) the *verbal formulation* of Article 14 of the ECHR, and comparing Article 2(1) to *what right-holders are entitled to according to the case law* of the European Court of Human Rights.

This may appear to be mere hair-splitting, until one considers that *interpretation* has multiple meanings. In its primary meaning, judges 'interpret' a legal text when they apply the traditional rules of legal interpretation, as, for instance, the rules of the Vienna Convention on the Law of Treaties. When judges 'interpret' in this sense, there will be relatively minor variations in the contents of rights that have identical verbal formulations. (For instance, this court might say that *race* includes 'caste', while that court says that it does not; or different courts will define 'caste' differently.) These kinds of variations in judicial interpretations will be important to the plaintiffs in the cases, but not to most right-holders, since they will not affect the essence of the right. But many people also use 'interpret' to refer to what would be more accurately described as judicial lawmaking, or a judicial re-writing of the law. This kind of 'interpretation' is a two-edged sword, since it can both enlarge the content of a right, and contract it. If a court *expands* the content of a regional right of non-discrimination, then the regional right would not clash with Common Articles 2. However, if the court *cuts back* on the meaning of the right, then the regional treaty would probably conflict with international human rights law: the regional law – as 'interpreted' by the judges – would allow States in that region to do things that the CRC and the Covenants forbid in rights that have a similar formulation.

21. Recognizing that the term *human rights* has multiple meanings can help us avoid ethnocentrism: it cautions us not to impute to the 'right of non-discrimination' in Common Articles 2 the meaning of the 'right of non-discrimination' in the particular regional treaty that one is most familiar with; and it reminds us that the judges on a sub-global court do not determine the 'common understanding' of human rights for the entire international community of States, or for the entire human race. So, in

order to avoid confusions stemming from the multiple meanings of *human rights*, this commentary makes a distinction between 'human rights under international human rights law', and 'rights in regional treaties'.

3.3. Built-in Anti-Discrimination Clauses

22. In addition to an umbrella right of non-discrimination, some of the sectoral rights have an anti-discrimination clause built directly into the right. When a society is having a problem with race, sex, etc. discrimination, there will be intense pressures on the State to discriminate in the allocation of those finite goods that are the most highly valued, like education, jobs, and 'participation in government' (*i.e.*, office holding, and employment in the public service). In order to emphasize that these finite goods must be enjoyed without adverse distinctions based on a person's race, sex, religion, etc., the UN lawmakers put anti-discrimination clauses directly in those sectoral rights.

For instance, participation in government must be free from 'unreasonable restrictions', but it also cannot be restricted by 'distinctions [on the grounds] mentioned in article 2' (Article 25 of the CCPR); higher education 'shall be equally accessible to all on the basis of merit', which rules out admissions and scholarships based on race, sex, etc. (Article 25(2) of the UDHR; also Article 13(2)(c) of the CESCR, and Article 28(1)(c) of the CRC); and job promotions must be based only on 'seniority and competence', again, ruling out race, etc. discrimination (Article 7(c) of the CESCR).

Other built-in clauses of particular note are the rights of children to protection 'without any discrimination as to race [etc.]' (Article 24(1) of the CCPR), and the requirement that 'equal protection of the law' be implemented 'without discrimination' (Article 26 of the CCPR).

In an ideal world, it would not be necessary for the sectoral rights to duplicate the prohibitions of discrimination contained in the treaty's Common Articles 2, but we do not live in an ideal world. (Indeed, everybody would spontaneously respect everyone else's human dignity in an ideal world, in which case there would be no need for international human rights law.) So the built-in anti-discrimination clauses are useful as reinforcements to the right of non-discrimination.

3.4. Prohibitions Inherent in 'Equality' Provisions

23. Finally, international agreements sometimes contain 'equality' provisions that inherently forbid certain kinds of discrimination. The duty to 'ensure the equal rights of men and women' logically prohibits state-imposed sex

discrimination (Article 3 of the CCPR; Article 3 of the CESCR). Moreover, the obligations in CEDAW are often framed in terms of 'same rights' and 'equal treatment' (*e.g.*, Article 11(1)[chapeau] and 11(1)(d) of the CEDAW); thus, while the treaty is primarily aimed at eliminating discrimination against women, many of its provisions protect males just as much as they protect females, a fact that is often overlooked.[14]

These 'equality' provisions overlap with the CRC in several ways. For one, older teenagers are 'young men' and 'young women' in ordinary speech, so the term-of-art definition (or legal fiction) of 'child' in Article 1 does not exclude them from the equality protections for men and women just mentioned. And for another, States cannot fulfil their 'equality' duties in regard to young or mature adults without addressing the problems that boys and girls face during the pre-natal, infancy, and childhood stages of their lives. CEDAW cannot do its job if the State begins fulfilling its obligations the day a girl becomes a woman, for example.[15]

24. To sum up this chapter: The *right* of non-discrimination in Article 2(1) cannot be authoritatively compared to anything until one has settled on a legal interpretation of the right. Until then, it is important to keep in mind that the terms *human rights* and *the right of non-discrimination* have multiple meanings; that support treaties like CERD, and regional treaties like the European Convention on Human Rights, are not, strictly speaking, human rights treaties; and that prohibitions of discrimination are also imposed within some of the sectoral rights, as well as through certain 'equality' provisions.

One of the themes of this commentary is that by making too much of the rhetoric of non-discrimination, people make too little of the right of non-discrimination in Common Articles 2. There are a variety of reasons for engaging in comparative law,[16] but for this commentary, the most important reason is to ensure that the CRC is used to protect children and adolescents from race, sex, religious, etc. discrimination. Being aware of shifts in the meanings of terms, and of shifts between bodies of law, will help us stay vigilant about the right of non-discrimination in Article 2(1).

---

[14] But 'equality before the law' and 'equal protection of the law' do not inherently prohibit race, etc. discrimination, as those phrases are understood in the domestic laws of various jurisdictions; see No. 182, and accompanying footnotes.

[15] Article 10(a) of the CEDAW makes it clear that 'equality' in education begins 'in pre-school'.

[16] *E.g.*, E. Örücü, *The Enigma of Comparative Law* (Leiden/Boston, Martinus Nijhoff Publ., 2004), pp. 1–3 (there is no settled opinion on the aims and utility of comparative law).

CHAPTER THREE

SCOPE OF ARTICLE 2(1): FREEDOM FROM DISCRIMINATION

1. *Introduction: What Is Discrimination?*

25. This chapter will conduct a detailed legal analysis of the right of non-discrimination, but first it will be helpful to ground the discussion in commonsense understandings that we can relate to the lived experiences of right-holders.

26. Let us say that Ahmed has reached the age for primary school and his mother goes to register him. There is a school fee, which officials can waive for families living below the poverty line. Ahmed's mother applies for the waiver, and the enrolment officer asks about his religion. She answers 'Muslim,' and the officer says, 'He is not eligible for a waiver; Muslims must pay the fee.' The mother cries, 'That's discrimination!' Is she correct?

It is safe to say that everyone will agree with the mother: Ahmed has been discriminated against on the ground of religion. Our shared understanding on this matter is rooted in the ordinary meaning of the word *discrimination*: 'to make a difference in treatment or favor on a class or categorical basis in disregard of individual merit.'[17] The authorities are treating students differently on the basis of membership in a group, rather than on merit: non-Muslims can get waivers, Muslims cannot: that's discrimination.

27. Discrimination is illustrated in the decision-tree models below, with Ahmed's case shown in Figure 1, and the general case in Figure 2.

In the school fee case, waivers are allocated according to the youngster's religious classification: they are denied to Muslims, but given to everyone else. The general case follows the same model of allocation: if the claimant belongs to Group A, the state allows the person to enjoy the opportunity, while members of Group B are excluded (where A and B stand for particular groups within the category of 'race', or 'sex', etc., according to the facts of

---

[17] *Webster's Third New International Dictionary* (London, Bell & Sons/Springfield, Mass., G. & C. Merriam, 1961), p. 648 (defining the verb; the noun *discrimination* is an act or instance of such treatment).

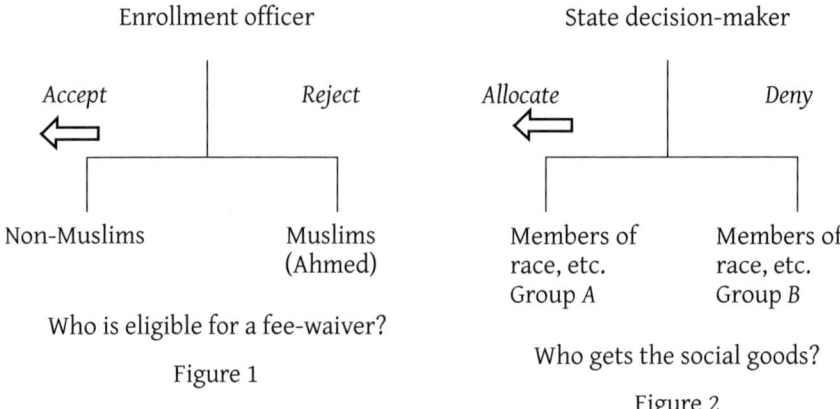

Figure 1

Who is eligible for a fee-waiver?

Figure 2

Who gets the social goods?

the case). During the apartheid era of South Africa, for instance, the pass laws allowed members of Group A ('whites') to move about freely, while members of Group B ('non-whites' – 'blacks' and 'coloureds') were restricted: so Frederik De Klerk was free to live in nice residential areas as he liked, while Steven Biko could not. Or during the fight for women's suffrage in the United Kingdom, voter-registration officials classified people according to their sex: they registered members of Group A (men), and rejected members of Group B (women): so Mr. Gladstone got to vote, while Mrs. Gladstone got to watch.

28. Although the decision-tree figure is simple, it is not an oversimplification: in all state-imposed discrimination, the government allocates important things in life according to one's membership in a category defined by race, sex, religion, or another ground named in Common Articles 2.

29. In the next several sections we will use the rules of legal interpretation to define the three elements of the right of non-discrimination. Subsequent sections will discuss the key concepts pertaining to discrimination, which will facilitate the application of the elements to real-life situations, and the last sections in this chapter will cover the main sources of confusion. But all of the detailed legal analysis to follow will just add precision to the ordinary understanding of discrimination outlined in this introduction.

2. The Rules of Legal Interpretation

30. To speak of the scope of a right is to talk about its content or meaning, and this calls for legal interpretation. The Vienna Convention on the

Law of Treaties lays down the primary rules of interpretation, and these mandatory rules are supplemented by principles of legal interpretation that have been developed by national and international courts over the course of many years.

31. The Vienna Convention has two main rules of interpretation. The first rule is the 'ordinary meaning rule':

> A treaty *shall* be interpreted [a] in good faith [b] in accordance with the ordinary meaning to be given to the terms of the treaty [c] in their context and [d] in the light of its object and purpose. (Article 31(1) of the VCLT, brackets and emphasis added.)[18]

Once an interpretation has been arrived at, a corollary to this rule allows the legislative records (the records of the negotiations, or *travaux préparatoires*) to be used to confirm the reading. But the records cannot be used to alter or over-ride the interpretation: the ordinary meaning rule requires that the interpretation be based on the text of the treaty, and on the commonsense inferences that can be drawn from the text.

32. If it is impossible to arrive at an interpretation using the ordinary meaning rule, then the secondary rule of interpretation, the 'legislative history rule', comes into play. Under Article 32 of the VCLT, the 'preparatory work' can be used to 'determine the meaning when the interpretation according to article 31 [either] (a) leaves the meaning ambiguous or obscure; or (b) leads to a result which is manifestly absurd or unreasonable'.[19] Since the ordinary meaning rule is sufficient for interpreting Article 2(1), this commentary will be focusing on the text of the CRC, and how the right of non-discrimination functions to promote the purposes of the treaty.

---

[18] 1155 UNTS 331 (1969; in force 1980).
[19] Brackets added. Article 32 of the VCLT reads in full:
Recourse may be had to supplementary means of interpretation, including the preparatory work of the treaty and the circumstances of its conclusion, in order
 [1] to confirm the meaning resulting from the application of article 31, or
 [2] to determine the meaning when the interpretation according to article 31:
  (a) leaves the meaning ambiguous or obscure, or
  (b) leads to a result which is manifestly absurd or unreasonable. (Brackets added.)
Article 32[1] of the VCLT is the corollary to the ordinary meaning rule in Article 31(1), and it cannot be used to replace or alter the meaning arrived at under that rule. It should not be confused with the legislative history rule in Article 32[2], the fallback rule that is used for producing an interpretation when the ordinary meaning rule fails. But if the interpretation produced by the ordinary meaning rule does not fall under the criteria in Article 32[2], then that interpretation must be accepted.

3. *The Three Elements of the Right of Non-Discrimination*

3.1. *Overview*

33. To specify the content of a right, one must define the right's elements or component parts. Once the elements are identified, the right can be applied to real-life situations. While most rights are framed in the positive, 'without discrimination' leads to expressing the elements of Article 2(1) as a prohibition. So if all of the elements of the right of non-discrimination are satisfied with respect to a particular law or practice, the State will not be in compliance with the CRC – it will have 'violated' the right, it will have 'breached' its international obligations.

34. The right of non-discrimination has three elements. Article 2(1) forbids the State Party to:

1. treat the right-holder differently on the basis of race, sex, or any of the other named grounds,
2. when doing so will impair the right-holder's enjoyment of,
3. another right in the CRC (*i.e.*, one of the sectoral rights).

These three elements follow logically from the ordinary meaning of *discrimination* – to treat a person differently on the basis of membership in a group or category unrelated to merit –, and from the inherent requirements of an umbrella prohibition.

35. We can find these three components embedded in any law that can be properly called an 'anti-discrimination law'. We can also see the three elements in the definition of discrimination given by the Human Rights Committee in General Comment 18. The elements may be difficult to see at first glance because the Committee's definition is extremely wordy, so brackets and italics have been added to highlight the components:

> '[D]iscrimination' as used in the Covenant [*i.e.*, Articles 4, 20, 24, and 26 of the CCPR] should be understood to imply [a] any *distinction*, exclusion, restriction or preference which is based *on any ground such as* race, colour, sex, language, religion, political or other opinion, national or social origin, property, birth or other status, and [b] which has the purpose or effect of nullifying or *impairing* the recognition, *enjoyment* or exercise by all persons, on an equal footing, of [c] all *rights* and freedoms.[20]

---

[20] HRC, *Gen. Com. No. 18* (1989) (UN Doc. HRI/GEN/1/Rev.8, 2006), para. 7. The HRC constructed its definition from those contained in Article 1(1) of the CERD, and Article 1 of the CEDAW.

36. The elements become even clearer when we strip the definition of its excess verbiage:

'[D]iscrimination' is
[a] a *distinction* based on the *grounds of* race, colour, sex [etc.],
[b] which *impairs* the *enjoyment* of
[c] *rights.*

In component [a], *distinction* inherently encompasses 'exclusion, restriction or preference'; the last three terms are merely different ways to make a differentiation in treatment: they are subcategories of the all-encompassing word, 'distinction'. In [b], *impairing* includes 'nullifying', and *enjoyment* covers 'exercise'. And as for [c], all of the 'freedoms' in the CCPR are *rights*. The Human Rights Committee has followed the old-fashioned style of legal drafting that piled synonym upon synonym, substituting complexity for clarity, and prizing inflated language over plain speaking. Pull the weeds out of the garden, and the three elements become visible: (a) differential treatment on a forbidden ground (b) that impairs the enjoyment (c) of a right.

37. It is important to note that the Human Rights Committee's definition does not contain a fourth component: the definition is not qualified by any terms like *disproportionate, unfair,* or *unreasonable – any* racial, etc. distinction that impairs the enjoyment of a recognized right is 'discrimination', and this corresponds exactly with the three elements of Article 2(1) in the CRC. All three of the elements will be elaborated on in the following sections.[21]

3.2. Element (1): Differential Treatment on Forbidden Grounds

38. In a more precise formulation, Element (1) forbids the State to:

1. treat a right-holder differently from one or more other persons on account of the right-holder's membership in any one of the named categories or groups (*i.e.*, race, sex, religion, language, and the other specified grounds).

---

[21] Compare to S. Besson, 'The Principle of Non-Discrimination in the Convention on the Rights of the Child', *International Journal of Children's Rights* 13, No. 4 (2005), pp. 433, 435 (claiming, without explanation, that the HRC's definition of discrimination contains a 'lack of proportionality of means to ends' element). Confusions arising from expressions like 'principle of non-discrimination' and 'proportionality' are discussed below in sections 8.1 and 8.2, respectively.

This element reflects the ordinary meaning of *discrimination*: 'to make a difference in treatment or favor on a class or categorical basis in disregard of individual merit.'[22]

39. In the school-fee case, Ahmed is treated differently because of his membership in the category 'Muslim', rather than according to his family's poverty, so Element (1) is satisfied. Note that Element (1) is an objective test: Ahmed was either treated differently on the basis of his classification as 'Muslim', or he was not: the matter is strictly a factual question. This follows from the fact that the ordinary meaning of *discrimination* is objective, that is to say, it does not contain any 'fairness' or 'reasonableness' component, which would require subjective judgements before using the word in a given situation.[23]

40. Before we move on to the other components, we need to refine the analysis of Element (1). Treating one person differently from another always involves *two variables*: there will always be (a) a *criterion* upon which the differential treatment turns, and (b) some particular *sphere of life* or *interest* to which the treatment pertains. When Ahmed complains about being

---

[22] *Webster's Third New International Dictionary*, *o.c.* (note 17).

[23] *Discrimination* has the same objective meaning in British English; *e.g.*, *The Oxford English Dictionary* (2nd ed., Oxford, Clarendon Press, 1989), vol. 4, p. 758. The author's survey of more than fifty American and British dictionaries found that the meaning of *discrimination* has remained stable for the period in which the UN human rights agreements were written; *e.g.*, *A New English Dictionary on Historical Principles* (Oxford, Clarendon Press, 1897), vol. 3, p. 436, and *The Concise Oxford Dictionary of Current English* (8th ed., Oxford, Clarendon Press, 1990), p. 334. While a few of the most recent British dictionaries show that a subjective usage of *discrimination*, containing a 'fairness' component, is emerging, this additional usage was not an ordinary meaning at the time of the creation of Common Articles 2.

The single most important publication concerning the right of non-discrimination in international law is United Nations, Secretary-General, *The Main Types and Causes of Discrimination: Memorandum submitted by the Secretary General* (UN Doc. E/CN.4/Sub.2/40/Rev.1, 1949) (Sales No. 1949.XIV.3). The study laid a foundation for moving from the Universal Declaration, where all the rights, including freedom from race, etc. discrimination, are principles of political morality (or 'common standards of achievement', last preambular paragraph), to the legally binding rights of the Covenants. The study has also been the foundation for this commentary.

The Main Types and Causes of Discrimination follows the objective meaning of 'discrimination' as seen in the above cited dictionaries and in the HRC's definition; *id.* paras. 31, 32, 33, and 87.

Terminology is discussed further in No. 45 (discrimination 'in favour of'/'against'); No. 47 ('distinction' and 'discrimination'); note 27 (translations of *discrimination*); Nos. 101–102 (*de jure/de facto* discrimination); Nos. 105–113 (principle of non-discrimination); note 73 (the differences between a word, a principle, and a right); note 74 (the bogus 'international' definition); Nos. 133–138 (direct/indirect discrimination); and No. 246 (expansions and contractions by Committee members).

discriminated against, we have to ask, 'Discriminated against on what ground? And in what area of life?' The answer: Ahmed was differentiated from other students (a) on the criterion of his religious classification, (b) in respect to the interest of receiving a waiver of school fees. The two variables of (a) *criterion* and (b) *interest* are logical components of the notion of differential treatment, so they must always be specified before the right of non-discrimination can be applied to specific cases.

41. Article 2(1) specifies the taboo (a)-variables: 'race, colour, sex, language, religion, political or other opinion, national, ethnic or social origin, property, disability, [and] birth'. There is no mystery why the framers of the CRC named these particular classifications. They have been singled out because of humanity's experiences with discrimination on these specific grounds. These particular characteristics are important to a person's identity; but race, sex, etc. classifications are virtually always arbitrary as a basis for the State to grant and deny fundamental things in life (like economic opportunities, education, political power, and all the other things now protected by international human rights law). Nevertheless, throughout history, authorities have used these particular classifications as the basis for depriving people of vital things in life: these discriminatory practices have caused enormous amounts of suffering and hardship to individuals. Moreover, people feel deeply offended when their enjoyment of basic things in life is conditioned on their belonging to 'the right' race, sex, religion, etc. And finally, discrimination on these particular grounds has often caused group-based violence and other social conflicts. On the positive side of the equation, the right of non-discrimination forces government officials to find other grounds for making differentiations between people, like financial need for waivers of school fees, and past achievement or demonstrated potential for scholarships and jobs.

In short, each of the (a)-variables has been included in the right of non-discrimination because of the realities of human nature and the human condition. Article 2(1) embodies the widely held belief that it is morally wrong to deprive people of vital things in life on the basis of the person's race, sex, religion, and the other forbidden grounds; the state must make distinctions only according to personal merit, or other non-arbitrary criteria. (Article 2(1) also names *or other status* as one of the prohibited variables, and this will be discussed later, in section 3.5.)[24]

---

[24] The main text discussion of the (a)-variables corresponds to *The Main Types and Causes of Discrimination*, o.c. (note 23), paras. 31, 32, 33, and 87.

42. Finally, we can see the two variables of Element (1) reflected in the decision-tree in Figure 2. State-imposed discrimination entails allocations of what can be called 'social goods'. The social good might be a finite resource (like a scholarship or a job), or it might be a sphere of liberty (like freedom of movement or voting), and the State treats people differently in the enjoyment of the social good on the basis of their race, sex, etc. classification. For example, when the law gives the right to vote exclusively to men, the (a)-variable is a 'sex' classification, with Group A defined as 'male' and Group B as 'female', and the interest at stake in the (b)-variable is exercising political power through the ballot box.

3.3. Element (2): Impairment

43. Under Element (2), the race-, etc.-based treatment is forbidden:

> 2. when the differential treatment will impair the right-holder's enjoyment of the interest in question, relative to the other person's (or persons') enjoyment of that interest.

The right of non-discrimination protects people from harmful conduct, with the harm being judged from the perspective of the right-holder who is being discriminated against. Notice too that the interest at stake in Element (2) is the same interest that we are concerned with in Element (1b).

44. In Ahmed's case, the interest at stake is obtaining a waiver of the school fee on the basis of financial need, and his enjoyment of that interest has obviously become inferior to that of non-Muslim students living in poverty: the law bars Muslims from applying for a needs-based waiver, so the law imposes an injury on Ahmed. The impairment aspect of Element (2) is seen immediately in the decision-trees in Figures 1 and 2: the deny-branch inflicts a harm, whereas the allocate-branch gives a benefit: members of Group B are given inferior treatment, relative to members of Group A.

45. Standing alone, the word 'discrimination' is neutral, so differential treatment in a given situation could be good or bad, legal or illegal, justifiable or unjustifiable. This is reflected in phrases like *unfair discrimination, unjust discrimination, arbitrary discrimination*, and *unlawful discrimination*. These expressions are not self-contradictions because 'discrimination' simply refers to differential treatment on the basis of membership in a class or category, unrelated to merit; decisions about the morality, legality, or pragmatic utility of the differential treatment are not built into the definition of 'discrimination'.

In everyday speech, however, the word 'discrimination' does not stand alone. The word is used in two ways. We can speak about distinctions that are favourable to a person – 'He discriminated *in favour of* his friends when he picked the team.' –, as well as about distinctions that are unfavourable – 'She discriminated *against* unpopular students when she formed the committee.' The right of non-discrimination is concerned only with discrimination *against*. This is made clear in Element (2): the differential treatment must impair the right-holder's enjoyment of the interest at stake.

In other words, it is not the race, religious, etc. differentiation *per se* that is forbidden; the differentiation must prejudice the welfare of the right-holder. So Article 2(1) might not be violated if the school asked about Ahmed's religion for statistical purposes. In our illustration, however, Ahmed has suffered a real injury: his interests in obtaining a waiver based on financial need are impaired, in comparison to non-Muslim students living in poverty.[25]

Preferences
46. Does that mean that Article 2(1) allows the State to give preferences to youngsters on the basis of their race, sex, religion, etc.? It is important to note that every act of discrimination *in favour of* is automatically an act of discrimination *against*: this is inherent in the notion of 'differential treatment'. This is also immediately apparent in Figure 2: every law that discriminates *simultaneously* discriminates *in favour of* members of A and *against* members of B. Most state-imposed discrimination involves finite social goods, like education, jobs, and seats in parliament. In these situations, the State 'rations' the resource on the basis of one's racial, etc. classification: the State denies social goods to members of B as the means for making them available to members of A.[26]

---

[25] *Webster's New Collegiate Dictionary* (Springfield, Mass., G. & C. Merriam, 1980), p. 324 (defining *discriminate* as, 'to make a difference in treatment or favor on a basis other than individual merit <~ in favor of your friends> <~ against a certain nationality>') (italics replacing boldface). In Asian countries, people often drop *against*, so one might hear, 'Dalits are discriminated in India.' In British and American English, however, one must say, 'Dalits are discriminated against.' For a misuse of language in a Western publication, see S. Besson, *o.c.* (note 21), 447 ('discriminate some children'); compare with the correct usage, p. 449 (children are 'discriminated against').

[26] *The Main Types and Causes of Discrimination* recognizes these two reciprocal dimensions of discrimination; *o.c.* (note 23), para. 87 (distinctions that are to the 'detriment of individuals belonging to a particular [race, sex, etc.] group'), and para. 89 ('granting privileges' on those grounds).

Article 2(1) is concerned with conduct that impairs the enjoyment of rights, so we must look at a law that gives 'preferences' from the perspective of the injured individuals: a preference to Group *A* is automatically discrimination against Group *B*: giving preferences to non-Muslims is discrimination against Muslims: it violates Ahmed's right to be free from religious discrimination.

'Distinction' v. 'Discrimination'
47. As mentioned earlier, the operative word in the Charter, the UDHR and the CCPR is 'distinction', while it is 'discrimination' in the CESCR and the CRC. This has caused a great deal of confusion. The confusion is unnecessary, however, because the two words are perfectly interchangeable in the context of Common Articles 2. Elements (1) and (2) are the same, regardless of which word is used. This is because 'treating the right-holder differently' captures the core meaning of both *distinction* and *discrimination.*

Some people are uncomfortable with the idea that the two words are interchangeable; when they say 'Discrimination!' they are referring to something bad, and 'distinction' does not express that condemnation. First of all, these people are forgetting the difference between the denotative meaning of a word and the connotative meaning. The word *discrimination* can carry a pejorative sting, while *distinction* never does, but the emotional bite is not in the word itself; the condemnation comes from the entire context of the particular usage, and this includes the attitudes and the feelings that the speaker wants to express or invoke, and the attitudes and feelings of the listener. For interpreting a legal text, however, we must use the denotative meaning, since an interpretation cannot vary according to each person's feelings. And secondly, the prohibited conduct is something bad in the context of Common Articles 2, and this is reflected in the second Element – the differential treatment hurts the interests of the right-holder. (In Figure 2, the injury is illustrated by the deny-branch *B*, which corresponds to 'discrimination *against'.*) So Element (2) is the same, regardless of whether the operative word is 'distinction' or 'discrimination'.[27]

---

[27] That the two operative terms are interchangeable in this context can be seen in a number of ways, in addition to the Elements and Figure 2. For instance, 'discrimination' is a type of (or subset of) 'distinction': *discrimination* is making a 'distinction' between people based on their membership in a group, rather than on merit – and race, sex, etc. are specific kinds of groups that are unrelated to merit. And, to make a *distinction* based on those grounds is to 'discriminate'.

The French cognates of the two operative terms are also interchangeable, and, in numerous treaties, there is a switching of the terms, and the use of equivalent terms, in the English and

48. To summarize the discussion so far: Element (1) reflects the ordinary meaning of *discrimination* – to treat a person differently on account of membership in a group or category, rather than according to individual merits. And Element (2) reflects the 'discrimination *against*' sense of the term – the treatment injures the right-holder in some particular aspect of life. Notice that neither of these elements contains any 'unreasonable', 'unfair', 'disproportionate', or 'unjustified' test.

3.4. Element (3): Protected Interests

49. Under Element (3), the State is forbidden to impair the right-holder's enjoyment of:

> 3. an interest that is protected by another right in the CRC (*i.e.*, a sectoral right).

The interest at stake in Elements (1b) and (2) must fall under the scope of one of the sectoral rights in the CRC (*i.e.*, Articles 6 to 40). Element (3) reflects the umbrella nature of the right of non-discrimination.

50. Whenever anyone claims that freedom from discrimination has been violated, it is essential to identify the sectoral right at stake.

In Ahmed's case, the fee wavier is an educational interest. Under the right to education, the State has to make primary schooling 'free for all' (Article 28(1)(a)). Free primary education is a 'progressive right', however, so the State does not have to give every primary student a free education if it cannot afford to do so (Articles 4 and 28(1)). But where the State charges a fee that is subject to the possibility of a needs-based waiver, then the interest

---

French versions of the same text. (For instance, in Article 7 of the UDHR, the English 'discrimination' reads *distinction* in the French text, while in Article 25 of the CCPR 'distinctions' is rendered *discriminations*. And, while 'discrimination' appears in both paragraphs of Article 2 of the CRC, the French text uses *distinction* in paragraph (1), and *discrimination* in paragraph (2).) Several studies have concluded that the choice of 'distinction' or 'discrimination' (and their cognates in French), and the switching in the translations, are only matters of style. E. W. Vierdag, *The Concept of Discrimination in International Law* (The Hague, Martinus Nijhoff, 1973), pp. 49–50, and M. Bossuyt, *L'interdiction de la discrimination dans le droit international des droits de l'homme* (Brussels, Emile Bruylant, 1976), p. 26.

Moreover, the same stylistic switching is seen in the other official translations of the four main UN human rights agreements: Spanish (switching two words: *distinción* and *discriminación*), Russian (two words: *razlichenie* and *diskriminatsia*), and Chinese (four terms, when one takes into account CEDAW: *fen, qū-bié, qi-shi,* and *chā-bié*), while the Arabic versions use the same word (*tamyiz*) for both operative terms.

None of these variations affects the three elements of Common Articles 2: the content of the right of non-discrimination remains the same.

in applying for and receiving a waiver must certainly be considered to fall under the scope of the right to education: a needs-based waiver is part of the progressive right to a free education. The religion-based discrimination that we identified in Elements (1) and (2) therefore pertains to an interest protected by Element (3). So the waiver law violates Ahmed's right of non-discrimination under Article 2(1) of the CRC, as read in conjunction with the right to education. (With respect to the general case in Figure 2, the State violates the right of non-discrimination when the social good is protected by one of the sectoral rights.)

51. The attentive reader may have noticed the shift in the formulations of the elements. The Overview spoke of '(1) a race-, etc.-based distinction that (2) impairs the right-holder's *enjoyment* of (3) a sectoral *right*', whereas the present discussion speaks of '(2) impairing *an interest* (3) that is *protected by* a sectoral right'. Why the difference?

Rights are social constructions for protecting the *interests* of people, and the elements have been reformulated so as to recognize the difference between the two concepts: the first two elements are now framed in terms of 'interests', while the third speaks of 'rights', and the reason for the change is to allow for precision in applying the right of non-discrimination to real-life cases.

While it is standard practice to speak of 'enjoying rights' and 'accessing rights', it is important to remember that these are metaphorical expressions. It is not wrong to use these metaphors, of course, but the fuzziness of metaphorical thinking is poison to a clear legal analysis. The right-holder is a human being who has suffered a harm, whereas a right is an abstraction, and abstractions cannot suffer. The word 'interest' is used to refer to the particular aspect of human dignity that is being injured. So the most precise way to talk about the differential treatment in Element (1) and the injury in Element (2) is to speak about 'interests', leaving legal arguments about the scope of the sectoral rights to Element (3).

52. Moreover, a good legal analysis requires us to speak of the interest at stake with the highest degree of particularity that the facts of the case and commonsense allow. For instance, one can say that the waiver law 'impairs Ahmed's well-being', but that is too abstract since 'well-being' is the sum total of all of a person's interests put together. And saying that the ban 'deprives him of a chance for an education' refers to a subsequent consequence of the discrimination, not to the discrimination itself. (And it is not absolutely certain that that consequence will happen, since future events depend upon other factors, none of which were specified in our statement

of Ahmed's case; his family might pay the fee by going into debt-bondage, for instance.) Both the discrimination in the first component, and the injury in the second, pertain to *eligibility for a needs-based waiver of the school fee*, which is the interest at stake at the highest degree of particularity.[28]

3.5. *The 'or other status' Clause*

53. Article 2(1) requires the State to ensure rights 'without discrimination of any kind, irrespective of...race, [etc.] or other status'. (There is also an *or other status* clause in the other three rights of non-discrimination in Common Articles 2.) There are two possible ways to interpret 'of any kind...or other status': (i) it includes *all possible* statuses, without limitation; or (ii) it includes *only* those statuses that are *similar in nature* to the specifically named characteristics. In both cases, 'or other status' is opened-ended, but in possibility (i) it is *completely* opened-ended, or *unbounded*, while in possibility (ii) it is *partially* opened-ended, or *bounded*. Deciding between the two possibilities calls for legal interpretation.

54. First of all, the unbounded interpretation leads to absurd results. Law by its very nature makes distinctions between people, and every differentiation rests on some type of a status distinction. As for the CRC, every sectoral right requires the State to make distinctions. The right to education makes a distinction between primary and secondary school students with respect to compulsory education (Article 28); the State cannot meet the distinctive needs of disabled youngsters without treating them differently (Article 23) – a blind student is given Braille textbooks, while a sighted student gets printed books, for instance; and so on. Indeed, the entire CRC is premised on distinctions – Article 1 requires under-18s to be treated differently to over-18s. Since it is absurd to say that a State Party cannot make distinctions between young people, and since legal interpretation rejects absurd constructions of legal texts, the completely opened-ended reading must be dismissed out of hand.

---

[28] *The Main Types and Causes of Discrimination, o.c.* (note 23), does not make the conceptual differentiation between 'interests' and 'rights', but it does recognize that the international prohibition of state-imposed discrimination pertains to 'human rights', para. 148, and 'legal rights', paras. 36, 100. For a short but helpful illustration of why an interests-based analysis is essential to legal reasoning about rights, see D. J. Harris, M. O'Boyle and C. Warbrick, *Law of the European Convention on Human Rights* (London/Dublin/Edinburgh, Butterworths, 1995), pp. 296–301.

55. Secondly, the legal profession has well-established principles for handling this kind of interpretation question. Professor Ian Brownlie has explained the rules in *Principles of Public International Law*: 'Thus general words following or perhaps preceding special words are limited to the genus indicated by the special words (the *ejusdem generis* doctrine); and express mention excludes other items (*expressio unius est exclusio alterius*).'[29] So, when an opened-ended term – in our case, 'of any kind...or other status' – is used in conjunction with more limited terms in a list – 'race, sex, religion', etc. – then the expressed examples limit the scope of interpretation of the open-ended term. In other words, *of any kind* is not to be read in isolation to mean 'every possible' ground of differentiation; it must be read in conjunction with 'race' and the other specified characteristics. New grounds can thus be added through the process of interpretation, on the condition that they bear a sufficient similarity to the specified characteristics. The bounded reading makes practical sense because it allows for an evolving consensus to expand the forbidden grounds of distinctions without the need for a formal amendment or new protocol to the CRC.

56. Thirdly, no commentator (as far as the present author is aware) has made a legal argument on behalf of the unbounded reading. One can find authors who give the impression that they believe Article 2(1) forbids every possible distinction, but no one has had the courage to make an argument in support of the absurd, unbounded reading.[30]

---

[29] I. Brownlie, *Principles of Public International Law* (3rd ed., Oxford, Clarendon Press, 1979), p. 626.

[30] *E.g.*, T. Hammarberg and A. Belembaogo, 'Proactive Measures Against Discrimination', in *Children's Rights: Turning Principles Into Practice* (Stockholm, Save the Children Sweden, 2000). 'But what exactly is meant by "discrimination" [in Article 2(1) of the CRC]? One authoritative international body [the Human Rights Committee] has defined it as *any distinction* that "has the purpose or effect of nullifying or impairing the recognition, enjoyment or exercise by all persons, on an equal footing, of all rights and freedoms".' *Id.* p. 15 (emphasis added), *quoting from* HRC, *Gen. Com. No. 18*, para. 7, *o.c.* (note 20). Note the selective quotation: The Human Rights Committee did not say 'any distinction'; it said 'any distinction...*based on* any ground *such as* race, colour, sex, [etc.]' (emphasis added); see quotation at No. 35. In addition, the authors have eliminated the (a)-variables, which are essential to preserving the core meaning of *discrimination*: a distinction based on assignment to a group or category, rather than on individual merit – like race, sex, etc.

For the CCPR, see M. Nowak, *CCPR Commentary*, *o.c.* (note 8), p. 47 ('In the final analysis, every conceivable distinction...' is covered by Article 2(1) of the CCPR, including 'shoe size'.). The 'final analysis' is disingenuous since Nowak did not conduct any analysis: he gives no reasons for adopting the absurd, unbounded reading. See note 67 below.

The records confirm that Common Articles 2 were not intended to forbid all possible distinctions. *E.g.*, *Travaux Préparatoires* for the CCPR (UN Doc. A/C.3/SR.1096, 1961), para. 37

57. And finally, monitoring committees have implicitly been adopting the bounded reading of their respective treaties, as, for instance, when the Committee on Economic, Social and Cultural Rights used the notion of an evolved consensus to say that 'disability' is a forbidden ground of discrimination.[31]

58. In short, the *ejusdem generis* principle of construction leads to the only viable interpretation of Article 2(1): *or other status* is partially open-ended, but not completely open-ended.

3.6. *Summary of the Elements*

59. To summarize the right of non-discrimination, Article 2(1) forbids a State to:

1. treat the right-holder differently from another person or persons (a) on the basis of the right-holder's membership in a named category (race, sex, etc.) (b) in respect to some specific interest,
2. if that differential treatment will impair the right-holder's enjoyment of that interest, as compared to the other person's or persons' enjoyment of the same interest, and
3. the interest is protected by another right in the CRC (*i.e.*, a sectoral right).

For convenience, the elements of the right of non-discrimination can be abbreviated as: (1) Differential treatment on a forbidden ground; (2) Injury; (3) Protected interests.

(Ceylon) (explaining that Article 25, which incorporates the prohibited grounds of distinction in Article 2(1), allows withholding the vote from minors, the mentally ill, and other categories of people); see also para. 64.

[31] Adding a ground under 'or other status' appears, on the surface, to be merely the product of reasoning by analogy. It is true that the starting place is comparing the proposed new ground to the named grounds. But since there are more points of dissimilarity than similarity in any analogy, the final step is actually a political decision. The Covenants and the CRC are framework treaties, not legal codes, and the ultimate authority to determine the meanings of the terms, which includes the adding of new grounds, and the ultimate responsibility to ensure treaty compliance, rests with the Parties collectively. Over the years, a consensus has developed among States that 'disability' must be included as a forbidden ground in the right of non-discrimination, which resulted in its being added to Article 2(1) of the CRC. Thus, when the CESCR Committee subsequently announced that 'disability' is included under 'other status', it was not engaged in lawmaking, it did not, by its own authority, 'add' that ground; instead, it was giving formal recognition to the political decision that the Parties had already made. CESCR Comm., *Gen. Com. No. 5: Persons With Disabilities* (1994) (UN Doc. HRI/ GEN/Rev.8, 2006), paras. 5, 6, and 7 (relying on the evolved consensus).

60. While the elements-approach is essential to a good legal analysis, most commentators have not used this methodology. Nevertheless, a few of the most prominent authors have, and, although they have not analysed the elements with the necessary precision, they are in agreement with this analysis on one crucial point: there is no fourth element requiring subjective opinions as to whether the discrimination is *fair, reasonable, just, or proportionate*.[32]

61. Although we have now identified the elements of Article 2(1), our interpretation task is not over. We still have to define the purposes of the right, and then determine whether or not freedom from race, etc. discrimination is an absolute prohibition.

4. The Three Functions of the Right of Non-Discrimination

4.1. Introduction

62. Human rights are 'tools' for promoting respect for human dignity. Each of the rights that are contained in the CRC, the two Covenants, and the Universal Declaration is concerned with some particular aspect of human dignity; and each right safeguards human dignity by trying to curb abuses of state power with respect to that particular aspect of dignity.[33] The inter-

---

[32] M. Craven, *The International Covenant on Economic, Social, and Cultural Rights* (Oxford, Clarendon Press, 1995). According to 'certain commentators', Craven writes, 'a universal "composite concept" of discrimination can be...characterized by the following elements: [A] a difference in treatment, [B] which is based upon certain prohibited grounds, [C] and has a certain purpose or effect, [D] in selective [sic] fields'. *Id.* p. 163 (bracketed letters substituted for the author's Arabic numerals). Craven's [A] and [B] correspond to Element (1a), and his [D] roughly corresponds to Element (1b). Oddly, his 'certain purpose or effect' in [C] omits the idea of impairment, which is the essence of Element (2). His [D] also corresponds vaguely to Element (3), although it fails to capture the idea of the umbrella nature of the right of non-discrimination. What is most strange is that, in a treatise on the CESCR, Craven has chosen to talk about a '"composite concept"' rather than interpret Article 2(2). Still, Craven's elements bear a family resemblance to the three elements as laid out in the main text.

Three of the five most frequently cited commentators on this topic have also spoken of elements, and they too are similar to those in the main text: W. A. McKean, 'The Meaning of Discrimination in International and Municipal Law', *British Yearbook of Int'l. Law* 44 (1970), p. 183; E. W. Vierdag, *o.c.* (note 27), p. 108 (grounds), p. 44 (impairment), and pp. 108, 109, 111 (protected interests); and M. Bossuyt, *L'interdiction de la discrimination dans le droit international des droits de l'homme, o.c.* (note 27), p. 227. None of these commentators say that there is an additional element that would allow a State to justify an adverse race, etc. distinction; indeed, Bossuyt expressly denies a 'reasonableness' element; *id.* p. 227.

[33] *E.g.*, T. Buergenthal, 'To Respect and to Ensure: State Obligations and Permissible Derogations', in: L. Henkin, *o.c.* (note 7), p. 90 (human rights protect 'the individual against the power of the state').

preter's task is not complete until the purposes or functions of the right in question have been identified. To interpret Article 2(1), we need to answer the following questions: How does freedom from race, etc. discrimination protect human dignity? How does it safeguard individuals from abuses of power? Since the right of non-discrimination is an umbrella right that works in conjunction with sectoral rights, what additional protection does it give to those rights? That is to say, why aren't the sectoral rights good enough on their own?

63. Probably most people intuitively sense the importance of the right of non-discrimination, but so many confusing things have been said about the right that commonsense understandings can become obscured. For instance, one publication explains Article 2(1) this way: 'governments must take measures to ensure' that all the rights apply to '*all* children within the jurisdiction of the state.... The rights laid down in the Convention extend equally to all children.'[34] But if this is what the right of non-discrimination means, then Article 2(1) is superfluous. This is because Article 1, the jurisdictional clause, has already defined the right-holders: '*every* human being below the age of 18 years' holds the rights in the Convention (emphasis added). If those authors are correct, then Article 2(1) can be removed without affecting the CRC right-holders. Another publication explains Article 2 as meaning 'Equal Treatment for All Children.'[35] We have already seen that this is completely opposite to what the CRC says, since every article requires the State to make distinctions. It is helpful here to remember that *equal* means 'same', and no one believes that all human beings should be treated in the same way. (When police arrest a person for assault, the victim does not want to be handcuffed along with the assailant.) It is absurd to say that the CRC requires the State to treat all under-18s the same, as if there were no differences between babies and teenagers, between boys and girls, or between youngsters in hospital for a broken leg and youngsters needing cancer treatment.

The Secretary General's study, *The Main Types and Causes of Discrimination*, addressed these misunderstandings about equal treatment. The bedrock requirement is 'equality in dignity', rather than 'material equality'.[36] Or, as it is usually put today, the State must have 'equal concern' or 'equal respect'

---

[34] International Save the Children Alliance, *Children's Rights: Equal Rights?* (London, International Save the Children Alliance, 2000), p. 26.

[35] UNICEF, *The Convention on the Rights of the Child: Human Rights Begin With Children's Rights* (UNICEF, undated [circa 2002]) (informational packet) (not paginated).

[36] *The Main Types and Causes of Discrimination*, o.c. (note 23), paras. 14, and 30.

for each human being, but not necessarily give 'equal treatment' or produce 'equal results' (or 'substantive equality') in all cases.[37]

64. In order to understand the functions of the right of non-discrimination, we must put the CRC promotional literature aside, and return to the concept of human dignity, and to the umbrella nature of Article 2(1). When we take this approach, we will find that Article 2(1) serves three interconnected functions: (i) the right of non-discrimination directly protects human dignity from assaults on the right-holder's humanity; (ii) it indirectly protects human dignity by being a 'trump' to racial, etc. politics; and (iii), the right of non-discrimination plays a socio-political function by affirming the moral norm that race, sex, religious, etc. discrimination is wrong.

4.2. Function One: Prevent Offences to Human Dignity

65. First of all, the right of non-discrimination directly protects human dignity. People are deeply offended when they are deprived of important things in life because of their race, sex, religious, etc. identification. (Indeed, they will be upset even if the discrimination pertains to something relatively minor, like being made to wait in a queue until the person standing behind them has been served.) This moral affront is recognized in numerous international agreements: Racial discrimination is an 'evil [...] perpetrated against the dignity of the human being', and 'a crime [...] against the conscience and dignity of mankind', in the words of the first World Conference against Racism;[38] and 'discrimination against women violates...respect for human dignity', as CEDAW puts it.[39] And similar things can be said about discriminating against people on the grounds of their religion, disability, and all of the other named characteristics in Common Articles 2.[40]

---

[37] Accord, L. Henkin, 'Introduction' in: L. Henkin, o.c. (note 7), p. 20.
[38] The World Conference to Combat Racism and Racial Discrimination, *Declaration* (UN Publ. Sales No. E.79.XIV.2, chap. II; *reprinted in* UN Doc. E/CN.4/1999/WG.1/BP.1, pp. 2, 3), fifteenth and ninth preambular paragraphs, respectively.
[39] CEDAW, seventh preambular paragraph.
[40] *E.g.*, Declaration on the Elimination of All Forms of Intolerance and of Discrimination Based on Religion or Belief, GA Res. 36/55 (1981), fourth preambular para. (religion is 'one of the fundamental elements in [a person's] conception of life'), and Article 3 (discrimination on the ground of religion 'constitutes an affront to human dignity and a disavowal of the principles of the Charter..., and shall be condemned as a violation of [...] human rights'); Convention on the Rights of Persons With Disabilities, preambular para. (f) (discrimination on the ground of disability 'is a violation of the inherent dignity and worth of the human person').

66. But while these formal documents have accurately articulated important moral sentiments, they cannot express the full range and depth of what the victims *feel* when they are discriminated against because of their race, sex, religion, and the other named grounds. Discrimination on these characteristics assaults the inner being or personhood of the individual in profound but inexpressible ways, and it is this sense of violation that international human rights law tries to capture by the notion of 'human dignity'. The right of non-discrimination has a protective function because it aims at stopping these assaults to dignity, whenever the enjoyment of other rights is at stake.

4.3. *Function Two: A Trump to Politics*

67. Secondly, the right of non-discrimination is a 'trump' on the political processes that would otherwise produce discriminatory laws, to use Professor Dworkin's famous metaphor.[41] The right of non-discrimination is an umbrella right that works in conjunction with the sectoral rights, and this raises an important question: 'Why isn't the sectoral right sufficient by itself?' The short answer is that lawmakers are often tempted to use discrimination as a tool for accomplishing policy goals, and the sectoral rights, standing on their own, cannot stop this. The sectoral rights need an anti-discrimination clause to protect them from the political processes. We will be devoting more attention to this topic than to most others because it is essential to fully appreciating the second, trumping function of Article 2(1).

68. The sectoral rights are highly 'vulnerable' to the political processes, but the root of the problem is usually overlooked in the human rights literature. The problem is that almost all human rights require the State to strike a balance between competing interests, and this is always a political judgment. Without some kind of non-discrimination clause, lawmakers would be free to use race, sex, etc. discrimination as a tool for governing society: 'The harm that the race, etc. discrimination in this law will do to the affected right-holders is reasonable in relation to the good that society will ultimately obtain, so we, the lawmakers, hereby adopt this law.' In one form or another, that is always the justification for state-imposed racial, etc. discrimination; the discrimination is always viewed as a reasonable

---

[41] R. Dworkin, *Taking Rights Seriously* (London, Duckworth, 1977), p. xi. The metaphor comes from the rules of card games where a designated card, say the ace of spades, will prevail over every other card.

means to a reasonable end. The right of non-discrimination in international human rights law is aimed at putting a block on the processes that result in these kinds of political decisions. As an umbrella right, Article 2(1) adds an extra layer of protection to the sectoral right: the State is free to make innumerable kinds of distinctions in the implementation of the sectoral rights, but there is one thing that it cannot do – the State cannot use race, sex, etc. discrimination, in the enjoyment of the sectoral rights, as a means for accomplishing political goals (in the absence of a valid reservation).

We need to fill in the sketch of the 'vulnerability' problem outlined in the preceding paragraph. The vulnerability of sectoral rights is built into the structure of international human rights law, and it lies at the root of most human rights controversies. While commentators sometimes acknowledge the need for balancing, there has not been a sufficient discussion of how the structure of international human rights law produces the vulnerability, and generates the conflicts.

69. There are two kinds of rights in the UN treaties: some are *context-dependent* rights, and some are *absolute* rights. The difference is the presence or absence of balancing decisions in the implementation of the right. Context-dependent rights always require trade-offs between competing interests, whereas absolute rights are concrete rules that are applied directly to real-life situations without any intermediate balancing decisions.

Context-Dependent Rights
70. Almost all human rights are context-dependent. For instance, freedom of expression is a context-dependent right. Article 13(1) of the CRC says that everyone under 18 years of age has 'the right to freedom of expression', and Article 13(2) says that the 'exercise of this right may be subject to certain restrictions', such as protecting the rights of other people, national security, morality, and public order. The scope of the freedom in the first paragraph is breathtaking, and it is matched by the equally expansive scope of permissible limitations.

Article 13 is actually made up of two competing principles: paragraph (1) says that young people can express themselves in any way that they like, without regard as to how it affects other people, and paragraph (2) says that they cannot, if other people will be adversely affected. What a youngster is actually entitled to enjoy in any real-life situation can only be determined by balancing the two opposing principles.

But since Article 13 contains two contradictory principles, *where exactly* is the right? Is it in paragraph (1), or in paragraph (2), or in the conjunction of the two together?

71. The most helpful way to look at the matter is to say that context-dependent rights exist at *two levels*: the abstract and the concrete. The *abstract level* of the right is the statement of the right as contained in the text of the treaty. Every youngster possesses the abstract right of free expression, as defined in the text of the Article 13(1): the youngster holds it at all times, in all places, and under all circumstances; the right is 'universal' – every CRC right-holder in the world holds the same abstract right.

A right cannot be exercised or enjoyed in the abstract, however; a right can only be exercised in concrete situations, which takes us to the next level. The *concrete level* of the right is what a person is actually entitled to enjoy in a real-life situation, and that legal entitlement is determined by a balancing of competing interests. For freedom of expression, this means the balancing of the two principles set out in paragraphs (1) and (2) of Article 13. The product of the balancing is the right at the concrete level.

72. Almost all CRC rights require balancing. For some of these rights, the balancing enters by way of a limitations clause (as in the freedom of expression example); for others, it enters by qualifying words or phrases, like, 'take all feasible measures' (Article 38(2), on participation in combat), or 'promote, where appropriate' (Article 21(e), on adoption). And for some rights, the balancing is a logical necessity of the right. (An absolute right to life in Article 6(1) would require the State to abolish all motor vehicles since these machines kill children; but that would result in the death of children because it would deprive them of ambulances, and it would bring the production and transport of food to a halt. An absolute right to life is therefore a self-contradictory notion; the right must be context-dependent.)

73. In order to 'implement' any of the context-dependent rights, State officials must 'translate' the abstract right into concrete entitlements, and they do this by making judgments about what constitutes a fair (or reasonable, just, appropriate) trade-off, taking all relevant factors into consideration. These balancing decisions are always subjective: among other things, decisions about trade-offs will depend upon opinions about the future consequences of the law, and, above all, they will hinge on value judgments.

Absolute Rights
74. By contrast, the hallmark of an absolute right is the absence of balancing: the statement of the right in the text of the treaty is applied directly to real-life situations without any intermediate decisions about trade-offs. Absolute rights can be said to exist at only one level: they are real trumps because they block balancing judgments. International human rights law

contains only a few absolute rights. Freedom from torture, a minor's right to be free from the death penalty, and freedom of religious belief (as distinct from practice) are examples of this rare species of right.[42]

A parenthetical note needs to be added here. One must be careful not to put too much weight on the word 'absolute'. 'Context-dependent' and 'absolute' are terms-of-art in a two-part classification scheme. Most importantly, this scheme does not take into account the possibility that a State could make a valid reservation, or that it could successfully invoke the doctrine of necessity in some extraordinary situation – two special cases in which the enjoyment of an 'absolute right' could be subject to balancing decisions.[43] In other words, 'absolute right' is not a claim that a UN treaty has set down a rule so fixed and final that it could never be modified at any time in the entire future course of human history, under any circumstance, to any degree. 'Absolute right' does not mean 'cosmic absoluteness'. In this taxonomy, an *absolute right* is a right that, when read in conjunction with the other sectoral rights and the umbrella provisions, is a concrete rule that admits to no intermediate balancing decisions; the validity of reservations, and the doctrine of necessity, entail other bodies of law, and are thus excluded from the classification scheme.[44]

75. Once one acknowledges that almost all human rights in the CRC and the two Covenants require balancing decisions, one comes face-to-face with the central features of international human rights law: (i) the treaties do not provide the test for determining what the correct trade-offs are when

---

[42] See, *e.g.*, W. A. Schabas, 'Public Opinion and the Death Penalty', in: P. Hodgkinson & W. A. Schabas (eds.), *Capital Punishment* (Cambridge, Cambridge Univ. Press, 2004), p. 326 (capturing the idea of a trump by saying that 'neither legislature or court may tamper with'); C. Tomuschat, *Human Rights: Between Idealism and Realism* (Oxford, Oxford Univ. Press, 2003), p. 44 (indirectly recognizing the trumping function of the right of non-discrimination in Article 2(2) of the CESCR).

[43] *E.g.*, International Court of Justice, *Legal Consequences of the Construction of a Wall in the Occupied Palestinian Territories*, No. 131, 2004, para. 135 (brief reference to necessity defence).

[44] The balancing metaphor is discussed further at No. 211.
A note on the 'universality v. relativism' controversy: Absolute rights, and the abstract level of context-dependent rights, are 'universal', in the sense that culture and other local particularities are irrelevant. But at the concrete level, context-dependent rights are not universal since they require consideration of particularities. But beware: all words have multiple meanings. Commentators who engage in the 'universality' debates typically shift to what are usually called 'natural rights'. The UN treaties create *legal rights*, and their content is determined by the rules of legal interpretation. But *natural rights* are philosophical (and often metaphysical, even quasi-spiritual) constructs, and their content is determined by the mind of the commentator who constructs them.

fulfilling the context-dependent rights; (ii) the 'correct' balance in a given case is a subjective opinion about fairness (reasonableness, proportionality, justice, or the like); (iii) each State Party, as a co-equal sovereign in the international community of States, has enormous latitude of discretion in deciding what is reasonable as it implements context-dependent rights; (iv) the State's sovereign exercise of discretion is not unlimited since it is subject to a system of international accountability (the treaty-monitoring bodies, the General Assembly, the Security Council, the special rapporteurs, and so forth); and (v) the accountability system is (very) weak, in comparison to the checks-and-balances that exist within the domestic systems of the States themselves.

In other words, the duty-bearer decides the scope of its own obligations at the concrete level where it matters most to individuals, subject to weak oversight by the international community. The very structure of international human rights law exposes the enjoyment of context-dependent rights to all of the dangers of the political processes within the State. And one of the gravest dangers is the risk of discrimination.

The Political Realities of Discrimination

76. When States enact discriminatory laws, they do so as a means for achieving policy objectives: race, sex, etc. discrimination is always a 'tool', a means to an end. Government officials nearly always frame the end-goal in attractive terms, like public order, development, homogeneity, diversity, or all-encompassing abstractions, like equity or social justice. The discrimination is thus justified as a means for promoting the welfare of society: officials say that the race, etc. discrimination is fair (just, reasonable, proportionate) in the light of those goals: the harm that the discrimination does to the individuals affected strikes a 'correct' balance with the good that the discrimination will eventually produce.

Whether or not the authorities actually use any particular discriminatory means to reach any particular objective will depend upon the political processes in the country concerned. People will have to fight battles in parliament and the courts to save themselves from state-imposed race, sex, etc. discrimination, and the battles will be never ending; if the pro-discrimination factions lose on one piece of legislation, they will try again on another. Unless there is a watertight anti-discrimination law.

77. The United Nations was created with the realities of discrimination in mind: without something to 'trump' the political processes, states *will* use race, sex, religious, etc. discrimination as a means for governing their

societies. The CERD 'is founded upon the lie that racial discrimination...can be *eliminated*',[45] writes Professor Michael Banton, one of its committee's most prominent members, and no doubt the same could be said about sex discrimination under CEDAW, or about the elimination of religious discrimination. The roots of discrimination lie in human nature and the human condition. Human beings are prone to dividing people into 'We' and 'the Other', and they can get deep psychological gratification in treating 'the Other' in inferior ways; due to human nature and the human condition, people find it hard to treat 'the Other' as they want themselves to be treated. Moreover, race, sex, etc. discrimination gives tremendous material advantages to members of the group being discriminated in favour of. And even 'people who believe discrimination to be wrong', writes Banton, 'do not always perceive differential treatment to be discrimination, and may think that particular circumstances constitute a justifiable exception, especially when their personal interests pull them in that direction'.[46] So the human urge to discriminate can never be eliminated, at best 'it can be reduced'.[47] States have always discriminated in the past, they are still doing it, and there is no reason to believe that they are going to stop doing it, unless non-discrimination becomes an absolute norm of international law.

78. The UN Charter took a major step in that direction by requiring Member States to respect human rights 'without distinction as to race, sex, language, or religion',[48] and the Members took even bolder steps by creating an individually-held right to be free from race, etc. discrimination in Common Articles 2, which they have supplemented with other treaties (like CERD and CEDAW), and with numerous other mechanisms. The right of non-discrimination, supported by these other tools in international law, serves a blocking function on national politics: State officials can (and must) make innumerable political judgments as they turn the ideals of 'human rights' into concrete enjoyments, but there is one thing they cannot do (in the absence of a valid reservation): they cannot discriminate against people on the grounds of their race, sex, religion, etc. as a means for attaining

---

[45] M. Banton, *International Action Against Racial Discrimination* (Oxford, Clarendon Press, 1996), p. 50.

[46] M. Banton, *Discrimination* (Buckingham/Philadelphia, Open Univ. Press, 1994), p. 36; also, Danish Institute for Human Rights, *Satellite meeting report* [World Conference Against Racism], (UN Doc. A/CONF.189/PC.2/Misc.1, 17 May 2001), p. 3 ('[W]e (almost) all agree in principle that discrimination is wrong, but we fail to connect this liberal, well-intending attitude with practices happening before our very eyes').

[47] M. Banton, *International Action*, o.c. (note 45), p. 50.

[48] Article 1(3) of the UN Charter, o.c. (note 2).

political objectives, if the differential treatment will impair a right-holder's enjoyment of a sectoral right. In short, the second function of the right of non-discrimination is to put a wall around the sectoral rights, protecting them from the political processes.

4.4. Function Three: Affirm the Moral Norm of Non-Discrimination

79. The third function of Common Articles 2 lies in the social-political domain: the right of non-discrimination affirms the ethical norm that race, sex, religious, etc. discrimination is morally wrong, a serious offence to human dignity.

Domestic legislation often serves this same socio-political function. When legislators turn an ethical norm into a legal right, the law *expresses* a moral value. When people can enforce the law through formal channels like courts, or through informal methods of social control, then society provides a means for rights to be *vindicated*. And all the informal and formal mechanisms work together to *transmit* the norms throughout society.

The right of non-discrimination in international law functions in similar ways. Common Articles 2 *express* the moral principle that it is wrong for the State to deprive people of important things because of their race, sex, religion, etc.[49] In addition, international human rights law requires States to transform human rights into enforceable legal entitlements, and to provide meaningful avenues of redress; when States do this in respect to Common Articles 2, they *vindicate* the moral norm. Moreover, each State is obligated 'to make the principles and provisions' of human rights law 'widely known' (Article 42), and when it does this for the right of non-discrimination, especially when it has also enacted anti-discrimination legislation, the moral principle of non-discrimination is *transmitted* throughout society.

80. In conclusion, Article 2(1) protects human dignity in three interconnected ways: (i) the right of non-discrimination directly protects human dignity by forbidding the State to make adverse distinctions between young people based on their race, sex, religion, etc., in all areas of life protected by the sectoral rights; (ii) the right to be free from discrimination indirectly protects human dignity by blocking actors who want to use adverse race, etc. distinctions in the enjoyment of sectoral rights as a means for achieving political objectives; and (iii), the right of non-discrimination helps express, vindicate,

---

[49] *E.g.*, C. Doebbler, *Introduction to International Human Rights Law* (Washington, DC, CD Publ., 2006), pp. 15, 26 (human rights express values).

and transmit the ethical norm that race, sex, religious, etc. discrimination is morally wrong. But if there were no right of non-discrimination, people would be at the mercy of all the things in human nature and the human condition that give rise to state-imposed race, sex, etc. discrimination.[50]

5. *Freedom from Discrimination Is an Absolute Right*

81. Since the rights in the UN human rights treaties are either absolute or context-dependent, which kind of right is Article 2(1)? Does it allow trade-off decisions? If it does, then a State can deprive young people of their rights because of their race, sex, religion, etc., subject to some sort of a balancing test. Or does Article 2(1) forbid balancing? In that case it is an absolute right. We have to conduct a legal interpretation under the Vienna Convention to determine which kind of right Article 2(1) is, reading the words of the CRC within their context, and in the light of how the right functions to promote the objectives of the CRC.

82. This commentary concludes that the right of non-discrimination is an absolute right. There are four considerations that support this interpretation.

The first consideration is that Article 2(1) has only three elements, and none of these contains a balancing test: (i) if a State treats a child or adolescent differently on account of race, sex, etc., (ii) and if that treatment harms the youngster's interests, and (iii) if those interests are protected by a sectoral right, then the action is unlawful under international law (provided that the State has not made a valid reservation). Article 2(1) would have to contain a fourth element in order to allow a State to engage in race, etc. discrimination, subject to some sort of a balancing test. The balancing element could be framed as a loose test – like, 'without *unreasonable* (or *disproportionate, inappropriate,* etc.) discrimination' –, or as a tough test – such as, 'without any discrimination . . . *unless necessary to save the life of the nation*' –, or it could be something in between. Article 2(1) does not contain

---

[50] While *The Main Types and Causes of Discrimination, o.c.* (note 23), does not expressly frame the prohibition of discrimination in terms of purposes, it clearly reflects the three functions identified in the main text: (i) to protect human dignity, paras. 11–14, 30–32; (ii) to prevent discrimination from arising by curtailing the underlying processes, *e.g.,* paras. 17–29 (psychosocial), 93 ('economic interests'), 94 ('group conformism'), 95 ('customs'), 98 ('vicious circle'); and (iii) to affirm-transmit-vindicate the moral norm, para. 140.

any such balancing element, however, and this leads to just one conclusion: the General Assembly intended Article 2(1) to be an absolute right.

83. To fully appreciate the wording of Article 2(1), we have to read it in its entire context. UN lawmakers are careful to ensure that the texts of human rights treaties indicate when a right is context-dependent. Altogether, the General Assembly employs *seven drafting devices* to subject rights to trade-off decisions.

Four of these devices are inserted directly into the article that defines the right. *Device (1): Balancing words.* Some sectoral rights are expressly qualified by balancing words, like 'appropriate' and 'feasible'.[51] *Device (2): Tailor-made exception.* Some rights allow balancing within a specified range of situations, such as, 'in accordance with their national laws', 'due regard [...] to the desirability of', and 'save in exceptional circumstances'.[52] *Device (3): Public-welfare override clause.* This clause allows the State to restrict the enjoyment of various 'civil and political rights' in order to protect other persons, and society as a whole. This is the device used to qualify freedom of expression, as we saw earlier. *Device (4): Words of aspiration.* Some rights are defined in terms of goals to strive towards, rather than here-and-now entitlements, as indicated by words like 'promote' and 'encourage'.[53]

There are also three kinds of balancing devices placed in the umbrella articles, thus qualifying the sectoral rights that they attach to: *Device (5): Umbrella progressive clause.* All of the so-called economic, social, and cultural rights are 'progressive rights' because an umbrella clause makes the right-holder's concrete entitlements dependent upon the State's resource capabilities.[54] To fulfil this category of sectoral rights, the State must ration finite social goods, and this calls for trade-off decisions. *Device (6): Umbrella public-welfare clause.* The CESCR has an umbrella clause that allows the State to put limitations on the sectoral rights 'for the purpose of promoting the general welfare'.[55] And finally, *Device (7): Umbrella national-emergency*

---

[51] Articles 2(2) and 28(2) of the CRC, respectively.
[52] Articles 20(2), 20(3), and 37(c) of the CRC, respectively.
[53] Articles 23(4) and 28(1)(b) of the CRC, respectively.
[54] Article 4 of the CRC, and Article 2(1) of the CESCR.
[55] Article 4 of the CESCR, in Part II, qualifying the sectoral rights in Part III.
The General Assembly did not recognize any absolute rights when it adopted the Universal Declaration, since Article 29(2) of the UDHR allows a public-welfare override of all rights, including freedom from discrimination and freedom from torture. This should not cause alarm, however, since the Universal Declaration was not intended to be legally binding, but was, in a manner of speaking, the warm-up exercise for the creation of the legally binding Covenants.

clause. The CCPR has an umbrella clause that allows most sectoral rights to be overridden during 'a public emergency that threatens the life of the nation'. The derogation clause also permits the State to suspend the right of non-discrimination with respect to five otherwise forbidden grounds of differentiation (political or other opinion, national origin, birth, property, and on the grounds added pursuant to the 'or other status' clause); but it can do this only when it is essential to saving the nation, and it must inform the United Nations of its derogations so that all of the accountability mechanisms can monitor the situation.[56]

These seven drafting devices all have the same function: the text itself tells us that the right is not a concrete rule that can be applied directly to a real-life situation without an intermediate balancing judgment: the lawmakers have expressly defined the right as context-dependent. Whenever we find one of these qualifying devices, we will have to add a separate balancing element when we break the right down into its component parts.

84. Now let us read the text of Article 2(1) in its full context. Given the meticulous attention that the General Assembly has paid to the drafting of human rights treaties, the absence of any of the seven balancing devices to qualify the right of non-discrimination points in just one direction: the General Assembly did not want to subject children and adolescents to adverse distinctions based on their race, sex, etc., if such action would impair their enjoyment of a sectoral right. When read in the light of the standard drafting practices, the text tells us that the lawmakers chose not to add a fourth element: Article 2(1) is an absolute prohibition.

85. The second consideration pertains to the purposes of Article 2(1) in relation to the purpose of the Convention. Treating Article 2(1) as an absolute right fulfils the three functions of the right of non-discrimination, and the overall objective of respecting the human dignity of each and every young person under the age of 18. Treating it as context-dependent, however, would defeat the three purposes of the right of non-discrimination, allowing race, etc. discrimination pursuant to some sort of a reasonableness test. Moreover, allowing a Party to use race, sex, religious, etc. discrimination as

---

[56] Article 4 of the CCPR, in Part II, allowing national emergency derogations of most sectoral rights in Part III, and of Article 2(1) on that limited set of grounds. According to S. Joseph, J. Schultz and M. Castan, *The International Covenant on Civil and Political Rights: Cases, Materials, and Commentary* (2nd ed., Oxford, Oxford Univ. Press, 2004), 'article 2(1) seems to allow no exceptions'; p. 9. That is true when Article 2(1) is read in isolation, and it is always true for race, sex, religious and language discrimination, even in Article 4 emergencies.

a tool for achieving political goals would rob boys and girls of the 'special care and assistance' that they need in their most vulnerable years, as they develop physically, mentally, morally, and socially (CRC, fourth preambular paragraph).

86. The third consideration is the need to make the CRC consistent with international law. Reading Article 2(1) as a context-dependent right would allow a State Party to act contrary to the purposes of the United Nations: ensuring that every State respects the human rights of 'all [including children and adolescents] without distinction as to race, sex, language, or religion'.[57] It would also conflict with the CESCR's prohibition of race, sex, etc. discrimination as the State goes about realizing progressive rights.[58] And it would conflict with the CCPR's absolute prohibition of discrimination on the grounds of race, sex, language, religion, and social origin, so absolute that the State cannot try to justify the discrimination by an appeal to 'saving the life of the nation'.[59]

The United Nations' position on racial discrimination is especially relevant to our analysis. The General Assembly has declared that 'there is no justification for racial discrimination, in theory or in practice, anywhere';[60] the prohibition of racial discrimination is widely considered a peremptory

---

[57] Article 1(3) of the UN Charter, o.c. (note 2).

The legislative records allow us to confirm the inference in the main text. While some States made vigorous efforts to insert a balancing device in Article 2(2) of the CESCR, other States successfully resisted, arguing that a relaxation of the prohibition would be contrary to the Charter. There were five references to the Charter in two meetings of the Third Committee alone (the 658th and 659th), for instance, showing its importance as a common reference point for all sides of the debates; see, *e.g.*, *Travaux Préparatoires* (UN Doc. A/C.3/SR.659, 1955), para. 35 (Costa Rica) (Article 2 without a balancing device is 'in harmony with the Charter'). Moreover, all sides treated Article 2(2) as an absolute prohibition; see, *e.g.*, (UN Doc. A/C.3/SR.657, 1955), para. 14 (Lebanon) (Article 2(2) 'could not be conditional'); see also, para. 15 (El Salvador); (UN Doc. A/C.3/SR.658, 1955), para. 22 (Egypt); para. 31 (China); para. 37 (Australia); (UN Doc. A/C.3/SR.659, 1955), para. 28 (Mexico), para. 34 (Turkey), para. 35 (Costa Rica), para. 38 (Dominican Republic).

[58] Discriminatory allocations are not permitted under the umbrella progressive clause of Article 2(1) of the CESCR, which is similar to Article 4 of the CRC; CESCR Comm., *Gen. Com. No. 13: The Right to Education* (1999) (UN Doc. HRI/GEN/1/Rev.8, 2006), para. 31 ('The prohibition against discrimination enshrined in article 2(2) of the Covenant is subject to neither progressive realization nor the availability of resources; it applies fully and immediately to all aspects of education and encompasses all internationally prohibited grounds of discrimination'.)

[59] Article 4 of the CCPR; see HRC, *Gen. Com. No. 29: Article 4: Derogations* (2001) (UN Doc. HRI/GEN/1/Rev.8, 2006), para. 8.

[60] CERD, sixth preambular paragraph (incorporating the Declaration on the Elimination of All Forms of Racial Discrimination, fifth preambular paragraph).

norm of international law;[61] and, when South Africa tried to invoke the principle of proportionality in its defence of apartheid in South West Africa, the International Court of Justice rejected the argument: racial discrimination 'is a flagrant violation of the purposes and principles of the Charter'.[62]

Treating the right of non-discrimination as context-dependent would make Article 2(1) a type of derogation clause in respect to the international ban on racial discrimination. On the other hand, treating Article 2(1) as an absolute right raises sex, religious, etc. discrimination to a level of protection similar to that of racial discrimination.[63]

87. The fourth consideration is the process of elimination. The right of non-discrimination is either context-dependent or absolute. If it were context-dependent, then, as an umbrella right that covers *all* of the sectoral rights, the State could use distinctions based on political belief, religion, race, etc., to deprive people of the enjoyment of the right not to be tortured, and the right of minors to be free from capital punishment, and so forth. So there would be no absolute rights at all – *everything* would be subject to balancing. Since that is unacceptable, we are left with the alternative: the right is absolute.[64]

88. All four considerations lead to the same conclusion: the CRC's right of non-discrimination is an absolute right. We are not finished with the analysis, however, because the Vienna Convention on the Law of Treaties contains a test for judging the validity of a conclusion arrived at under the

---

[61] *Report of the International Law Commission: Fifty-third session* (UN Doc. A/56/10, Supp. 10, 2001), p. 208. Under Article 53 of the VCLT, a treaty is void if it 'conflicts with a peremptory norm'.

[62] International Court of Justice, *Namibia (South West Africa) Case (Advisory opinion)*, I.C.J. Rep. 1971, para. 131.

[63] While this section has used the legislative records for the UDHR and the Covenants to confirm the conclusions from the ordinary meaning rule, the only relevant material from the records for the CRC is the desire for consistency with the other treaties. *Travaux Préparatoires* (UN Doc. E/CN.4/L.1575, 1981), para. 43 ('bring the formulation…more closely into line' with the corresponding articles in the other treaties); (UN Doc. E/CN.4/1989/48, 1989), para. 148 ('make the text consistent with' the earlier treaties); *reproduced in* Office of the United Nations High Commissioner for Human Rights, *Legislative History of the Convention on the Rights of the Child* (New York/Geneva, United Nations, 2007), pp. 321, 332. The *Legislative History* is available on-line at www.ohchr.org. Also in S. Detrick (ed.), *The United Nations Convention on the Rights of the Child: A Guide to the "Travaux Préparatoires"* (Dordrecht/Boston/London, Martinus Nijhoff Publ., 1992).

[64] *The Main Types and Causes of Discrimination, o.c.* (note 23), does not recognize any situation that justifies state-imposed race, sex, etc. discrimination, either as a means to combat discrimination, *e.g.*, paras. 17, 138–156; or to protect minorities, paras. 6–10; or to promote social justice, *e.g.*, paras. 86 (for women), 99–137 (for any segment of society).

ordinary meaning rule: the interpretation must not be 'manifestly absurd or unreasonable'.[65] If our interpretation of Article 2(1) fails that test, we must reject it, and start all over again. (This is when the fallback rule, the legislative history rule, would come into play: if the ordinary meaning rule fails to yield a coherent result, then, and only then, can the interpreter use the negotiating records – the *travaux préparatoires* – to try to determine the lawmakers' intentions.) So we must apply the test to our interpretation: Is it *absurd* to demand that a State Party never intentionally deprive an adolescent or child of the enjoyment of a CRC right because of that youngster's race, sex, religion, or other named characteristic? Is an absolute prohibition *manifestly* absurd?

89. An ordinary citizen may very well say, 'Yes. There could be historical, cultural, or other situations in a country that could justify an exception to the right of non-discrimination on some particular ground, in regard to various rights. A categorical prohibition would deprive states of the flexibility that they may need to respond to these special situations.'

That answer is not really a rejection of Article 2(1) being absolute, but an argument against the idea of there being any absolute rights at all. People have 'justified' torture, the execution of minors, and punishing people for their religious beliefs, for instance, by the same plea of 'special circumstances' and 'necessity'.

More importantly, the answer overlooks the fact that 'absolute right' is a term-of-art; interpreting Article 2(1) as 'absolutely' forbidding race, etc. discrimination does not preclude a State from making a reservation (under Article 51). If a particular State is facing a special set of circumstances, and if it formulates a reservation that is tailored to address those problems, while leaving the rest of the right intact, then the law on reservations provides the necessary flexibility. Furthermore, an absolute right does not preclude the doctrine of necessity being applied in a truly extraordinary situation.

In the light of these two safety valves – reservations and the necessity defence – it is not manifestly absurd to say that the CRC categorically forbids the State Party from practicing race, sex, discrimination against children and adolescents.[66]

---

[65] Article 32 of the VCLT, quoted in full, *o.c.* (note 19).

[66] The legislative records also confirm the point about reservations. While States sometimes boasted that there is no discrimination in their countries, there were times when they candidly admitted that an absolute prohibition in Article 2(2) of the CESCR would cause them problems, particularly in regard to the kinds of sex discrimination against women in employment that was lawful under their domestic laws. But no balancing device was inserted into

90. One final note before we conclude this section. Our legal analysis did not consider any arguments in support of reading Article 2(1) as context-dependent. There is a simple explanation for this. The research for this commentary found no author who has put forward a legal argument for interpreting Article 2(1), or its counterparts in the two Covenants, as having a balancing element.[67]

6. Justiciability

91. The three elements of Article 2(1) are also the basis for solving the justiciability question. 'Justiciable' is legalese for the authority of judges to use a right in some particular legal source as a direct basis for invalidating or upholding a state law, and the source could be either a national law or a treaty. At the heart of the question is the political issue of allowing judges to make balancing decisions on political or policy matters. For instance, modern constitutions contain a number of so-called civil and political rights, like freedom of expression. Generally speaking, these legal systems allow judges to make the final balancing decisions in translating the abstract right of expression into concrete entitlements, thus overriding the policy judgements of the legislature. Some constitutions also recognize a number of so-called economic, social and cultural rights, like health and social security. And generally speaking, most of these legal systems do not permit state court judges to make the balancing decisions for most aspects of these

---

Article 2(2): the remedy for such problems is the right to make reservations. *E.g., Travaux Préparatoires* (UN Doc. A/C.3/SR.657, 1955), para. 14 (Lebanon) (weakening Article 2(2) is 'inadmissible' since 'individual cases' can be 'covered by means of specific reservations').

  The brilliant study, S. Bunn-Livingstone, *Juricultural Pluralism vis-à-vis Treaty Law* (The Hague/Boston, Martinus Nijhoff Publ., 2002), demonstrates how reservations play a vital role in the creation and ratification of treaties by accommodating the needs of a diverse world.

  [67] This is not to say that all commentators treat the right of non-discrimination as absolute; indeed, many do not. But one cannot engage in legal discourse with a commentator who has not presented a line of legal reasoning. For instance, Manfred Nowak says, '[CCPR] Art. 2(1) prohibits every distinction on the basis of the above-mentioned criteria...[I]n ensuring the rights of the Covenant, States may not differentiate among their sovereign subjects on the basis of certain personal qualities.' But on the next page, at eye level with that passage, he says just the opposite: 'distinctions on the basis of race or sex may be permissible when they can be justified with objective and reasonable criteria. A determination can be made only on a case-by-case basis and is ultimately dependent on value judgments....' M. Nowak, *CCPR Commentary, o.c.* (note 8), pp. 45–46 (first quotation), and p. 47 (second quotation). Nowak gives no explanation of how the absolute right on the left-hand page turned into a context-dependent right on the right-hand page.

rights, since they depend upon complex administrative systems that have to be built up and maintained over long stretches of time, and that require innumerable, and continuing, trade-off decisions about the redistribution of wealth in society. These constitutional rights are sometimes called 'programmatic rights' to indicate that they are not legal entitlements that can be enforced in court; parliament must make the policy decisions that translate them into judicially enforceable entitlements. Plaintiffs can bring cases directly on the entitlements contained in legislation, and sometimes upon constitutional guarantees of procedural fairness, but not directly upon the abstract 'programmatic' rights in the constitution; these rights are not justiciable.

When it comes to the justiciability of human rights in international law, each jurisdiction creates its own rules for when a court can directly use a right in a UN treaty as a basis for a ruling. Here, too, the ultimate concern is the proper allocation of authority for making policy decisions.

The right of non-discrimination does not contain any balancing element, so the concerns about the allocation of authority have been removed. The political organs have already made the policy decisions about freedom from discrimination when they ratified the treaty, including their decisions about reservations. When Article 2(1) is an absolute obligation (*i.e.*, when there is no valid reservation or necessity defence), there are no political judgments for the courts to make in applying the right to actual cases, and thus no intrusions on the policy-making prerogatives of the other branches. The right to be free from race, sex, etc. discrimination, as with all absolute rights, should be considered justiciable in every legal system.

92. While this brings to a close our legal analysis of the elements, there are a number of topics that still need discussing in order to avoid confusion when applying Article 2(1) to real-life situations. For one thing, there are three concepts that are indispensable to implementing the right of non-discrimination (discussed in the next section), and for another, there are several terms and concepts in the legal literature that are frequent sources of confusion (as we will see in section 8).

7. The Key Concepts Pertaining to Discrimination

93. People tend to make too much of the right of non-discrimination, while simultaneously making too little of it. One way that they make too much of it is by denouncing a statistical disparity as 'discrimination' without

bothering to find out the causes of the imbalance. Walk into a science class, and one might see a handful of girls in a room full of boys. 'Sex discrimination!' someone exclaims. But is discrimination really the explanation? Visit a juvenile court, and all the people in handcuffs are boys, with no girl in sight. 'Sex discrimination!' But is that really so?

We cannot know the cause of an event by looking only at the event itself; we have to go upstream in the causal chain to identify the thing or things that have caused the event to happen. A statistical disparity is a complex collection of events; the presence of each boy in the courtroom, the presence of each girl in some place other than the science class, is an event with its own antecedent chain of causes. So as with any complex sociological phenomenon, one has to speak in the plural about 'causes' of a statistical disparity, and one has to make generalizations about the relative frequencies of each of the multiple causes. 'This research study found that ten per cent of the imbalance is due to sex discrimination, and the rest is caused by the following...,' for instance.

94. In order to analyse the multiple causes of disparities, one needs to have a set of conceptual tools pertaining to discrimination that can be applied across the board. There are three concepts that are particularly important: (i) the phrase 'an act of discrimination' is a shorthand expression for a sequence of acts; (ii) the paired concepts of 'overt discrimination' and 'covert discrimination'; and (iii) the paired concepts of '*de jure* discrimination' and '*de facto* discrimination'.

7.1. 'An act of discrimination' Is a Shorthand Expression

95. Whenever we are looking for 'an act of discrimination', it is important not to take the phrase literally. Element (1) of the right of non-discrimination speaks of 'treating the right-holder differently from another person': the actor treats A one way and B another way, depending on the race (or sex, etc.) of each person. So there are two actions, not just one. Moreover, each treatment is a part of a sequence of acts. And finally, discrimination always begins in a 'mental event': the actor perceives people as belonging to either a Group A or a Group B, and then assigns different levels of valuation to the well-being of the two groups.

For instance, parliament passes a law that gives fee waivers to non-Muslims living in poverty. The law comes into effect at a specified date in the future. The law is printed and distributed to all the ministries and to the public. The enrolment officials are instructed on how to implement the law. And then, when Ahmed's mother requests a waiver, a particular state employee tells her 'No.' The state's 'treatment of Ahmed' is all of those things taken together. Looking only at parliament's adoption of the law will give us an incomplete analysis because the act of voting 'Yes' did not actually do anything to Ahmed. And if we look only at the last event in the chain, the action that impacted him, then we will fail to see that the employee who denied the waiver was not acting alone, but in obedience to a chain of orders that ultimately traces back to that fateful Yes-vote in parliament. In Ahmed's case, we say the state is the actor that committed the religious discrimination, not the enrolment officer personally, and the entire chain of events – from the passage of the law to its implementation against Ahmed – is one sociological event, one 'act of discrimination'. And the state's differential treatment of Ahmed began in the legislators' mental act of dividing people into 'Muslim' and 'Non-Muslim', and valuing the well-being of Muslim children less than that of other children.

In a different scenario, a state employee might commit discrimination acting on personal initiative, in defiance of the law. Let us say that a waiver law is based solely on need, but the officer rejects a girl's application because she is a girl, in violation of the fee-waiver rules and the state's anti-discrimination legislation. In this case, the 'act of discrimination' is not a sequence of actions working their way down the chain the command, but the actions of one person – the enrolment officer's own differential treatment of girls and boys. We hold this employee personally accountable as the actor who committed the discrimination, and we hold the state liable, not because it committed the discrimination, but because the state is responsible for how its agents exercise their delegated authority, even when the agents violate the law.

96. The point is that 'an act of discrimination' is a shorthand expression that can be used for both simple and complex scenarios when applying Article 2(1). When we find a state employee allocating a finite resource or a sphere of liberty on a discriminatory basis (as shown in Figure 2), we will often have to investigate the situation before we can determine where in the government hierarchy the causal chain begins, and thus decide which behaviours go together to constitute 'the act of discrimination'.

7.2. 'Overt Discrimination' and 'Covert Discrimination'

97. Commentators often speak of 'forms' of discrimination, but unfortunately most of the 'forms' that they have come up with actually interfere

with the analysis (as we will see in section 8). Of all the ways to talk about 'forms', there are two pairs of concepts that are essential for applying anti-discrimination laws in situations of statistical disparities: 'overt and covert' discrimination, and '*de jure* and *de facto*' discrimination.

98. *Overt discrimination* is where the differential treatment is expressly mandated in the law. The discrimination is 'overt' because it is open, or readily seen: the discrimination is said to exist 'on the face' of the statute or regulation. (A law that says, 'School fees can be waived on the basis of financial need for all students except Muslims,' is overt religious discrimination, for example.)

99. *Covert* means 'hidden', and *covert discrimination* occurs when lawmakers write a neutral-looking law with the aim to either give an advantage to a particular Group *A*, or impose a disadvantage on a particular Group *B*. When a covertly discriminatory law produces a differential impact on racial, etc. groups, the statistical imbalance is not an accidental by-product of a measure aimed at some other objective: the lawmakers *design* the law so that it will produce the differential impact, and they *hide* that intention behind innocent-looking language. Covert discrimination is therefore a double evil: there is the moral wrong of the race, etc. discrimination, and the moral wrong of the deception, of trying to hide one's wrongful intentions behind the facade of a 'facially-neutral' law.

The concept of covert discrimination entered American law many years ago in the battles over racial equality. For instance, national law would require states to give the right to vote to people of all races, but state officials in some localities would then impose a literacy test with the aim of depriving Negroes (African Americans) of political power. The local laws hurt poor people of all races as they were written in race-neutral language, but since a large percentage of the black population lived in poverty, the laws had the effect of keeping one race politically subjugated to the other. And since the lawmakers intended that effect, the entire sequence – from the decision to impose literacy tests to the actions of the voter-registration officers – constituted an act of covert discrimination. Fortunately, these attempts to circumvent national law did not succeed. The courts had no difficulty striking them down as acts of racial discrimination, and legal action was so swift and sure that covert discrimination did not become a major problem in the overall struggle for racial justice.

Because covert discrimination is a form of discrimination, it comes under the scope of Common Articles 2. An actor who designs a facially-neutral law in order to produce a differential impact on members of a targeted race (or sex, etc.) is treating people differently on the basis of group membership, which satisfies Element (1). And Element (2) is satisfied because the impact is detrimental to members of the targeted group.

100. While covert discrimination is well established as a legal concept in American law, the situation is different in Europe. The terms 'overt' and 'covert' appear occasionally in discussions about discrimination in the European literature and in UN documents, but commentators usually do not define the terms, and it can be difficult to deduce an author's precise meaning. In some respects this lack of clarity is not a problem. When one examines court cases in Europe and North America, or looks at empirical studies on race and sex discrimination in the governmental and private sectors, covert discrimination is seldom an issue, or at least not a serious issue. And since covert discrimination is not a widespread problem, there is no need for conceptual clarity to resolve most discrimination cases. Nevertheless, the conceptual difference between overt and covert discrimination is fundamental to understanding and applying anti-discrimination law in situations of statistical disparities, and the failure to have the concepts clearly in mind leads to serious problems, as we will see later.

7.3. 'De Jure *Discrimination' and* 'De Facto *Discrimination'*

101. The other important way to classify discrimination is the paired concepts '*de jure* discrimination' and '*de facto* discrimination'. *De jure discrimination* refers to differential treatment that is imposed by law. (Overt and covert discrimination are the two ways that a State engages in *de jure* discrimination.) By contrast, *de facto discrimination* occurs when state agents practice discrimination on their own initiative, rather than in obedience to a law, acting either voluntarily or as a result of work or social pressures. The term is not used for individual instances of discrimination, but for a pattern of discrimination that is wide enough to produce a statistical disparity between groups, in a manner analogous to the imbalances that are produced by *de jure* discrimination. Ahmed's case illustrates *de jure* discrimination since the enrolment officer is applying a law that dictates the differential treatment of Muslims. But if a law gives fee waivers to all students on the basis of financial need, and government employees are routinely denying waivers to members of a particular religious, racial, etc. group in disobedience to the law, then it would be *de facto* discrimination.

There can be a number of scenarios lying behind *de facto* discrimination. The discrimination could be the initiative of the employees who are doing the face-to-face allocating of social goods, in defiance of the law and their supervisors' orders. Or the initiative could come from lower-level department heads that order or pressure subordinates to discriminate. Or the initiative could come from the mid-level or even the highest reaches of the state hierarchy. In all of these situations, the end result is a disparity between racial (etc.) groups in the enjoyment of the social good in question. And all of these scenarios will come under Common Articles 2: the impairment that each right-holder suffers – which collectively add up to the statistical imbalance – is caused by an act of discrimination; the discrimination is *de facto* because the causal chain does not begin in a written law; and the State is responsible, since it is always liable for the conduct of its agents.

102. Figure 3 shows the two main ways to classify acts of discrimination. The large rectangle contains all acts of State discrimination, with overt discrimination represented by area x, and covert discrimination by area y. *De jure* discrimination is x and y together, and *de facto* discrimination is area z.

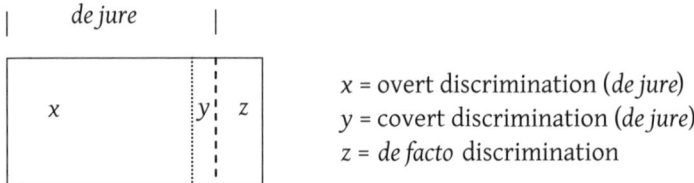

x = overt discrimination (*de jure*)
y = covert discrimination (*de jure*)
z = *de facto* discrimination

Figure 3. Main forms of discrimination

These forms of discrimination all concern Element (1). 'Overt and covert' and '*de facto* and *de jure*' describe ways that a State can treat people differently on the basis of their race, sex, etc. (And Element (2) pertains to the individuals who are hurt by that differential treatment.)

103. So far this commentary has concentrated on defining what the right of non-discrimination is; another way to understand the content of Article 2(1) is to identify what the right is not. In the next section, we will examine the main sources of confusion about freedom from race, etc. discrimination under international human rights law.

8. *The Main Sources of Confusion about the Right of Non-Discrimination*

104. This section will look at seven of the most frequent causes of confusion about Common Articles 2: (i) shifting from a *right* of non-discrimination to a *principle* of non-discrimination; (ii) shifting from the right of *non-*

discrimination to the principle of *proportionality*; (iii) confusing international human rights law with European regional law; (iv) the CRC Committee's shifting from 'rights' to the 'four general principles'; (v) trying to fit the doctrine of 'direct discrimination and indirect discrimination' into Common Articles 2; (vi) the *purpose or effect* clause that is found in some definitions of 'discrimination'; and (vii) allowing 'affirmative action' and other buzz words to obscure the realities of race, etc. discrimination.

8.1. *The* Right *of Non-Discrimination v. The* Principle *of Non-Discrimination*

105. When talking about the CRC and the two Covenants, commentators frequently shift from the right of non-discrimination to 'the principle of non-discrimination'. Unfortunately, this undermines Common Articles 2 in a number of ways.

106. First of all, replacing the language of 'rights' with the language of 'principles' defeats the fundamental aim of the international human rights movement – to get people to believe that every human being on the face of the Earth, including the youngest child, is a right-holder of internationally recognized human rights. (We have the 'Convention on the *Rights of* the Child,' not the 'Convention on *Principles Concerning* Children.')

107. The second problem pertains to the difference between a *moral principle* and a *legal right.* Many laws have their origins in moral principles. For example, the moral principle that race, sex, etc. discrimination is wrong was the basis for the General Assembly to create a right of non-discrimination in international law; and, as we have seen, the third function of this right is to express, vindicate, and transmit that moral principle. But the legal right, and the moral principle that gave rise to the right, are two different things. So the second problem with 'the principle of non-discrimination' is that it makes the legal right disappear.

108. The third problem pertains to the difference between two kinds of rights: some rights are *legal rules*, and some rights are *legal principles.* As Ronald Dworkin explains in *Taking Rights Seriously*, a legal rule is a concrete 'do or don't' that controls behaviour. A legal principle, on the other hand, is only a guide to behaviour.[68] A principle is a generalization about what should or should not be done; as another commentator has put it, 'a legal principle [...] is the expression of a meta-value which the law-giving community wishes to

---

[68] Dworkin, *o.c.* (note 41), pp. 22–28.

observe, but its abstract formulation does not order a *specific* conduct for its implementation'.[69] The fact that a principle is a generalization means that there can be exceptions. However, the generalization will not specify the concrete circumstances that will justify acting contrary to the principle; the principle leaves the exceptions unspecified. That is the opposite of a legal rule, which orders a specific action, unimpeded by considerations of the particularities of each situation, unless there is another rule to cover the special cases. Thus, the prohibition against under-age military recruitment is a rule (in Article 38(3)) – a concrete don't –, while freedom of expression is a generalized statement (in Article 13(1)) – a principle that has to be balanced against other principles.

In the field of international law, we can speak of a moral principle of 'no torture': 'It is wrong for a State to inflict severe pain on people for the purpose of obtaining confessions, or for achieving any other objective.' And we can speak about a moral principle of non-discrimination: 'It is wrong for a State to treat people in an inferior way on the ground of their race, sex, etc. classification.' These are important principles, without a doubt, but, as principles, they inherently admit to unspecified exceptions. By contrast, freedom from torture and freedom from race, etc. discrimination are legal *rules*: they are *concrete* commands, not mere guides that are subject to unspoken exceptions; they are *absolute* commands; and they are absolute *human rights* – absolute legal entitlements held by every human being under international law.

109. Shifting from the right of non-discrimination to 'the principle of non-discrimination' has an important psychological effect on perceptions about the content of Common Articles 2. This commentary has argued that the right of non-discrimination in the CRC and the Covenants is an absolute right – a concrete rule that is applied directly to real-life situations without any intermediate balancing decisions –, and it has laid out several pages of legal reasoning to support that conclusion. By shifting from a legal right to a (legal or a moral) principle, an author can induce people to believe that the right of non-discrimination allows States to practice race, sex, etc. discrimination. And the author does not need to give any legal arguments to achieve this perception, simply because the word *principle* contains the idea of exceptions. A small change in language – replacing 'right' with 'prin-

---

[69] K. Zemanek, 'Basic Principles of UN Charter Law', in: R. St. John Macdonald & D. M. Johnston (eds.), *Towards World Constitutionalism* (Leiden/Boston, Martinus Nijhoff Publ., 2005), p. 401.

ciple' – affects the reader's understanding of Common Articles 2 without the commentator having to give any reasons, or the reader having to engage in any conscious thinking about the matter.

8.2. The Proportionality Principle v. The Right of Non-Discrimination

110. There is an even more profound way that a shift in language alters the perception of the contents of Common Articles 2. Many commentators do not mean the principle of *non-discrimination* when they say 'the principle of non-discrimination'. What they really mean is the principle of *proportionality*. The two are very different things.

The right of non-discrimination in Common Articles 2 embodies a moral principle, or normative value: it is morally wrong to deprive people of important things in life on the basis of their race, sex, etc. And the right is a legal rule: the State shall not impair the enjoyment of rights on the basis of race, sex, etc. But commentators frequently do not mean either of these things.

When commentators say 'the principle of non-discrimination', many of them mean: 'It is wrong for a State to engage in race, sex, etc. discrimination *only if* "there is no reasonable relationship of proportionality between the [discriminatory] means employed and the aim sought to be realized".'[70] That is the opposite of the moral principle of non-discrimination that underlies Common Articles 2.

111. The interior quotation in the above paragraph is from the case law of the European Court of Human Rights. It is most often referred to as the proportionality principle, but people also call it the principle of non-discrimination, and the principle of equality. But however it is labelled, and regardless of the variations in the verbal formulation, the result is to shift from a rule to a principle – from an absolute ban against race, etc. discrimination to a context-dependent prohibition.

112. There are three important things to note about the Court's 'proportionality' test for the lawfulness of race, etc. discrimination. First, the 'proportionality principle' is a misnomer. In the test, 'there is no reasonable relationship

---

[70] ECtHR, *Case 'Relating to Certain Aspects of the Laws on the Use of Languages in Education in Belgium' (Merits), judgment of 23 July 1968,* 6 ECtHR (ser. A) 1, at para. 10 (1967–68), 1 EHRR 252. While usually referred to as the 'Belgian Linguistics' case, the dispute was not about linguistics, and that word does not appear in the official title. This commentary will abbreviate it as the *Belgium Languages* case.

of proportionality between the [discriminatory] means employed and the aim sought to be realized', the key word is *reasonable*: the discrimination must have a 'reasonable relation' to the ends. Adding *of proportionality* is a cosmetic gesture, since it contributes nothing grammatically to the meaning of the sentence, and the phrase plays no role in the Court's handling of cases. It would be more accurate to call it the 'principle of reasonableness'. (It could also be called the 'principle of appropriateness' or the 'principle of fairness', since these expressions convey the same basic idea.) But regardless of the name that we give it, the so-called proportionality principle is about reasonableness.[71]

The second important point is that the reasonableness test is the lowest standard known to modern-day law. And since human beings have an extraordinary capacity to disagree about what is reasonable, it is also the most subjective test, and hence the most arbitrary test, that the Court could have devised.[72]

Third, the reasonableness (proportionality) principle is more of a friend to discrimination than a foe. Not only does it allow the State to practice race, etc. discrimination under the lowest possible standard, it makes the moral norm disappear. Under the proportionality principle, what is wrong is seeking to achieve an unreasonable aim, or, if the aim if reasonable, using an unreasonable means: what is wrong is acting unreasonably. But there is nothing wrong with the race, sex, etc. discrimination itself. As we saw earlier, it is an offence to human dignity to deprive a person of something important on account of the person's race, sex, etc., and the first function of the right of non-discrimination is to protect people from these assaults on their human dignity. Also, the third function of the right of non-discrimination is to express, vindicate and transmit the ethical norm that adverse distinctions on the grounds of race, etc. are morally wrong. But this is not the norm that is embodied in the proportionality principle. In fact, State-imposed discrimination is now a good thing: race, sex, etc. discrimination are legitimate tools for achieving good things for society. Political calculations about 'reasonableness' now replace the moral principle that race, sex, etc. discrimination is an offence to human dignity. And without the

---

[71] *See, e.g.*, P. van Dijk, and F. van Hoof, *Theory and Practice of the European Convention on Human Rights* (3rd ed., The Hague/London/Boston, Kluwer, 1998), p. 719 (explaining the proportionality principle in terms of 'reasonableness'), p. 723 ('fair balance').

[72] Nowak, who shifts to the reasonableness principle for the right of non-discrimination, tacitly admits that it is arbitrary: 'A determination can be made only on a case-by-case basis and is ultimately dependent on value judgments....'; see note 67.

moral norm of non-discrimination to govern the balancing decisions, the pro-discrimination actors in society gain the advantage in the judicial and legislative battles. Proponents of discrimination could not ask for a better ally than the proportionality principle.[73]

113. In short, the expression 'the principle of non-discrimination' does not officially remove Common Articles 2 from the UN treaties, but the contents – or rather the perception of the contents – changes. Article 2(1) absolutely forbids the State from targeting adolescents and children because of their race, sex, etc., whenever the right-holder will suffer an impairment of a right (in the absence of a valid reservation). Shifting to 'the principle of non-discrimination' induces people to believe that the State has the right to practice race, etc. discrimination against right-holders, subject to the lowest, most subjective, and therefore the most arbitrary, test known to modern-day law. Instead of *individuals* having a *right not* to be discriminated against, the *State* has the *right to discriminate*, as long as it is acting 'proportionately'.[74]

---

[73] Three of the five most frequently cited commentators shift to the principle of non-discrimination, by which they really mean the principle of reasonableness: W. A. McKean, 'The Meaning of Discrimination in International and Municipal Law', *l.c.* (note 32), and W. McKean, *Equality and Discrimination Under International Law* (Oxford, Clarendon Press, 1983); B. G. Ramcharan, 'Equality and Nondiscrimination', in L. Henkin, *o.c.* (note 7), pp. 246–269; A. Bayefsky, 'The Principle of Equality or Non-Discrimination in International Law', *Human Rights Journal* 11, 1–34 (1990).

Numerous others have followed in their footsteps; see, *e.g.*, O. M. Arnardóttir, *Equality and Non-Discrimination Under the European Convention on Human Rights* (The Hague/London/ New York, Martinus Nijhoff Publ., 2003); S. Besson, *l.c.* (note 21); W. Vandenhole, *Non-Discrimination and Equality in the View* [sic] *of the UN Human Rights Treaty Bodies* (Antwerpen/ Oxford, Intersentia, 2005). An indication of the confusion is the tendency of authors to shift back and forth between the singular 'the principle of equality and non-discrimination' and the plural 'principles of equality and non-discrimination', even in the same sentence; *e.g.*, W. Vandenhole, p. 3.

[74] McKean has injected considerable confusion into the literature by his claim that the word *discrimination* has a special meaning in international law: an 'unfair, improper, unjustifiable or arbitrary distinction': W. A. McKean, 'The Meaning of Discrimination in International and Municipal Law', *l.c.* (note 32), p. 178. In other words, he turns the right of non-discrimination into the principle of reasonableness by inserting (or smuggling) a reasonableness element into the definition of 'discrimination'. However, McKean cites no real life example of such a usage to substantiate his assertion. In fact, all of his examples contradict his claim; *e.g.*, the footnote to the above quotation reads: '*The Random House Dictionary of the English Language* (New York) defines the verb "to discriminate" as "to make a distinction in favour [sic] of or against a person . . . on the basis of the group, class or category . . . rather than according to actual merit".' That, of course, is the ordinary meaning that this commentary has been using, and the meaning reflected in the HRC's definition in General Comment No. 18. Although McKean is probably the most frequently cited author in this field, no commentator, to the present author's knowledge, has pointed out McKean's self-refutation. For a contemporary author who makes the same claim, and has the same problem with lack of substantiation, see

8.3. *Confusing International Human Rights Law with European Regional Law*

114. One of the most common sources of confusion is using regional law, in particular the case law on the European Convention on Human Rights, to understand the right of non-discrimination in Common Articles 2.

The regional treaties are said to be 'higher' law than national law, and the UN treaties are even higher than the regional ones. The CRC and the Covenants are 'universal' treaties that impose obligations on all States, without limitation as to geography, culture, or anything else. Subsets of the entire community of States are free to create their own treaties, of course, and they can set tougher standards if they wish; but the sub-global agreements must not conflict with the universal obligations agreed to in the UN treaties (unless those States have made valid reservations). Regional law must 'bend' to international law: regional treaties should be interpreted so as to conform to the UN treaties whenever possible, and States still have to comply with the higher UN standards if a regional treaty has set a lower or conflicting standard.

115. But when it comes to freedom from discrimination, many commentators are doing just the opposite: they are bending the UN human rights treaties to conform to regional and national laws. In particular, they are using the 'proportionality' jurisprudence of the European Court of Human Rights to define the scope of Article 2(1), and the corresponding rights in the two Covenants. This leads to a serious problem: for all practical purposes, the European Court has nullified the right of non-discrimination in the European Convention, and it has filled the empty space with the proportionality principle. Nowadays, when commentators look at Common Articles 2 in the UN treaties, many of them are seeing 'proportionality' rather than a right to be free from discrimination. Since this problem has not been adequately discussed in the legal literature, we need to examine

---

M. Bossuyt, 'The Concept and Practice of Affirmative Action' (UN Doc. E/CN.4/Sub.2/2000/11, 2000), para. 52(a) (citing only himself and McKean).

It is helpful to remember that there are differences between a *word*, a *concept*, a *right,* and a moral or political *principle*. McKean, Bossuyt, B. G. Ramcharan, *l.c.* (note 73), and A. Bayefsky, *l.c.* (note 73) are blurring the difference between a *word* and a *principle*: what they actually mean is the 'principle of reasonableness', which they have inaccurately called the 'principle of non-discrimination'. See also S. Besson, *l.c.* (note 21), p. 435, and W. Vandenhole, *o.c.* (note 73), p. 33 (explicitly confusing the definition of a *word* with the statement of a *principle*). And finally, astute readers will have noticed that the HRC did not define the word *discrimination*, but identified the elements of a prohibition of discrimination (see Nos. 35–36); try substituting its so-called definition into Article 24(1) of the CCPR, and you will get absurdity. Query: What causes the absurd result? (Hint: Follow the elements.)

it closely in order to understand the present day confusions about the right of non-discrimination.

116. Article 14 of the European Convention on Human Rights is almost identical in wording to the rights of non-discrimination in Common Articles 2:

> The enjoyment of the rights and freedoms set forth in this Convention shall be secured without discrimination on any ground such as sex, race, colour, language, religion, political or other opinion, national or social origin, association with a national minority, property, birth or other status.

If Article 14 of the ECHR is interpreted in accordance with the ordinary meaning rule, it will contain a right of non-discrimination that has the same three elements as Article 2(1) of the CRC.[75]

117. However, in 1978, in the *Belgium Languages* case, the European Court redefined the contents of Article 14. The holding reads:

> A difference of treatment in the exercise of a right laid down in the Convention must not only pursue a legitimate aim: Article 14 is likewise violated when it is clearly established that there is no reasonable relationship of proportionality between the means employed and the aim sought to be realized.[76]

The Court's statement of the content of Article 14 bears no relation to what the European Convention says. In effect, the Court removed the right of non-discrimination, and then filled the gap by adding the reasonableness principle, as we will be seeing below.

118. *Belgium Languages* was the Court's first Article 14 case, and it has never deviated from that ruling. As the judges have been applying the holding, Article 14 has four elements:

(a) the State treats a person differently on the basis of membership in an enumerated classification (race, sex, religion, etc.),
(b) that action injures the person's interests,

---

[75] We need to insert brackets to make the comparison:
The [a] enjoyment [b] of the rights and freedoms set forth in this Convention [c] shall be secured [d] without discrimination on any ground such as sex, race, colour, language, religion, political or other opinion, national or social origin, association with a national minority, property, birth or other status. (Brackets added.)
Element (1) of Common Articles 2 corresponds to [d] in Article 14 of the ECHR. Element (2) corresponds to [a] and [c] combined. Element (3) corresponds to [b], reflecting the umbrella or accessory nature of the right of non-discrimination.
[76] *Belgium Languages, l.c.* (note 70), para. 10 (second internal paragraph).

(c) the impaired interest is protected by a sectoral right in the ECHR, *and*

(d) *either*

(i) the State is using the race, etc. discrimination in question to achieve an *unreasonable goal,* or

(ii) it has a reasonable goal, but the race, etc. discrimination is *not a reasonable means* to reach it.

Component (d) is the so-called proportionality principle, and it has no counterpart in the right of non-discrimination in the CRC and the Covenants. If the Court believes that all four elements are satisfied, it will declare that the State has contravened the European Convention; otherwise, the race, etc. discrimination is permissible, pursuant to the new component (d).

119. The introduction to this section said, 'for all practical purposes, the European Court has nullified the right of non-discrimination in the European Convention'. That this is so can be seen in five ways.

120. First, it can be seen by comparing the way that the Court handles two categories of complaints. (i) When a case is brought for violating a context-dependent sectoral right, the judges use the proportionality principle: the Court will strike the law down if *either* the limitation on the enjoyment of the sectoral right is an unreasonable means to the aim of the law (*i.e.,* the means is not proportionate to the ends), *or* the aim is not reasonable. (ii) When the law uses a race, sex, etc. classification to limit the enjoyment of a context-dependent sectoral right, the complaint is brought for violating Article 14 (in conjunction with the sectoral right). And in these cases the judges will also use the proportionality principle: the Court will invalidate the law if *either* the race, etc.-based limitation is an unreasonable means to the aim of the law (*i.e.,* the race, etc. discrimination is a disproportionate means to the ends), *or* the aim is unreasonable. So the test is always proportionality. Whereas Common Articles 2 in the UN treaties add an extra layer of protection to the sectoral rights by giving people an absolute right to be free from race, etc. discrimination, 'amended' Article 14 gives no substantive protection to the rights in the European Convention. If the Convention were officially amended to remove Article 14, it would make no difference to the case law: with or without Article 14, the test is the reasonableness principle (*i.e.,* 'proportionality').[77]

---

[77] Some commentators seem to have reached the same conclusion about *Belgium Languages,* but have not stated it as clearly; *e.g.,* C. Hillgruber & M. Jestaedt, *The European Convention on Human Rights and the Protection of National Minorities* (Köln, Germany, Verlag Wissenschaft und Politik, 1994) (S. Less & N. Solomon, transl.), p. 36 (the case law 'reduces Art. 14 of the

121. A second way to see that the judges nullified Article 14's right of non-discrimination is to look at the elements. Before the *Belgium Languages* ruling, a State would have violated Article 14 if its actions satisfied components (a), (b), and (c) – the same three elements that define the right of non-discrimination in Common Articles 2. But since the Court added component (d), the first three elements now function as procedural requirements: (a) *if* a State treats someone differently on account of race, etc., and (b) *if* that impairs the person's interests, and (c) *if* that interest is protected by a sectoral right, *then* (d) the Court will apply the proportionality principle. If the law is not reasonable, it will invalidate it; if it is reasonable, it will uphold it. So components (a) to (c) are procedural requirements that a plaintiff must satisfy to get to the Court's balancing decision in (d).

122. There is a third way to see how *Belgium Languages* nullified the right of non-discrimination. The three procedural components give a person *the right to ask the Court* if it disapproves of the discrimination in question under component (d). This means that the holding in the case has a unique kind of substantive function: fulfilment of (a) to (c) *gives the Court the right* to authorize the State to commit race, etc. discrimination under (d). The practical effect of *Belgium Languages* is to give judges the right to deprive people of the enjoyment of their sectoral rights on account of the person's race, sex, etc.

From the glass-half-full perspective, a State cannot use discrimination to deprive people of their enjoyment of sectoral rights, unless the judges give their permission. From the half-empty perspective, a State can target people on account of their race, etc., unless, and until, the judges say that the discrimination is unreasonable. Either way, the impacted individual has *no right to be free from discrimination*: Article 14 is not a right in the sense of being a 'trump'. Instead, as a matter of practical reality, the injured person and the State have the same right – the *right to ask the judges to make the political decision regarding state-imposed discrimination*: 'Is it reasonable (or appropriate, or fair) for the State to use *this* race, etc. discrimination as a means for reaching *this* policy objective?'

In other words, the Court sits in a hierarchical position to the Contracting States with respect to discriminatory laws; it is the judges' policy decision

---

ECHR to a mere ban on arbitrary treatment.... [This] robs the ban on discrimination of any real definitive character' (interior quote and cite omitted)); and even less clearly, P. van Dijk, et al., *o.c.* (note 71), p. 726 (the proportionality principle has 'deprived [Article 14] of much of its meaning').

about 'reasonableness' that authorizes Governments to engage in race, etc. discrimination. Thus, an individual's right to be free from discrimination has been transformed into the right of the judges to commit race, etc. discrimination, acting through the States parties. And the judges have given themselves that right by inserting component (d).

123. A fourth way to see what the Court did is by examining the holding of *Belgium Languages*. It is made up of two steps. (i) In the first step, the Court effectively removed the right of non-discrimination from the Convention. The judges did not give an interpretation of Article 14 during this step, they did not even try to interpret it, and they did not give their reasons for these failures; they simply treated Article 14 as if it had no substantive content, as if it did not contain an umbrella right of non-discrimination.[78] (ii) In the second step, the Court filled the vacuum: it invented the so-called principle of proportionality, and then used that to fill the hole.[79] As a matter of practical reality, *Belgium Languages* revised the European Convention by replacing the right of non-discrimination with the proportionality principle.[80]

124. A fifth way is to make a hypothetical comparison. The Convention Against Torture absolutely prohibits torture, and the treaty gives a crisp definition of the term. In simplified form, '"torture" means any act by which severe pain is intentionally inflicted on a person for such purposes as obtaining information or a confession' (condensing Article 1 of the CAT). Now let us 'interpret' the treaty: '"Torture" means any act by which severe pain is intentionally inflicted on a person for such purposes as obtaining

---

[78] *Belgium Languages, l.c.* (note 70), para. 10 (first internal paragraph) (ignoring the rules of interpretation, and removing, *de facto* if not *de jure*, the right of non-discrimination).

[79] *Id.* para. 10 (second internal paragraph) (inventing the principle, and making the substitution).

[80] G. Schwarzenberger, *International Law* (London, Stevens & Sons, 1957), pp. 489–497 (making the distinction between 'interpretation and revision' of a treaty, with the latter referring to judicial 'law-creating' (or 'amending', in the language of this commentary), which he considers an 'overstep[ping]' or 'abuse' of prerogatives.) The Court did not interpret Article 14 because it did not apply the rules of interpretation; it revised the ECHR when it replaced the right of non-discrimination with proportionality.

There is a large literature on judicial law-making in American law, and an increasing attention to it in the European literature; *e.g.,* M. de S.-O.-L'E. Lasser, *Judicial Deliberations: A Comparative Analysis of Judicial Transparency and Legitimacy* (Oxford, Oxford Univ. Press, 1999). A former judge of the European Court has asked, 'Can the Court Limit Human Rights?'; his answer is yes, because 'the Court feels that it has the right to curtail' rights, and because 'the judges themselves are not unaffected by turbulence in society', such as 'the growth of racism' in Europe. I. Foighel, 'Reflections of a former judge of the European Court of Human Rights', in: S. Lagoutte, H.-O. Sano, and P. S. Smith, *Human Rights in Turmoil* (Leiden/Boston, Martinus Nijhoff Pulb., 2007), pp. 271, 278.

information or a confession, *when the act is not proportionate to the aim, or the aim is not legitimate.*' The new language rewrites the law: instead of CAT prohibiting torture, the 'interpretation' allows States to use torture as a means to an end, subject to the most arbitrary test known to the law. And the same is true for the European Convention: adding the proportionality test to Article 14 rewrites the treaty.

125. What have other authors said about these five ways of looking at *Belgium Languages*? Commentators have been highly critical of how the Court applies Article 14; as one author recently summarized the literature, the case law 'is typically considered to be unclear and confusing'.[81] The root of the problem lies in component (d): the proportionality principle is a 'reasonableness' test, and that is the lowest, most subjective, and hence most arbitrary test that the Court could have invented. Of course the Court's decisions are confusing and confused; it cannot be otherwise with a rule that calls for ad hoc opinions about the reasonableness of using race, etc. discrimination as a means to an end. But while the legal literature is replete with minute analysis of 'proportionality' at work in the case law, the commentators have not been using their legal talents to discuss how component (d) got into Article 14.

Rather than explain what the Court did in *Belgium Languages*, commentators seem to go out of their way to maintain the pretence that there is still a right of non-discrimination in the Convention. For instance, the decision contains this dictum: 'a measure which in itself is in conformity with the requirements of the Article enshrining the right or freedom in question [*i.e.*, the sectoral right] may however infringe this Article [the sectoral right] when read in conjunction with Article 14...'.[82] When that statement is put into plain language, its absurdity becomes immediately evident: 'Race, etc. discrimination in the enjoyment of a sectoral right can be proportionate (under the sectoral right), and, at the same time, disproportionate (under Article 14): the discrimination can simultaneously be a reasonable and an unreasonable *means* to achieve the aim, and the *aim* can simultaneously be legitimate and illegitimate.' Although commentators are fond of quoting that dictum, they avoid discussing it.[83] But if the truth of the statement were put to the test, it would require an admission that the judges nullified the right of non-discrimination in the European Convention.

---

[81] O. M. Arnardóttir, *o.c.* (note 73), p. 1.
[82] *Belgium Languages, l.c.* (note 70), para. 9.
[83] See, *e.g.*, P. van Dijk, et al., *o.c.* (note 71), pp. 715–716; compare with the quotation in note 77.

126. To summarize the discussion, there is a marked tendency for people to view Common Articles 2 through the jurisprudence of the European Court, bending universal human rights treaties to the case law on a regional treaty. But the full significance of this mistake in vision cannot be appreciated until one confronts what the Court did in *Belgium Languages*: the judges in effect nullified the right of non-discrimination, keeping 'Article 14' in the treaty, like a town's name might be kept on a map after the town has vanished, but replacing its content with the reasonableness test. And when people look at Article 2(1) and see 'proportionality', the effect is to deprive boys and girls of their right of non-discrimination in the CRC.[84]

8.4. *The CRC Committee's 'four general principles'*

127. The Committee on the Rights of the Child has added to the confusion by its vigorous promotion of the so-called 'four general principles of the CRC' – non-discrimination, best interests, life-survival-and-development, and respect for the views of the child (paralleling Articles 2, 3, 6, and 12, respectively). The 'four general principles' has now become a central fixture in the CRC literature, a ritual incantation that is almost as obligatory as standing up when judges enter the courtroom. But we need to ask some questions: Why did the Committee reduce the CRC to four principles, and why these particular four? (For instance, Article 4 – the duty to utilize resources to the 'maximum extent' for economic, social and cultural rights – is vital to children given the life-or-death importance of those rights; so why is the Committee against treating Article 4 as a general principle?) Why does the Committee place so much emphasis on 'principles' when the CRC is about 'rights'? (In its concluding observations, for example, most of the time the Committee does not speak of the 'right' of non-discrimination.) And most importantly, what does the Committee mean by 'the general principle of non-discrimination'?

Although the Committee has never explained itself, we can deduce a few answers.

128. First, as for why the Committee chose 'four general principles', and why it picked these four, we can find partial answers. Over the years, the present

---

[84] Nowak appears to be reading the right of non-discrimination in Article 2(1) of the CCPR through the lens of the case law of the European Court; see M. Nowak, *CCPR Commentary*, *o.c.* (note 8), pp. 45–46, and p. 46 n. 89 (first bending Article 2(1) to the 'equality' clauses in Article 26, then treating 'equality' as the proportionality principle, coinciding with the Court's case law).

author has asked these questions of members who joined the Committee after the original members had departed. Their replies boil down to, 'We speak of the four general principles because the Committee has always spoken of the four general principles.'

By digging into the UN archives, we find that 'the four principles' was invented by the members of the original Committee when they were drafting the guidelines for state reports in 1991. The initial draft was framed in terms of subject headings or themes, rather than 'principles', with Articles 2, 3 and 12 placed under the heading 'The Child and the Law.'[85] The heading was then changed to 'Basic Principles' (and Article 6 was added).[86] The records don't tell us what the Committee meant by 'principles', however; all they show is that the discussion was limited to such comments as, the 'headings...might appear artificial at times', and the 'headings were not substantive in nature'.[87]

So why did the original Committee transform 'Basic Principles' – a non-substantive, even superficial heading – into 'the four general principles of the CRC', and why did it make that the cornerstone of its promotional activities for the Convention?

While the records are silent on these questions, discussions with original members indicate an answer: since the Convention was so unfamiliar to government officials and the public in those early days, the Committee wanted to simplify the CRC for didactic reasons. The 'four general principles' were like the trainer-wheels on a child's bicycle.

Unfortunately, leaving the trainers on for so long has led to two problems: first, understandings of CRC rights have not matured (for instance, people remain confused about the difference between a rule and a principle, and the stress on 'general principles' is undermining the idea of children as right-holders); and second, 'the four general principles' has become a vacuous cliché.[88]

---

[85] CRC Comm., *Matters Relating to the Committee's Methods of Work* (UN Doc. CRC/C/L.2, 1991), para. 7.

[86] *Summary records* (UN Doc. CRC/C/1991/SR.11), para. 58 (Santos Pais).

[87] *Summary records* (UN Doc. CRC/C/1991/SR.11), para. 63 (Hammarberg), and (UN Doc CRC/C/1991/SR.12), p. 6 (Kolosov), respectively.

[88] E.g., M. Nowak, *Article 6: The Right to Life, Survival and Development*, in: A. Alen, J. Vande Lanotte, E. Verhellen, F. Ang, E. Berghmans and M. Verheyde (eds.), *A Commentary on the UN Convention on the Rights of the Child* (Leiden/Boston, Martinus Nijhoff, 2005), pp. 2, 5, 14–17. Nowak insists that the 'general principle' of 'life, survival and development' adds something important to the realization of CRC rights, that the principle 'ensur[es] a common philosophical approach to the broad spectrum of areas addressed by the Convention', and that it 'defin[es] decisive criteria to assess the progress' in realizing CRC rights, *id.* p. 17. Those

129. Second, in the phrase 'general principles', the Committee is using *general* to express the idea of 'overarching principles of the Convention, which should be read together with every right contained in it'.[89] This commentary speaks of 'umbrella' provisions to convey the same idea.

130. Third, the word *principle* indicates that members are confused about the contents of the CRC articles, and about the differences between rules and principles: Article 6 is a principle – a generalized statement of the end-goals of the Convention –, while Articles 2(1), 3(1), and 12 are rules – concrete do's and don't's.[90]

131. Fourth and last, what does the Committee mean by 'the general principle of non-discrimination'? The one definitive thing that we can say is that the Committee does not mean anything by that phrase. The Committee on the Rights of the Child is just that, a committee; it is not a human being with a single mind of its own, but a group of changing composition, with each member giving his or her own meaning to the expression, and perhaps even giving it multiple meanings.

Based on the author's observations of how individual members have used 'the principle of non-discrimination' in the dialogues with States, in meetings, in conversations, and in other settings, all of the following meanings have been deduced: it means the right of non-discrimination, which is conceived more or less along the lines presented in this commentary; it means a principle of political morality; it means the principle of proportionality; it means that the member who is speaking does not like a particular

---

are bold claims, but since he gives no examples to back them up, we must ask: How does he know that those wonderful things are the result of a general principle rather than a right? Indeed, since Article 6 is not a legal *rule* but a legal *principle*, the right and his general principle could be the same thing, without his realizing it. (See note 90, below.)

[89] CRC Comm., *Report of the Committee on the Rights of the Child* (UN Doc. A/57/41), para. 38.

[90] Briefly: (i) Articles 1 to 5 are umbrella provisions. (ii) Article 6 is a principle, but a special kind of principle because it expresses the end-goal of the Convention. In fact, Article 6 can be called a mega-right, since life-survival-and-healthy-development embrace every non-trivial interest that make up a youngster's well-being or human dignity: all the rights in Articles 7 to 40 can be deduced from that end-goal. (iii) Article 3(1) is a procedural rule (prescribing a step in the decision-making process – the actor must consider the impact on young people). If it were a substantive provision, then it would function as a derogation clause to all of the sectoral rights, including freedom from torture. (iv) Article 12 – the 'right to be consulted' – functions like an umbrella provision because it applies whenever the State is making a decision about a particular youngster that will affect that youngster's other CRC rights. And the right is a *procedural rule* (prescribing a step in the decision-making process – the state actor must give the youngster an opportunity to express views, and must take the views into account), with a substantive sub-component (the age-and-maturity test).

disparity in treatment or well-being; and, finally, it is a clichéd utterance, without any concrete thought behind it at that moment. But most of the time, there are not enough clues to make an educated guess about what the member is thinking.

Until the Committee members can agree amongst themselves on what the 'general principle of non-discrimination' is, and then tell us in a joint statement, it has no particular meaning: people are free to understand it in whatever way they like.

132. We conclude by noting an irony. The Committee insists that States educate the public about the Convention so that everyone will fully understand CRC rights. But the Committee has only added to the confusion that surrounds the absolute human right to be free from race, sex, etc. discrimination; in particular, by speaking of a mysterious 'general principle', some people are forming the impression that States are permitted to discriminate against children and adolescents – because principles are generalizations, and generalizations admit to unspecified exceptions. (We will see how the confusions are multiplying, in Chapter Six on the Committee's concluding observations.)

8.5. 'Direct Discrimination' and 'Indirect Discrimination'

133. After the case law of the European Court and the 'principle of non-discrimination', the next greatest source of confusion is the paired notions of 'direct discrimination' and 'indirect discrimination'. Each jurisdiction writes its own definitions of these terms, but they are all essentially the same. We will use one of the most widely cited formulations, those of the European Union:

> *Direct discrimination* is defined as treating one person less favourably than another person on the ground of race (or sex, etc.).

> *Indirect discrimination* is defined as (a) an *apparently neutral* provision (b) that puts members of one race (or sex, etc.) at a *disadvantage* in comparison to members of the other race (or sex, etc.), and (c) that cannot be objectively *justified* by having a legitimate aim, and by using a means that is appropriate and necessary for achieving that aim.[91]

---

[91] These definitions are the author's adaptations of those in the 'equal treatment' directives pertaining to sex and race: Council Directive 2002/73/EC (men and women), Article 1, OJ, L269 (amending Council Directive 76/207/EEC, Article 2(2)), and Council Directive 2000/43/EC (race), Article 2(2), OJ, L180.

134. The paired terms are overlapping categories, as can be seen in Figure 4.

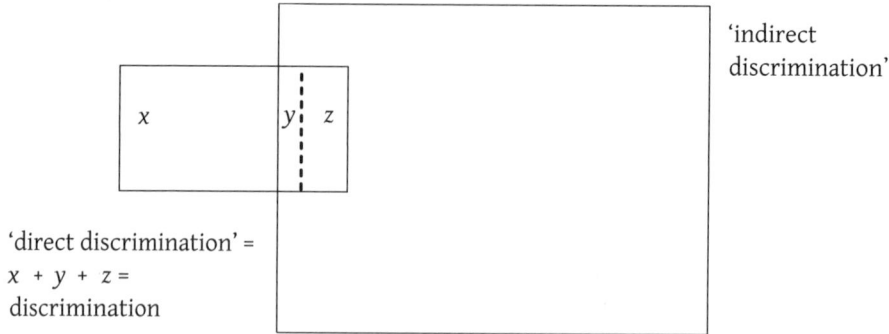

Figure 4. 'Direct discrimination' and 'indirect discrimination'

'Direct discrimination' is a confusing neologism for *discrimination*. The two definitions coincide exactly, so nothing is gained by adding 'direct' except mystification. As for 'indirect discrimination', the large majority of acts that the law punishes as 'indirect discrimination' do not involve discrimination. The only acts of discrimination in the 'indirect discrimination' box are where it overlaps with the box 'direct discrimination'. They overlap because two forms of 'direct discrimination' – *covert* discrimination (area y) and *de facto* discrimination (area z) – are 'apparently neutral': the law does not, on its face, require differential treatment on account of race (or sex, etc.). So 'indirect discrimination' is a legal fiction. It is no more a species of discrimination than a hot dog is a species of dog.

135. There are three important points to note about the word 'indirect discrimination'. The first important point is the way that it functions as a legal fiction. The concept that underlies the term was invented in the United States, where it is known as unlawful 'disparate impact' (or 'adverse impact'):

An 'indirect discrimination' (disparate-impact) law has four components: The rule or practice is unlawful when: (a) it does not *on its face* differentiate (i) on the ground of race (sex, etc.) (ii) with respect to some particular interest; (b) it adversely affects a significantly higher percentage of members of one race (sex, etc.) than of another, with respect to that interest; (c) it is not reasonable (*e.g.*, the rule cannot be justified on the grounds of a legitimate business necessity, or it is not proportionate); and (d) the interest affected is covered by the indirect discrimination law in question. Component (c) is the balancing element. Component (d) is not in the definition; it comes from the directive's scope of application, which is defined in another article.

an employment rule is unlawful when (a) it is neutral on its face, (b) it has different statistical consequences for groups defined by race or sex, and (c) it lacks a reasonable business justification. When an employment rule has differential impacts on groups defined by race or sex, American law allows people to challenge the rule in administrative and judicial forums. (For instance, a rule that requires police officers to meet physical requirements like a minimum height test will adversely affect 'women' more than 'men' because women as a group are smaller in stature than men as a group; so women can challenge the height rule.) The issue before the judge is whether the rule is reasonable under component (c), not whether the actor has committed covert discrimination. (If the judge believes the particular height limitation is not reasonable, the rule will be deemed 'unlawful disparate impact'. But if the facially-neutral height rule was designed to keep women from being police officers, then the anti-discrimination laws will apply, along with their tougher punishments, under the legal concept of covert discrimination.) In short, the disparate impact laws are about reasonableness, not discrimination.

European lawmakers adopted the political idea of allowing people to challenge the reasonableness of employment and other rules in disparate-impact situations, but they did not borrow the terminology. Instead, they created the legal fiction of *indirect discrimination.* People generally feel hostile to those who engage in race and sex discrimination, and the lawmakers capitalized on that feeling when they coined 'indirect discrimination'. When the public hears a charge of 'Indirect discrimination!' they tend to attach the stigma associated with race and sex discrimination to the actor and the act. The fiction plays the same psychological function as in other situations where a pejorative label is used to smear an entire group. For instance, foreigners are stigmatized as 'illegals' (or 'prone to crime', or 'disloyal', etc.). The indiscriminate labelling of the group allows the anger-arousing things that may be true for a small number of the group to produce negative feelings towards the group as a whole. There is a double psychological effect here: the labelling 'blinds' people to the fact that what may be true for a small number of cases is false as applied to the group, and it transfers stigma to people and situations where the stigma does not belong. While fictions are used routinely in the law, *indirect discrimination* is unique because no other legal term is used to produce similar psychological effects on the public.

Closely related to 'indirect discrimination' are terms like *structural discrimination, systemic discrimination*, and *institutional racism* (sexism, etc.). Originally, 'structural discrimination' was used for situations of widespread *de facto* discrimination, so the 'discrimination' was real, and 'structural' ('systemic', 'institutional') referred to its prevalence and intransigence. But nowadays, people typically apply these words to any statistical disparity that they do not like, without regard to the prevalence of, or even existence of, race, etc. discrimination. Rather than factual descriptions, these terms are now metaphorical expressions. The statistical disparity *looks something like* a situation where an actor is discriminating. An abstraction – 'police', 'society', 'the work place' – is turned into an actor, and all of the chains of cause-and-effect behind the observed events are reduced to one reified actor doing one thing: the abstraction is guilty of (metaphorically) treating individuals differently on the basis of their race, etc. Moreover, the term is a pejorative label: the speakers use the metaphorical 'structural discrimination' to smear their targets. The difference is that 'indirect discrimination' is used to stigmatize a specific rule or practice, whereas *structural discrimination* is used to vilify innumerable, unidentified actors and actions. The commonality is that all of these expressions are forms of question begging and name-calling.

136. The second important point about 'indirect discrimination' is the test in component (c): 'The provision cannot be objectively justified by having a legitimate aim, and by using a means that is appropriate and necessary for achieving that aim.' This test is an alternate formulation of the proportionality principle in *Belgium Languages*.[92] As discussed earlier, these verbal formulas are a fancy way to say that the provision must be reasonable. What is most important about the legal test is not the wording but the political function. The function of 'indirect discrimination' laws is to shift the power to make employment policies to judges; instead of business managers and parliamentarians deciding what is and is not a reasonable employment rule, the power is transferred to the courts. And, as we have seen, the test for the judges' exercise of this power is the most subjective, and thus most arbitrary, test known in contemporary law.[93]

---

[92] The formulations in the directives trace back to the Court's 'no objective and reasonable justification' test, which is an alternative formulation of the proportionality principle; *Belgium Languages, l.c.* (note 70), para. 10 (second internal paragraph). Note the importance of calling the 'indirect discrimination' definition a 'formulation', or verbal test. If taken seriously as a legal test, no law could ever pass it because 'objectively justified' is an oxymoron: a justification always depends on value judgments, which are subjective. The real test is the arbitrary 'reasonableness' test.

[93] The 'indirect discrimination' laws of the European Union lead to a 'highly intrusive form of judicial review and lawmaking', according to A. S. Sweet, *The Judicial Construction of Europe* (Oxford, Oxford Univ. Press, 2004), p. 159.

Moreover, a judicial determination of 'indirect discrimination' is retroactive lawmaking, for the defendant in the case.

137. The third important point about 'indirect discrimination' is the way that it makes too little of discrimination. As they are written and applied, indirect discrimination laws are acts of 'direct discrimination', and they violate the right of non-discrimination in international human rights law. This is because the aggrieved person has to be a member of the 'disadvantaged' group to have a right to challenge the disputed rule.

Sally is one centimetre short of the required height to be a police officer, so she has the right have a judge decide if that particular cut-off is or is not reasonable. Sam is just as tall as Sally, but he cannot challenge the rule because he is not a woman. The impaired interest is Sam's ability to obtain redress before an administrative or judicial tribunal for an unreasonable rule, and it is protected by international law (*e.g.*, Article 2(3) of the CCPR, access to justice). So the 'indirect discrimination' law satisfies all three elements of Common Articles 2, and Sam is a victim of sex discrimination.

The problem could be easily fixed by allowing both men and women to bring a case if either sex is adversely affected, but so far no commentator has pointed out the contradiction between the 'indirect discrimination' laws and the 'direct discrimination' laws (or the conflict with international human rights law, for that matter). Ironically, the intense focus on rooting out and destroying all acts of 'indirect discrimination' has allowed real discrimination to escape undetected.

138. To sum up, the case law on 'amended' Article 14 of the ECHR and the law on 'indirect discrimination' share a common core: the idea of 'discrimination' is replaced by political calculations based on 'reasonableness'; the linguistic symbol *discrimination* is retained while its meaning is changed; and, amidst the verbal and conceptual confusions, the right of non-discrimination begins to disappear. 'Indirect discrimination' is a dramatic example of making too much of non-discrimination, while at the same time making too little of it.

8.6. *The 'purpose or effect' Clause*

139. We began the discussion of the elements of the right of non-discrimination with the definition of the Human Rights Committee: 'Discrimination' is 'any distinction [...] based on any ground such as race, colour, sex [etc.] which has the *purpose or effect* of [...] impairing' the enjoyment of rights (emphasis added, quoted in full at No. 35). The phrase *purpose or effect* was borrowed from the definitions in CERD and CEDAW, and it has come to be one of the sources of confusion in the literature. The problem occurs when

commentators say or imply that *purpose* makes the definition apply to 'direct discrimination', and *effect* makes it cover 'indirect discrimination'.[94]

140. Nothing could be further off the mark. The best place to start is by breaking the definition down into its components:

'Discrimination' is
    (1) a distinction based on race, etc.
    (2) that has
        [a] the *purpose* or
        [b] the *effect*
        of impairing the enjoyment
    (3) of human rights.

The *purpose or effect* clause is part of component (2), which means that there must always be an act of discrimination (in the ordinary sense of that word) under component (1). So the word *purpose* does not make the Committee's definition cover 'direct discrimination', because component (1) has already done that. And the word *effect* cannot make the definition cover 'indirect discrimination', because, as we saw in the previous section, there is no discrimination at all in the large majority of 'indirect discrimination' cases. And the few cases where there is discrimination will either be *de facto* or covert discrimination, which are already covered by component (1).

141. This leaves us with a mystery. If the *purpose or effect* clause does not cover 'indirect discrimination', then what exactly does it add to CERD and CEDAW?

The clause is a part of component (2), so 'purpose' and 'effect' are two different ways that the impairment element can be fulfilled. This implies that there are some real-life cases of race, etc. discrimination where (i) the actor has the objective of injuring people of one race, etc., but the harm does not materialize (the purpose without the effect), and other cases where (ii) the actor has no aim to harm members of the affected group, but the differential treatment injures them anyway (the effect without the purpose).

142. And that is correct. While an aim to impair and actual impairment go together in the vast majority of real-life cases, there are scenarios where

---

[94] *E.g.*, A. Conte, S. Davidson, and R. Burchill, *Defining Civil and Political Rights: The Jurisprudence of the United Nations Human Rights Committee* (Hants, UK, Ashgate, 2004), p. 165 (claiming, without explanation, that in the HRC's definition, '"purpose or effect" comprehends the two categories of discrimination which are usually known as direct and indirect discrimination').

one occurs without the other. A couple of hypothetical examples will illustrate the point.

First, the purpose to injure can exist without the injury. For instance, a hotel clerk, acting out of racial spite, purposely gives a customer a room where the shower does not work. But the clerk does not know that the pipes have been fixed, and since the room has the best view in the hotel, the customer ends up being benefited, rather than being injured as the clerk had intended. In legal language, the clerk is guilty of *attempted* racial discrimination, and the attempt has failed due to *a mistake of fact*. The failed-attempt/mistake-of-fact scenario does not happen very often, so adding 'purpose' to component (2) is of marginal practical importance.

Second, impairment can exist without an aim to harm. This can happen in several ways. It occurs when the actor honestly believes that the differential treatment is good for the affected people, as in bygone days in Europe when legislators banned women from working at night. The objective was to bestow a benefit on the 'weaker sex', but the effect was to hurt women by depriving them of freedom of choice, and a chance to earn a livelihood. It can also happen when the actor has the conscious intention to do good for members of Group A, or for society as a whole, but the unavoidable consequence is to harm members of Group B. A race-based quota in hiring new employees has the *purpose* of helping race A, but the inevitable *effect* is to impair the right to work of members of race B (as illustrated in Figure 2). So there are many real-life cases where the *effect* sub-component has application, but all of these cases would still come under component (1) if the 'purpose or effect' clause did not exist: adding *effect* to component (2) of the definition is only cosmetic.[95]

143. To sum up the discussion of 'purpose or effect': One must first show that a state actor is treating people differently on the basis of their race, sex, etc. under component (1) before getting to the 'purpose or effect' clause in component (2). (In other words, one must first show an act of race, etc. discrimination, in the ordinary meaning of that word.) And, 'purpose or effect' does not refer to 'direct discrimination' and 'indirect discrimination' respectively; it refers to alternative ways to satisfy component (2).

144. The trend in talking about 'discriminatory effects' is making too much and too little of international anti-discrimination law. Too much, because

---

[95] And it is not an attractive cosmetic addition: 'the effect of impairing' is a tortured way to say 'impairs'.

political actors are allowed to point to a statistical disparity and cry 'Discriminatory effects!' where there is no discrimination. But 'discriminatory effects' without an act of discrimination is as nonsensical as 'murderous effect' without a murder. What these actors mean is that there is a *disparity* that they do not like; but since they cannot show that discrimination is the cause of the difference in well-being, they resort to an innuendo: the word 'discriminatory effects' is enough to plant a false idea of causation in the audience's mind.[96]

And the trend simultaneously makes too little of the right of non-discrimination, because the rhetoric of 'discriminatory effects' leads to the same destination as 'indirect discrimination': people end up reading a 'proportionality' or 'reasonableness' test into the definitions of discrimination in CERD and CEDAW, and into Common Articles 2. Moreover, since the political issue is a disparity that the speaker does not like, the arbitrary 'proportionality principle' is the perfect vehicle for selectivity in choosing one's targets.

8.7. *Affirmative Action*

145. Of all the words in contemporary political debates, one of the most confusing is *affirmative action*. This is partly because the term has multiple meanings. But it is also because affirmative action is one of the most challenging issues in all of human rights law. The challenges are legal, political, moral, psychological, and social, and the challenges only increase when the issues are viewed from a 'children's rights perspective'. The commentary will therefore spend more time on this topic than any other. We will begin by defining the two kinds of 'affirmative action' measures, and then relate the two types of measures to a young person's right of non-discrimination under Article 2(1).

8.7.1. *The Multiple Meanings of* 'Affirmative Action'
146. There are two kinds of 'affirmative action': there is (i) *non-discriminatory* affirmative action, and (ii) *discriminatory* affirmative action. Discriminatory

---

[96] According to A. Conte, et al., *o.c.* (note 94), pp. 165–166, 'indirect discrimination' occurs when 'a rule which is neutral on its face [has] the effect of discriminating in fact'. Translated into ordinary speech: 'the rule has the effect of discriminating' means, 'The rule results in differential outcomes that I do not like.' And labelling it as 'indirect discrimination' means, 'I want the courts to make the policy judgements.' (In addition, their definition has left out the balancing element. The authors have also omitted the race, etc. subcomponent, but that is implied in their discussion.)

affirmative action uses race, sex, religious, etc. discrimination as the means for reaching policy objectives, while non-discriminatory affirmative action does not. It is the presence or absence of discrimination that distinguishes the two, not the goals of the measures.

147. 'Affirmative action' entered the political vocabulary of the United States in the early 1960s, where it first referred to *non-discriminatory* measures aimed at ensuring social justice for certain social groups, particularly African Americans, and later women. The idea was that no matter how rigorous the anti-discrimination laws are, non-discrimination by itself will not be enough to raise the group's overall well-being to that of its counterpart, not when history and culture have combined to produce serious imbalances in society. Something more has to be done – *affirmative action* has to be taken: the government must take *action*, as opposed to relying on the current set of measures, and the action must be *affirmative*, as opposed to only being prohibitions. But 'affirmative action' does not entail race or sex discrimination: it does not conform to Figure 2.

148. Within a few years 'affirmative action' took on a second meaning. People increasingly began to use it to refer to *discriminatory* measures to promote the well-being of the various groups. In this usage, 'affirmative action' is a euphemism for discrimination. Examples of the second kind of affirmative action are quotas (whether overt or covert, fixed or variable), and bonus points, where members of Group A are given an inflated score in competitive exams. (In popular speech and learned journals alike, *reverse discrimination* was a common synonym for the new usage of 'affirmative action'.)

149. Many countries in the world today are engaged in controversies about the respective merits of the two kinds of affirmative action, and a number of other terms are also heard in these debates, like *positive action*, *special measures*, and *positive discrimination*. Each of these words can be used in the same two ways as *affirmative action*, so people must continually decode what they are reading and hearing.

Affirmative Action for Girls
150. We can use the right to education to make our discussion concrete. Every school age youngster under 18 years of age has the right to an education under the CRC, so the government cannot rest until each right-holder is actually receiving an education of the kind and quality described in Articles 28 and 29. However, 'In many countries, girls are less likely to attend school

than boys,' as UNICEF says in *State of the World's Children*.[97] The statistical imbalances are not the result of sex-discrimination in the country's laws but are the combined product of a number of things in society, so perfect implementation of Article 2(1) will not correct the situation; and even the most vigorous campaign to end societal discrimination against women and girls will not ensure that every girl in the here-and-now is getting an education. So, whenever girls as a group are lagging behind boys as a group in educational attainments, anti-discrimination is not enough. Something more must be done: the Government must take *affirmative action*: it must take *special measures*, since its ordinary measures have proved insufficient to ensure that the well-being of girls is at the same level as that of boys.

There are two kinds of affirmative action. *Non-discriminatory* affirmative action comes in many shapes and sizes. A State takes 'affirmative action' when it conducts a national survey to determine the various causes of girls not being in school, and it takes 'affirmative action' every time it creates a programme to remove a barrier. Among other things, the State can make school hours flexible to accommodate the time-demands that are placed on girls in the home. It can build latrines to ensure that adolescent girls have the required levels of privacy. The State can work with local communities to promote the importance of educating girls, and to help create local solutions to specific problems (*e.g.*, parental concern with the safety of the girls, and helping families free their daughters from domestic chores). It can conduct a nation-wide campaign to promote the value of girls' education. And it can make school more attractive to girls by ensuring that the contents of the curriculum, and the range of school-related activities (like sports, music, and girls clubs), are relevant to their needs and interests. Each of these 'affirmative action' measures will help close the statistical gap between girls' and boys' educational attainments, but none of them deprives a boy, on account of his being a boy, of an education. They are all *non-discriminatory* affirmative action: they do not satisfy the three elements of Common Articles 2: they do not conform to Figure 2.[98]

---

[97] UNICEF, *State of the World's Children 2006: Excluded and Invisible* (New York, UNICEF, 2005), p. 8.

[98] For these and other non-discriminatory measures to promote girls' education, see N. Stromquist, *Increasing Girls' and Women's Participation in Basic Education* (Paris, UNESCO, 1997); UNICEF, *Educating Girls and Women: A Moral Imperative* (New York, UNICEF, 1992). For an excellent summary of non-discriminatory affirmative action for girls across the sectoral rights, written by a Committee member, see S. Chutikul, 'Helping the Girl Child', *Global Futures* (2nd Quarter, 2003), p. 16.

Discriminatory affirmative action, by contrast, takes an educational opportunity away from individual boys as the means for giving individual girls more opportunities, with the aim of up-lifting girls as a group. Giving scholarships, fee-waivers, and other subsidies to girls on terms not available to boys, and imposing quotas against boys in admittance to educational programs or in awarding scholarships, are examples of discriminatory affirmative action. Each of these measures falls under the decision-tree model of resource allocation in Figure 2: the state deprives a boy of an educational benefit as the means of making it available to a girl, with the criterion of allocation being the student's sex. These and other discriminatory affirmative action measures will satisfy the elements of Common Articles 2.[99]

Affirmative Action for Boys

151. What about the global situation of boys' education? The same thing that UNICEF said about girls can be said about boys: in many countries, there are fewer boys in school than girls. For instance, boys are under-represented in secondary schools in ninety-one countries, or nearly half of the world's total.[100] Moreover, the problem of under-representation is on every continent, the dropout-rates increase going up the educational ladder, and the trend of boys' under-representation is getting worse over time. And, here

---

State reports are generally weak on concrete measures to promote girls' education. This is probably due in significant part to the failure of the reporting guidelines to ask concrete questions about the multi-pronged measures that need to be undertaken, and the Committee's lack of concreteness in its dialogues and recommendations. As in many other areas, however, the Committee's performance has improved over time, but is still far short of its full potential for promoting the right to education for girls as a group. For a better than average set of recommendations, see CRC Comm., *Concl. Obser.: Equatorial Guinea* (UN Doc. CRC/C/143, 2004), para. 366 (while not framed in terms of cither girls or boys, its multi-pronged recommendations will benefit any group that is lagging behind). For an impressive report on non-discriminatory affirmative action measures for girls, see *Pakistan* (UN Doc. CRC/65/Add.21, 2003), paras. 67–86, 277–326; note para. 81 ('...female medical students protested admission quotas for girls. They demanded admission based on merit, not gender.... [T]he Punjab High Court issued a writ abolishing the quota limitations.... Recent trends...show larger number of girls winning merit scholarships than boys.'), and para. 80 ('Girl students excel in higher education.') For the multi-pronged approach, without the concrete details, see *Zambia* (UN Doc. CRC/C/11/Add.25, 2002), para. 344.

[99] E.g., *India* (UN Doc. CRC/C/93/Add.5, 2003), para. 821, discussed in section 9.3 below; see also, *Summary Records, Gambia* (UN Doc. CRC/C/SR.740, 2001), para. 36 (educational scholarships for girls only); *Bangladesh* (UN Doc. CRC/C/65/Add.22, 2003), para. 52 (tuition waived for girls).

[100] UNICEF, *State of the World's Children 2006: Excluded and Invisible, o.c.* (note 97), pp. 114–117 (Table 5). However, UNICEF does not make the parallel statement about boys not being in school.

too, anti-discrimination is not enough: the State must take *affirmative action* in favour of boys.

And again, there are two kinds of affirmative action. *Non-discriminatory* affirmative action aims at preventing or mitigating the things that are creating problems for boys. There are a number of well-known risk factors for boys dropping out of school: boys have learning disabilities at rates five times that of girls, and they are diagnosed as suffering from Attention Deficit and Hyperactivity Disorder (ADHD) at a rate three times greater – all of which precipitate difficulties with teachers, social exclusion, and self-rejection; the increasing absence of fathers in the family is keeping boys from bonding with a loving, male authority-figure – which affects their social and psychological development; boys also experience high rates of violence and rejection from the non-biologically-related males that replace their fathers in the home; the effects of the loss of male role-models at home are not being offset at school when there is an overrepresentation of female teachers in the early grades; and bullying at school, and gangs in the community, which are overwhelming male, have push-pull influences on dropping out. There are also gender-specific family duties that can keep boys out of school, like taking care of livestock, or going to work to help support the family. *Non-discriminatory* affirmative action would address these problems without depriving individual girls, on the basis of being a girl, of educational opportunities.

Discriminatory affirmative action, on the other hand, would give a preference to individual boys at the expense of individual girls in the allocation of educational goods, like giving boys scholarships and other subsidies on preferential terms, and quotas to ensure that boys as a group are enjoying the same rates of attainments as girls as a group. And since there are fewer boys in school than girls in almost half of the countries of the world, that could entail a great deal of sex discrimination against girls.

Preferential Treatment
152. The confusion begins with the existence of the multiple meanings of 'affirmative action', but commentators add to the problems by not defining their usage, or, when they do, their definitions are ambiguous. For instance, according to one popular definition, *affirmative action* is a measure that 'gives preferences to a disadvantaged group'.[101] This description fails to bring out the critical difference.

---

[101] *E.g.*, A. Eide, 'Possible ways and means of facilitating the peaceful and constructive solution of problems involving minorities' (UN Doc. E/CN.4/Sub.2/1993/34), para. 172 ('Affirmative

Both non-discriminatory affirmative action and discriminatory affirmative action have the same ends – they both aim at helping a disadvantaged group, and anything that does that will 'give a preference to the group'; where they differ is in the means. When state officials spend money and political capital on conducting a national survey on the barriers to girls' education, those resources are not available to tackle other problems, like building a bridge, or remodelling prison facilities. So the state is giving *priority* to solving the problems of girls; it is treating girls (as a group) with *favouritism*; it is giving the group 'girls' a *preference*, relative to the attention it is giving to other needs of other segments of the population. But that preference to the group is not sex discrimination against individual boys. The national survey on girls' education does not deprive any boy, on the ground of his being a boy, of any educational opportunity. (The money spent on the national survey is not available to spend on separating boys from adult men in detention facilities, for instance, but it does not come under the Figure 2 model of discriminatory allocation of social goods between individuals.)

The verbal difference is subtle: *Non-discriminatory affirmative action* is 'Preference to Group A, without discriminating against individual members of B,' while *discriminatory affirmative action* is 'Preference to Group A, by the means of giving preferences to individual members of A at the expense of individual members of B' (the Figure 2 situation). The difference in wording is slight, but the conceptual and legal differences are profound.[102]

153. The first step in the legal analysis is to define the multiple meanings of 'affirmative action'. Now that we have done that, we can relate the multiple meanings to the right of non-discrimination.[103]

---

action is preference, by way of special measures, for certain groups...typically defined by race,.,.'); S. Joseph, et al., *o.c.* (note 56), p. 728 ('Affirmative action denotes positive steps taken...to improve the status of disadvantaged groups.').

[102] Ambiguity is the common practice in the implementation reports, where the State Party does not give information about the means being used; see, *e.g.*, *Bangladesh* (UN Doc. CRC/C/65/Add.22, 2003), paras. 48, 49, 51; *Mauritania* (UN Doc. CRC/C/8/Add.42, 2001), paras. 33, 35.

[103] Some additional fine points about terminology. First, people also use 'affirmative action' as an umbrella word for programmes that combine non-discriminatory and discriminatory measures. Second, there are a total of seven usages of *affirmative action*. The present author uses the following system to decode other authors' meanings: 'AA1' = non-discriminatory affirmative action; 'AA2' = discriminatory affirmative action; 'AA3' = the umbrella usage (AA1 and AA2 combined); 'AA4' = any dedicated effort to solve a problem; 'AA5' = term-of-art in a statute or learned work; 'AA6' = an author's idiosyncratic usage; and 'AA7' = too ambiguous to decode.

For an AA6 (idiosyncratic) usage, see S. Joseph, et al., *o.c.* (note 56), p. 730 (in regard to the HRC's decision in *Stalla Costa v. Uruguay*, No. 198/1985, using both *positive discrimination* and *reverse discrimination*, which is always AA2, for a normal judicial remedy of reinstating

8.7.2. *Affirmative Action and Article 2(1)*

154. There are three essential points about the relation of affirmative action to international human rights law: (i) The State has an inherent duty to take affirmative action: the State *must take action* to fulfil each right – it cannot remain passive, relying on evolutionary processes alone; and the action must be *affirmative* – the State cannot rely on just prohibitory measures. (ii) *Discriminatory* affirmative action is absolutely prohibited by the absolute right of non-discrimination – when it entails race, sex, etc. distinctions that impair the enjoyment of sectoral rights (unless there is a valid reservation). And (iii), *non-discriminatory* affirmative action is not only lawful, it's mandatory – whenever the well-being of any segment of society is lagging behind the rest of the nation.[104]

---

employees unlawfully discharged). Since the individuals who were benefited by the reinstatement had been actual victims, the remedy did not entail any 'discrimination', in the ordinary sense of that word. Note that the HRC did not say either *positive* or *reverse discrimination* in its decision. For an AA4 (any dedicated effort) usage, see R. Hodgkin and P. Newell, *Implementation Handbook for the Convention on the Rights of the Child* (2nd ed., New York/Geneva, UNICEF, 2002), p. 26.

Third, some generalizations about patterns of usage: In Europe, *positive action* usually means AA1, but sometimes it is AA2 or AA3. In British English, *positive discrimination* has been preferred over 'affirmative action' for the AA2 meaning, but sometimes people use it to refer to AA1 or even AA4, and there are a few notable AA6 usages in the human rights literature (see S. Joseph, et al., in the preceding paragraph). With respect to minority rights, *special measures* has historically been used to refer almost exclusively to AA1, but nowadays activists frequently use it for AA2, AA3, and AA4.

[104] Commentators frequently quote the following statement from the HRC's General Comment No. 18: '[T]he principle of equality sometimes requires states parties to take affirmative action in order to diminish or eliminate conditions which cause or help to perpetuate discrimination prohibited by the Covenant.' HRC, *Gen. Com. No. 18, o.c.*, (note 20), para. 10. Curiously, some commentators represent that statement as endorsing *discriminatory* affirmative action. *E.g.*, A. Conte, et al., *o.c.* (note 94), pp. 178–179 ; E. Evatt, 'The Practical Relevance of Article CEDAW', in: I. Boerefijn, F. Coomans, J. Goldschmidt, R. Holtmaat, and R. Wolleswinkel (eds.), *Temporary Special Measures* (Antwerpen/Oxford/New York, Intersentia, 2003), p. 48. However, when the statement is read carefully, it can only be referring to AA1 measures (*i.e.*, *non-discriminatory* affirmative action): *action to eliminate conditions which cause discrimination* refers to steps that remove the underlying causes of discrimination, rather than to discriminatory allocations under Figure 2 (*i.e.*, AA2).

Moreover, the summary records confirm that the HRC was not using *affirmative action* as a code word for discrimination. *Official Records of the Human Rights Committee 1988/89* (UN Doc. CCPR/8, 1995): Wennergren (explaining that 'affirmative action and preferential treatment' in the general comment means things like 'measures on behalf of minorities to enable them to learn the language of the country and thus have easier access to higher education'), 914th mtg., p. 328, para. 33; see also, Pocar, 901st mtg., p. 270, para. 66; Ando, 914th mtg., p. 327, para. 13; *Official Records of the Human Rights Committee 1989/90* (UN Doc. CCPR/9, 1995): Lallah (explaining that 'affirmative action' simply means 'specific legislative or administrative measures' to 'guarantee equality of rights'), 938th mtg., p. 81, para. 42; Movrommatis (stating that 'affirmative action' does not mean the kinds of measures that are sometimes

155. Before we conclude our discussion of discriminatory affirmative action, we need to examine two other matters – one is to view the issues from a children's rights perspective, and the other is the 'special measures' clauses in the support treaties.

8.7.3. The 'Children's Rights Perspective'

156. Debates about discriminatory affirmative action have been going on for years, and by now most people have formed their basic opinions. But regardless of which side of the fence the person is on, the views have probably been formed in reference to national or regional law, without regard to international human rights law. This commentary has filled the gap in the literature by looking at discriminatory affirmative action from the international law perspective, and, while our topic is Article 2(1) of the CRC, everything that has been said so far applies equally to children's and adults' human rights. Furthermore, the opinions were probably formed in debates about adults imposing discrimination against other adults as a means for achieving political goals. In order to take a true 'children's rights perspective', we need to supplement the legal analysis. The premise of the CRC is that children and adolescents are entitled to 'special care and assistance' (fourth preambular paragraph). In this section, we will briefly discuss four ways that discriminatory affirmative action harms the healthy development of children and adolescents, in addition to impairing the immediate interest at stake.

157. The first problem is that discriminatory affirmative action usually inflicts a more serious harm on youngsters than on adults. Most of the discrimination against CRC right-holders occurs in developing countries, and it impairs education, usually in the form of denying waivers of school fees, scholarships, and other benefits because the student is the 'wrong' sex, etc. (The discrimination predominately injures boys, but the 'special care and assistance' problems are the same regardless of the (a)-variable.) In the first place, because primary and secondary education lay a foundation for life, discriminatory affirmative action can damage the youngster's entire future. In the second place, these children will not have alternative ways to obtain a basic education. By contrast, discriminatory affirmative

---

called 'reverse discrimination'), 948th mtg., p. 113, para. 62; see also Higgens, 948th mtg., p. 113, para. 58. Despite the many statements that the HRC was not approving of discriminatory affirmative action, the research for this commentary found no author who informed readers of the summary records.

action against adults does not harm a person's future in the same way. For example, a popular form of sex discrimination in Europe is using a person's sex as a 'tie-breaker' in competitions for jobs. The 'victim' is not barred from competing for other jobs, however, and the financial harm suffered is likely to be modest, given the number of employment opportunities in the robust economies of Europe, and the State can easily remedy the human rights violation by paying compensation.[105] But school fees and scholarships have an all-or-nothing impact in developing countries: using sex, etc. discrimination to deprive youngsters of a primary or secondary education can effectively deny the right to education altogether.

158. Second, people usually justify discriminatory affirmative action as a 'necessary' means for achieving statistical equality between Group A and Group B. The justification rests on three premises: the discriminatory measures really do lift Group A up to the level of B; they do a better job of producing that result than non-discriminatory affirmative action; and the harm done to the individual 'victims' is less than the benefits that society gains. The first two are empirical claims, and the third is a mixed claim of fact, conjecture and values, but the debates virtually never put the claims to the test. As noted by Thomas Sowell, an authority on discriminatory affirmative action measures around the world, when people argue about these policies, they usually argue 'for or against the *theory* of affirmative action' rather than about the empirical evidence of how it works in actual practice.[106] Fortunately, there is abundant research on discriminatory affirmative action; unfortunately, the evidence does not substantiate the factual claims.

Three problems stand out: (i) Discriminatory affirmative action against individual members of sex (race, etc.) Group B helps individual members of Group A obtain the social good in question, but those measures do not remove the barriers that have been holding back Group A as a whole. By contrast, all of the non-discriminatory measures mentioned earlier address either the root or the proximate causes of A's problems. (Working with community groups to identify and overcome the barriers to girls' education helps all girls; a quota limiting the number of scholarships given to boys does not, for example.) (ii) The number of individual members of A that get the social good as a result of discriminatory affirmative action is small. (Governments

---

[105] *The Main Types and Causes of Discrimination* identifies the use of race, sex, etc. for tie-breaking as a form of impermissible discrimination, *o.c.* (note 23), para. 167.

[106] T. Sowell, *Affirmative Action Around the World: An Empirical Study* (New Haven/London, Yale Univ. Press, 2004), p. ix.

allocate only a small amount of money for the scholarships and fee waivers reserved for girls, for instance.) (iii) When a State says, 'We are taking affirmative action for [whatever group in society]!', the buzz word *affirmative action* has a powerful psychological effect: people feel that the Government is committed to ending the disparities, so they do not press officials about their failures to have concrete programs to correct each of the underlying barriers. (Generally speaking, the CRC implementation reports show a weak array of measures for promoting the education of girls – or of boys, where they are lagging behind.) In short, children are being denied their human rights on the unexamined *assumption* that discriminatory affirmative action delivers on its promises, in disregard of the evidence to the contrary.[107]

159. There is a third aspect of the 'special care and assistance' perspective: children and adolescents are dependent upon adults for the realization of their rights. When political actors in a society are trying to create discriminatory laws, the adult targets of the discrimination will have adult capacities to mobilize against those efforts; sometimes they will be successful in stopping discriminatory measures, and sometimes not, but at least they can be political actors. But when children and adolescents are the victims, they will not have the same ability to defend themselves in the political arenas. Youngsters must depend on their parents, and on the altruism of other adults, to protect them. Unfortunately, not only do adults often fail to protect the interests of young people in the general case, but the psycho-socio-political dynamics of discrimination put children and adolescents at special risk. As UNICEF says, 'Children are easy targets for discrimination.'[108]

160. To understand discriminatory affirmative action from this perspective, we can listen to a story told by Dick Gregory, a stand-up comic and prominent figure in the American civil rights movement in the 1960s. The story went something like this:

> The captain of a trans Atlantic flight came out of the cabin, and announced to the passengers: 'We've developed engine problems and we're losing altitude fast. I'm sorry, but in order to save the lives of everybody on board this plane, I'm going to have to ask one of you to jump.' Then a man stood up, and said, 'I'm from England, and in order to save the lives of everybody on board, I'll jump!' And he went to the door, cried, 'God save the Queen!' and jumped out.
>
> A few minutes later the captain came out again. 'I'm terribly sorry, but we're still losing altitude, so in order to save the lives of everyone on board, I

---

[107] *Id.* (reviewing the empirical evidence from many countries).
[108] UNICEF, *The Convention on the Rights of the Child, o.c.* (note 35), not paginated.

must ask one more person to jump.' Another man got up and said, 'I'm from France, and in order to save the lives of everyone on this plane, I'll jump.' And he went to the door, cried 'Vive la France!' and jumped.

The captain came out a third time. 'I'm terribly, terribly sorry, but we're still losing altitude, and in order to save the lives of everybody on board this plane, I must ask just one more person to jump.' A giant of a man stood up and said, 'I'm from Texas, and to save the lives of everyone on board ...,' then he picked up a Mexican, shouted 'Remember the Alamo!' and threw him out the door.

161. Fee waivers and scholarships are finite resources, like all educational goods, and adults must make sacrifices in order for these goods to be available to young people. Under discriminatory affirmative action against boys, adults are in effect saying, 'In order to ensure that girls get educated, I will sacrifice the futures of disadvantaged boys, rather than make financial sacrifices by redistributing my wealth for their education.' Like the Texan who is willing to 'altruistically' sacrifice the Mexican, discriminatory affirmative action against CRC right-holders is an abuse of power of the strong over the weak.[109]

162. The fourth problem is that discriminatory affirmative action harms the moral development of children and adolescents. (i) Using discrimination as a means for achieving political goals teaches young people that sex, race, etc. discrimination is good (provided, of course, that it's 'reasonable'). This lesson contradicts the moral norms underlying the Charter and the right of non-discrimination. (ii) Using 'affirmative action', 'special measures', and 'positive discrimination' as euphemisms to refer to sex, race, etc. discrimination has the same moral effect as using 'enhanced interrogation' to refer to torture: it teaches children and adolescents to lie when their behaviour raises serious moral questions. (iii) Changing *discrimination* to mean 'unreasonable distinctions' (or 'the right of non-discrimination' to mean 'the principle of proportionality') deprives young people of the vocabulary they need to

---

[109] *E.g.*, K. Buhman, 'Administrative Law Reform in the PRC', in: H.-O. Sano and G. Alfredsson, *Human Rights and Good Governance* (The Hague/London/New York, Martinus Nijhoff Publ., 2002), pp. 230–232 (rights protect individuals from abuses of power).

The right to education is progressive, so the State can ration resources, including fee waivers and scholarships, and this requires innumerable distinctions, each one of which puts some kind of sacrifice, or impairment, on someone. But the right of non-discrimination is not subject to the lack of resources escape clause; CESCR Comm., *Gen. Com. No. 13: The Right to education* (1999) (UN Doc. HRI/GEN/1/Rev.8, 2006), para. 31 ('The prohibition against discrimination enshrined in article 2(2) of the Covenant is subject to neither progressive realization nor the availability of resources....'). Basing the sacrifice on the right-holder's race, sex, etc. would be an abuse of power, and against the CESCR.

Incidentally, Gregory's joke had a second punch line: 'And the man was really Hawaiian.'

make moral judgments. This is the essence of George Orwell's warning when he called political euphemisms 'double-think': when the words for moral wrongs have been 'strip[ped] of undesirable meanings', it is no longer possible to even think about the moral issues.[110] Substituting *affirmative action* for *discrimination* has the same psychological impact as substituting *peace* for *war*: take away the language tools, and there can be no moral clarity.

163. To sum up the 'children's rights perspective', while children and adults have essentially the same human rights, young people need 'special care and assistance' in the fulfilment of CRC rights. But in examining the literature, one never sees the proponents of discriminatory affirmative action mentioning these four injuries to healthy development.

8.7.4. *The CRC and CEDAW*

164. Our discussion of affirmative action in education is not complete until we have examined the relation between the right of non-discrimination in the CRC and the 'special measures' clause in the CEDAW. Before beginning the legal discussion, however, it is important to recall that people hold human rights under the Covenants and the CRC, and that CEDAW (and CERD) are support treaties that help States fulfil their human rights obligations.

165. Article 4(1) of the CEDAW says that 'special measures aimed at accelerating *de facto* equality between men and women shall not be considered discrimination as defined in [Article 1 of] the present Convention, but shall in no way entail as a consequence the maintenance of unequal or separate standards;...'. There are two ways to read that: (i) it is an exception to the definition of discrimination, or (ii) it is not an exception; it's a clarification cause.

It is not unusual to find people treating the 'special measures' clause in CEDAW as an exception that allows discriminatory affirmative action against men and boys. However, the treaty is about discrimination against women, so if the clause is an exception, then it would allow the State Party to discriminate against individual women in the here-and-now in order to advance the long range goal of equality between women as a group and men as a group. (For example, the State could use quotas or other discriminatory affirmative action measures against women to force women out of 'traditionally female-dominated' occupations into male-dominated jobs, thereby accelerating statistical parity.) But despite the widespread assump-

---

[110] G. Orwell, *Nineteen Eighty-Four* (Harmondsworth, Penguin Books, 1975), p. 249.

tion that it is an exception, and despite the oddity that a treaty devoted to eliminating sex discrimination against women would contain an exception that allowed discrimination, commentators have not been addressing the interpretation issues. This section will now fill that gap, using the ordinary meaning rule of the Vienna Convention on the Law of Treaties. (CEDAW's special measures clause is patterned after the one in CERD, and it will be discussed in the margins.)[111]

The Concept of a Clarification Clause

166. A clarification clause is a non-substantive provision – it neither adds to nor takes away from the State's obligations, as defined in the other provisions. A clarification clause is used to help avoid misunderstandings about what the terms of a treaty mean, but it does not change those terms.

167. We have already seen the extensive confusion that is caused by the multiple meanings of affirmative action and related terms, and especially the difficulty of making mental and verbal distinctions between non-discriminatory affirmative action and discriminatory affirmative action. The 'special measures' clause in CEDAW is a clarification clause in response to those confusions: Article 4(1) was inserted to help prevent confusion about *non-discriminatory* affirmative action. It is saying, in paraphrase: '*Just because* a measure aims at helping women as a group obtain equality with men as a group, it must not, *on that ground*, be considered as falling under the definition in Article 1.' That is all that the special measures clause in CEDAW is saying.

Officials might claim that a particular *discriminatory* affirmative action measure is not 'discrimination against women' because it is aimed at helping women. Or political opponents might claim that a certain *non-discriminatory* affirmative action programme violates the Convention because it is treating the group 'women' differently to 'men'. But the truth of any legal claim must always be tested by carefully applying Article 1's definition to the facts in the case – to the particular measure that the government is using, in all its specific details.

---

[111] Article 1(4) of the CERD says, in condensed form, that [a] 'special measures' aimed at advancing particular racial groups so that they can have 'equal enjoyment' of human rights, 'shall not be deemed racial discrimination, [b] provided, however, [i] that such measures do not, as a consequence, lead to the maintenance of separate rights for different racial groups and [ii] that they shall not be continued after the objectives...have been achieved' (brackets added).

Some examples will illustrate how 'special measures' functions as a clarification clause. Article 4(1) is defined in terms of an end-goal: 'special measures <u>aimed at</u> accelerating *de facto* equality between men and women shall not be considered discrimination as defined in the present Convention' (underlining added). There are two ways to go about reaching that objective: *non-discriminatory* affirmative action, and *discriminatory* affirmative action. Both kinds of affirmative action have the same end-goal – de facto equality; where they differ is in the use of sex discrimination as a means to the end.

Let's start with a *non-discriminatory* affirmative action measure: family-friendly workplace policies that help parents combine their child-rearing roles with their occupational roles; these policies will make it easier for women to pursue business careers, thereby advancing equality of results. As a clarification clause, Article 4(1) is saying, '*Just because* a family-friendly policy is "aimed at accelerating" equality, it "shall not be considered", *on that ground*, to be "discrimination against women" under Article 1.' So how do we decide if it is discrimination? We apply the definition in Article 1: a family-friendly measure is not a 'distinction…made on the basis of sex', and it certainly doesn't impair the women's enjoyment of the right to work. So no exceptions are necessary for non-discriminatory affirmative action.[112]

Now let's consider a *discriminatory* affirmative action measure: a ban on scholarships to women who want to go into elementary school teaching, in a country where females are over-represented in that profession; the ban will pressure women into traditionally male careers, thereby accelerating *de facto* equality. As a clarification clause, Article 4(1) is saying, '*Just because* this ban on scholarships is "aimed at accelerating" equality of results, it "shall not be considered", *on that ground*, to be "discrimination against women".' And how do we determine if it is discrimination? We apply the definition in Article 1: a ban on giving scholarships to women is a 'distinction…made on the basis of sex', and it obviously will impair their enjoyment of the right to education. But Article 4(1) does not authorize this act of discriminatory

---

[112] See, M. Freeman, 'Temporary Special Measures', in: I. Boerefijn, et al., *o.c.* (note 104), pp. 97, 99 ('This ['special measures'] caveat is necessary because measures to accelerate…*de facto*…equality will appear to advantage women over men…', and 'Opponents…characterise them as "reverse discrimination"…'.), p. 100 (citing 'child care' and 'curriculum and textbook reviews' as examples of Article 4(1) measures). A 'caveat' is a warning or caution, so it is not as accurate as 'clarification clause', but Freeman's point is still correct: the clause guards against mistaken opposition to non-discriminatory affirmative action.

affirmative action, and that is because 'special measures' is not an exception to the definition.

168. In short, the aim of a clarification clause is to help minimize the chances of misunderstanding the terms of a treaty, but it does not change those terms. Unfortunately, experience has shown that these clauses can create more misunderstandings than they prevent, so it is probably best if lawmakers did not use them. Nevertheless, the General Assembly has used them,[113] so we must use legal methodology to interpret 'special measures' with two possibilities in mind: (i) it is an exception, so States can use discriminatory affirmative action against women to promote the interests of women as a group, or (ii) it is a clarification clause, as was described in the preceding paragraphs.

The Legal Analysis
169. In the discussion below, we will consider five reasons why 'special measures' can only be read as a clarification clause. The first reason is that the special measures clause does not use the word 'exception' or any equivalent term. In a treaty dedicated to ending 'all forms of' sex discrimination against women, the absence of express words of exception can mean only one thing: the General Assembly did not create an exception: it did not intend to allow States to use discriminatory affirmative action against individual women as a way to advance *de facto* equality for women as group. This commonsense conclusion is supported by several considerations.

(i) To begin with, the way that the General Assembly wrote the CEDAW must be viewed in the context of how it has written the human rights agreements. When the Universal Declaration and the Covenants were being created, States often said that they must be written in language that is

---

[113] *E.g.*, Article 1(1) of the CERD defines 'racial discrimination', and Articles 1(2) (pertaining to citizens/non-citizens) and 1(3) (pertaining to citizenship) are clarification clauses: they do not create exceptions to Article 1(1); they cannot create exceptions because 'citizenship' is not a named ground in the definition. Accord, CERD Comm., *Gen. Recom. No. 30: Discrimination against non-citizens* (2005) (UN Doc. HRI/GEN/1/Rev.8, 2006), para. 2. See also *Travaux Préparatoires* for the CERD: *e.g.*, GA, 3rd Comm. (UN Doc. A/C.3/SR.1299, 1965), para. 10 (United States) (explaining that Article 1(2) 'was aimed at clarifying the meaning of the expression "national origin"'). Compare to T. Meron, *Human Rights Law-Making in the United Nations* (Oxford, Clarendon Press, 1986), pp. 44–46 (asserting, without explanation, that Article 1(2) is an exception, and being unclear about Article 1(3)). Meron provides one of the most extensive discussions of CERD, but, unfortunately, he tends to give conclusory opinions rather than conduct a legal analysis, as will be seen in the footnotes to follow.

not only legally precise,[114] but also so that ordinary people will be able to understand them.[115]

(ii) The General Assembly kept to those principles by clearly indicating exceptions through unmistakable language; for example, the CCPR says that the State Party 'may take measures derogating from their obligations...' under specified circumstances.[116]

(iii) State-imposed discrimination on the basis of sex (or race) is an extremely serious matter. The Charter says that Member States are to realize human rights 'without distinction as to race [and] sex', and, when CEDAW announces that 'all forms of discrimination against women' are to be 'eliminated', it would be strange for the General Assembly to have allowed any exceptions. (And the same is true for CERD with regard to allowing racial discrimination.) On the other hand, *if* the General Assembly were to permit States to use sex discrimination under CEDAW as a means to *de facto* equality (or race discrimination under CERD), *then* it would have done it in clear, unambiguous language. (The clearest way is for a treaty to

---

[114] For statements in reference to the non-discrimination articles, see, *e.g.*, *Travaux Préparatoires* for the CESCR: GA, 3rd Comm. (UN Doc. A/C.3/SR.562, 1954), para. 6 (United Kingdom) ('cardinal importance' that rights 'be stated with utmost precision'); (UN Doc. A/C.3/SR.567, 1954), para. 15 (Philippines) ('should be precise it its wording'); (UN Doc. A/C.3/SR.571, 1954), para. 21 (Poland) (defined 'with a maximum of precision'); (UN Doc. A/C.3/SR.659, 1955), para. 28 (Mexico) ('provision on discrimination' must be 'clear and unequivocal' to have 'moral weight and practical value'), and para. 38 (Dominican Republic) ('drafted with the utmost clarity'); (UN Doc. A/C.3/SR.1183, 1962), para. 13 (Italy) (must be 'technically perfect').

[115] For statements in reference to the non-discrimination articles, see, *e.g.*, *Travaux Préparatoires* for the UDHR: *Official Records of the Third Session of the General Assembly, Part I: Third Committee: 21 September – 8 December 1948* (Lake Success, New York, United Nations, 1948): 176th mtg. (6 Dec. 1948), pp. 875–876 (Mrs. Roosevelt, United States of America) (rights must 'be intelligible to the person who reads the document [the UDHR]'); and *Travaux Préparatoires* for the CESCR: (UN Doc. A/C.3/SR.1183, 1962), para. 10 (India) (drafting of CESCR must 'not be done with only jurists in mind' but so that 'average men and women' can read the non-discrimination provisions and find them 'clear').

[116] Article 4(1) of the CCPR; also: Article 8(3) ('Paragraph 3(a) shall not be held to preclude....', 'the term "forced or compulsory labour" shall not include...'), Article 13 ('shall, except where compelling reasons of national security otherwise require,...'), Article 14(1) ('[E]veryone shall be entitled to a...public hearing....The press and the public may be excluded...for reasons of....'), Article 15(2) ('Nothing in this article shall prejudice....'), Article 19(3) ('The exercise of the rights...may therefore be subject to certain restrictions....'), and Article 22(3) ('This article shall not prevent the imposition of lawful restrictions on....'). See also: Article 14(2) of the UDHR ('This right may not be invoked in the case of....'), and Article 29(2) ('shall be subject only to such limitations...'). Also: Article 4 of the CESCR ('may subject such rights only to such limitations...'), and Article 8(2) ('shall not prevent the imposition of lawful restrictions...').

(1) define 'discrimination', then (2) prohibit 'discrimination', and then (3) make an exception to the prohibition, not to the definition. For instance: 'Article 3. The State Party may derogate from the prohibitions in Article 2 in the following circumstances..., provided that it observes the following safeguards....' That structure and language make the intention crystal clear.) But CEDAW does not use any of the established techniques for creating exceptions (and neither does CERD).

(iv) Due to a fairly widespread assumption that the special measures clause is an exception, there is a tendency for people to read Article 4(1) quickly with that presupposition in mind, without looking closely at the language. But when the article is read carefully, it is clear that it is not a derogation provision. The key words are: 'special measures...shall not be considered discrimination'. *Shall not be considered* is different than *shall be considered not to be*. The latter phrase makes an exception, which it does by creating a legal fiction. But the former phrase, the one used in CEDAW, is not grammatically an exception.

Consider these two hypothetical statutes:

> Law (1): 'Dogs are prohibited in restaurants. Seeing-eye dogs shall be considered not to be dogs.'
> Law (2): 'Dogs are prohibited in restaurants. Cats shall not be considered to be dogs.'

The statement about seeing-eye dogs is a legal fiction. No one denies that a seeing-eye dog is a 'dog', but the statute issues a positive command to give an artificial meaning to the word. It is saying, in paraphrase: 'When enforcing this Law, *consider* seeing-eye dogs *not to be* "dogs"; treat these particular dogs *as if* they were not dogs; do not exclude these particular dogs from restaurants, even though the Law says "Dogs are prohibited".' *Shall be considered not to be* creates a legal fiction, and the fiction makes an exception to the prohibition. In Law (2), on the other hand, 'Cats shall not be considered to be dogs' is not a fiction. Quite the contrary; it issues a negative command not to read the words of the Law contrary to their normal meaning. In paraphrase it is saying: 'Do not interpret *dogs* to include cats; despite good reasons for also forbidding cats in restaurants, cats shall not be treated as if they were dogs, in disregard to the ordinary meaning of the word *dog*.' *Shall not be considered to be* is a clarification clause aimed at preventing misapplications of the law.

If the General Assembly had intended the special measures clause in CEDAW to allow derogations, *then* the language would have to have been, 'shall be considered not to be discrimination' – a positive command that creates a legal fiction. But the grammatical construction of the phrase used – *shall not be considered* – does not create a fiction, and it does not permit exceptions. Moreover, if the General Assembly had intended to allow States to use sex discrimination as a tool for advancing equality, it would have said so in crystal clear language, as it has done when making other kinds of exceptions in the human rights treaties.

To summarize the first point, the General Assembly's decision not to expressly say that 'special measures' is an exception to the definition of in Article 1, in a treaty dedicated to eliminating 'all forms' of sex discrimination against women, leads to just one conclusion: Article 4(1) of the CEDAW does not create an exception; it is only a clarification clause.[117]

170. The second reason is that Article 4(1) contains a proviso that no discriminatory affirmative action measure could pass: a special measure 'shall in no way entail as a consequence the maintenance of unequal or separate standards'. Let us say that parliament authorizes sex-based waivers of school fees, and the law is to come into effect on 1 January 2008. From that day forward, the State is 'maintaining unequal standards' for the award of educational benefits. Regardless of which sex is being discriminated against, a sex-based criterion is an 'unequal standard' of allocation. By its very terms,

---

[117] Accord, E. Evatt, 'The Practical Relevance of Article 4 CEDAW', in: I. Boerefin, et al., *o.c.* (note 104), p. 52 (the General Assembly made a policy decision not to frame special measures 'as exceptions'); R. Cook, 'Obligations to Adopt Temporary Special Measures [Under CEDAW]', in: I. Boerefijn, et al., *o.c.* (note 104), p. 123 ('Article 4(1) is explanatory in nature.'); R. Holtmatt, 'Building Blocks for a General Recommendation on Article 4(1)', in: I. Boerefijn, et al., *o.c.* (note 104), p. 215 (Article 4(1) 'is an *explanation* instead of an *exception*').

CEDAW's *shall not be considered* is a variation of *shall not be deemed* in Article 1(4) of the CERD. Based on the same four considerations, the absence of clear words of exception in Article 1(4) of the CERD, a treaty devoted to eliminating 'all forms' of racial discrimination, leads to a similar conclusion: the General Assembly did not intend to allow discriminatory affirmative action.

While CERD's framers gave only a few generalized examples of 'special measures', none entailed racial discrimination, and most referred to protecting indigenous peoples; the most concrete of all the examples was the restoration of land after unjust dispossession. *Travaux Préparatoires* (UN Doc. E/CN.4/Sub.2/SR.411, 1964), p. 9 (Cuevas Cancino). The restoration of land to indigenous owners (or descendants) is a particular application of normal legal principles, such as restitution and inheritance, and is not based on racial discrimination.

Compare to T. Meron, *o.c.* (note 113), pp. 14–17, 36–38 (claiming that 'special measures' is an exception, but not addressing the lack of words of exception, or discussing the possibility that it is a clarification clause). He also claims that Article 4(1) in the CEDAW allows 'affirmative action', but he is silent about it being an exception that allows discriminatory affirmative action against individual women, for the benefit of all women, even though it is nearly identical to the special measures clause in the CERD; *id.* p. 63.

the special measures clause rules out the use of sex discrimination as a means for achieving CEDAW's objectives.[118]

171. The third reason is that discriminatory affirmative action measures cannot survive the requirements laid down in CEDAW's sectoral articles. For instance, the treaty expressly forbids a sex-based quota on school enrolment: 'access to studies' must be on 'the same conditions' for males and females. And a sex-based preference in financial aid is expressly outlawed: males and females must have the 'same opportunities to benefit from scholarships'. (Article 10(a) & (d) of the CEDAW, respectively.)[119]

172. The fourth reason is that CEDAW is a support treaty to the human rights treaties, so it must be read in harmony with the Covenants, the CRC, and the UN Charter. The right to an education, and the right not to be dis-

---

[118] Accord, R. Cook, *o.c.* (note 117), p. 125 (Article 4(1) prohibits 'unequal or separate standards, where those standards would prove detrimental to men'); A. W. Heringa, 'Comments on the Contribution by Professor Cook', in: I. Boerefin, et al., *o.c.* (note 104), p. 145 (Article 4(1) 'assume[s] that unequal or separate standards are inherently wrong').

Likewise, racially discriminatory affirmative action cannot pass the 'no maintenance of separate rights' test in Article 1(4) of the CERD. Compare to T. Meron, *o.c.* (note 113), p. 16 (pretending that the no-separate-rights test applies only after the measure has achieved its objective).

In both treaties, 'special measures' has two sub-clauses: no-separate-rights/standards, just discussed, and a separate statement that a measure is not to continue after its objective has been achieved. People often think that the second sub-clause is a safeguard, but that is not so: it's trivial to say that an action must stop if it loses its justification. This sub-clause first appeared in the Draft Declaration on the Elimination of All Forms of Racial Discrimination, but it was removed because it added nothing of substance. *Travaux Préparatoires* (UN Doc. A/C.3/SR.1214, 1963), para. 44 (Farhang) (sub-clause is 'pointless'), (UN Doc. A/C.3/SR.1224, 1963), para. 26 (sub-clause removed). And even though it was later put into the CERD, it's superficiality was still noted; (UN Doc. E/CN.4/SR.784, 1964), p. 10 (Benites) ('obviously' an 'obsolete' law 'should not be maintained'). But since 'special measures' is not an exception, the superficiality is not legally important. On the other hand, people have abused these sub-clauses by claiming that the treaties allow race and sex discrimination as long as it is 'temporary', as if the General Assembly could have thought that was morally relevant. (Apartheid was temporary, even shorter was the Nazi liquidation programme, and shorter still the ethnic cleansings in Bosnia and Rwanda – all 'special' measures using discrimination to obtain a goal.)

[119] Article 5 of the CERD obligates the State 'to prohibit and eliminate racial discrimination [as defined in Article 1]... *and to guarantee* to everyone, *without distinction as to race* [etc.] to equality before the law, notably in the enjoyment of the following rights...' (emphasis added). If Article 1(4) of the CERD is read as an exception to the definition of 'discrimination' in Article 1(1), then the State is still forbidden to make adverse racial distinctions by virtue of the 'without distinction as to race' requirement. The only way to avoid the treaty being self-contradictory is to read Article 1(4) as a clarifying clause. Compare to T. Meron, *o.c.* (note 113), p. 11 (acknowledging that Article 5 is relevant to interpreting the definition in Article 1(1), but, since he does not conduct a legal analysis or provide an interpretation, he does not address this issue).

criminated against on account of sex (race, etc.) in enjoying that right, are held by individuals pursuant to the human rights treaties, not the support treaties. If a support treaty were to carve out an exception to the human rights treaties, there would have to be a clause that made the necessary cross-reference. (For example: 'A State Party to this Convention [CEDAW] can derogate from its obligations under Article 2(1) of the CCPR for the following purposes...under the following circumstances....') The clause would amend the crossed-referenced human rights treaty.[120] But CEDAW contains no provision that amends the Covenants or the CRC. In fact, it does just the opposite. CEDAW expressly reaffirms the non-discrimination requirements in the UN Charter, the Universal Declaration , and the two Covenants: States must fulfil human rights without 'distinction[s] based on sex'.[121]

173. The fifth reason is because the special measures clause has to be read in the light of the 'object and purpose' of the CEDAW (Article 31(1) of the VCLT).[122] If something can be interpreted in two ways, then the reading that best fulfils the purpose of the treaty is the one to be adopted. We are

---

[120] The third main rule of interpretation, the 'subsequent acts rule', allows the terms to be altered by subsequent agreements (Articles 31(3), 40, 57 of the VCLT), or events (Articles 61 and 62 of the VCLT). Also, see note 56 (CCPR forbids sex and race discrimination even in national emergencies).

[121] Preambular paragraph two of the CEDAW, citing the UDHR; see also preambular paragraphs one and three of the CEDAW. Likewise, CERD reconfirms the UN's non-discrimination norms (preamble, all seven paragraphs). At its adoption, the UN Secretary General said that CERD's terms must be 'carried out precisely' and 'in accordance with' the Charter and the Universal Declaration. GA, 1406th mtg. (21 Dec. 1965), para. 143. Compare to T. Meron, *o.c.* (note 113), pp. 7–41 (referring to the Charter and Covenants, but not addressing the conflict between their prohibitions of race discrimination and his reading Article 1(4) as an exception that allows discriminatory affirmative action).

Discriminatory affirmative action is also ruled out by the two built-in anti-discrimination clauses in the right to education: 'on the basis of equal opportunity', and 'on the basis of capacity', in Article 28(1) [chapeau] and (c) of the CRC. 'Equal opportunity' is normally understood as referring to non-discrimination, and we must read in the relevant forbidden grounds from Article 2(1). 'Capacity' is referring to the youngster, not the school, and equates with 'merit' in Article 26(1) of the UDHR. See, *e.g.*, UNICEF, *Educational For All?* (Florence, UNICEF, International Child Development Centre, 1998) (Regional Monitoring Report No. 5), p. x ('A well-run national system of school examinations also helps ensure that selection is on the basis of merit rather than any other criterion.').

The Main Types and Causes of Discrimination, o.c. (note 23), identifies numerous 'forms' of impermissible discrimination against people on the basis of their race, sex, etc. These include: employment policies that 'limit the number' of members of a particular race, etc. group that can be hired, trained or promoted, paras. 111, and 124; rules that restrict access to educational opportunities of members of any race, etc. group, including 'quota or percentage systems', para. 114; and restrictions upon 'the right of individuals to vote or to be elected because they belong to' a particular race, sex, etc. group, paras. 118, and 124.

[122] Quoted in full, No. 31.

confronted with choosing between reading Article 4(1) as either (i) a legal fiction that allows exceptions, or (ii) a clarification clause. The overarching purpose of CEDAW is to eliminate 'all forms' of sex discrimination against women, and the preamble says that 'discrimination against women violates the principles of equality of rights and respect for human dignity'. That settles the matter: Article 4(1) must be read as a clarification clause rather than an exception.[123]

174. All five reasons lead to the same conclusion that 'special measures' is not an exception, but our task is not finished. We still have to consider the 'absurd results' test in the ordinary meaning rule. If a text-based interpretation 'leads to a result which is manifestly absurd or unreasonable', then we can reject that reading, and turn to the legislative history to try to discover what the lawmakers had meant to say (Article 32 of the VCLT[124]). So we must ask: 'Is it manifestly absurd to read the special measures clause as a clarifying clause?' The answer is 'No,' for the same reasons that an absolute right of non-discrimination is not manifestly absurd: (i) The State can promote equality in well-being through an extraordinary range of *non-discriminatory* affirmative action measures; (ii) the clarification-clause reading is consistent with the UN Charter and the human rights treaties, while the legal-fiction/ exception reading is not; and (iii) a State that feels it must use discriminatory affirmative action can file a carefully written reservation, and then defend itself under the laws on reservations (Article 28 of the CEDAW).[125]

175. In conclusion, we have used the ordinary meaning rule to decide between two possibilities: Article 4(1) is either (i) a legal fiction that creates an exception, thereby allowing States to use sex discrimination as a means

---

[123] Using CEDAW to discriminate against men would also violate those two principles.

CERD's statement of purpose is even stronger: 'there is no justification for racial discrimination, in theory or in practice, anywhere'. (Preamble, para. 6; repeating the condemnation in the Declaration on the Elimination of All Forms of Racial Discrimination, fifth preambular paragraph.) This is as categorical a condemnation as possible. Article 1(4) of the CERD cannot be an exception when read in the light of that statement, or the rest of the preamble. Moreover, international law is widely recognized as absolutely forbidding state-imposed racial discrimination; see No. 86. Compare to T. Meron, *o.c.* (note 113), pp. 12–14 (claiming that CERD's objective is 'equality', ignoring its stated paramount purpose to eliminate all forms of racial discrimination, and ignoring the problem that discriminatory affirmative action is *de jure* inequality of treatment, and hence, inequality of results between competitors, as shown in Figure 2).

[124] Quoted in full, note 19.

[125] For the same reasons, it is not absurd to read Article 1(4) of the CERD as a clarifying clause.

to an end, or (ii) it is a clarification clause. All of the considerations have led to the same conclusion – it is a clarifying clause.

176. For a commentary to be authoritative, we usually expect the author to discuss the reasons in support of Proposition A, then the reasons in support of the countervailing Proposition B, and then decide between the two after examining their relative merits. This section has not discussed the positive case for reading the special measures clause as a legal fiction that allows derogations from the prohibition of sex discrimination against women, or for reading CEDAW as authorizing sex discrimination against men. The reason for this is simple: no commentator has given the legal arguments for such interpretations. Many people have acted as if CEDAW authorizes discriminatory affirmative action, but none have opened up their reasoning to public scrutiny.[126]

---

[126] The CEDAW Committee wrote a lengthy comment 'aim[ed] to clarify the nature and meaning' of Article 4(1): CEDAW Comm., *Gen. Recom. No. 25: Article 4, paragraph 1* (2004) (UN Doc. HRI/GEN/1/Rev.8, 2006), para. 2. The Committee drew upon a legal memorandum by the present author covering the same points as in this section, and upon numerous other legal papers, some of which are collected in I. Boerefijn, et al., *o.c.* (note 102). After being fully briefed, the Committee did not say that 'special measures' is an exception, or that CEDAW, or anything else in international law, permits States to use sex discrimination against either women or men as a means to promote equality. Oddly, however, the comment does not give a legal interpretation, and it contains several mystifications; *e.g.*, it mentions 'quotas' and 'preferential treatment' without any explanation of what is meant, *id.* para. 22, and it says, 'Measures taken under article 4, paragraph 1' are 'not [...] an exception to the norm of non-discrimination'; *id.* para. 18. But it does not say what that 'norm' is.

To oversimplify, the literature on CERD can be divided into three categories. (i) Some commentators do not say that the special measures clause creates an exception, in contexts where, if they believed that it did, they would have said so; *e.g.*, M. Banton, *o.c.* (note 45); P. Thornberry, *International Law and the Rights of Minorities* (Oxford, Clarendon Press, 1991), pp. 265–268; P. Thornberry, 'The Committee on the Elimination of Racial Discrimination – Questions of concept and practice', in: R. F. Jørgensen & K. Slavensky (eds.), *Implementing Human Rights: Essays in Honour of Morten Kjærum* (Copenhagen, Danish Institute for Human Rights, 2007), pp. 318–336. (ii) Some commentators are ambiguous, which allows readers to see what they want to see; *e.g.*, L.-A. Sicilianos, 'L'actualité et les potentialités de la Convention sur l'élimination de la discrimination raciale', *Revue Trimestrielle des Droits de L'Homme* 64 (2005), pp. 869–921. Sicilianos correctly identifies the issue as whether or not Article 1(4) of the CERD is a legal fiction, but instead of addressing the question, he makes declaratory statements in favour of using racial discrimination as a means to an end; *id.* p. 899. By contrast, he applies legal analysis to other, less important matters; *id.* p. 883. (iii) Some commentators say, either directly or by implication, that 'special measures' are exceptions, but without giving their lines of reasoning; *e.g.*, T. Meron, *o.c.* (note 113); and International Labour Office, *Equality at Work: Tackling the Challenges* (Geneva, ILO, 2007), categorically condemning race, sex, etc. discrimination as wrong and a human rights violation, using the same definition of 'discrimination' as in this commentary, *e.g.*, pp. x, 2, 7, 9, 50, but then endorsing discriminatory affirmative action, without acknowledging the self-contradiction, *e.g.*, pp. 2, 10 (calling 'quotas' 'affirmative action'), 61–64 (masking the discrimination).

177. But all of this detailed legal analysis must not distract us from our task, which is to define the relation of 'special measures' in CEDAW (and CERD) to Article 2(1) of the CRC. In a sense, it ultimately does not matter whether 'special measures' is an exception or not because young people hold human rights under the CRC and the two Covenants, not the support treaties. In the (unlikely) event of a conflict, the right of non-discrimination in Common Articles 2 must prevail, in the absence of a cross-referencing provision in a support treaty that derogates from the 'inalienable rights'[127] in the human rights treaties. States must take *affirmative action* to secure the enjoyment of the sectoral rights (and to fulfil their obligations in the support treaties), and it must be *non-discriminatory* affirmative action (unless there is a valid reservation).

Conclusion to Section 8: 'The Main Sources of Confusion'

178. This section has been the longest in the commentary because we have had to deal with so many sources of confusion about the right of non-discrimination: the 'principle of non-discrimination'; the so-called proportionality principle; the case law on the European Convention; the Committee's 'four general principles'; 'indirect discrimination'; 'purpose or effect'; 'affirmative action'; and the 'special measures' clauses in CEDAW and CERD. Three points have emerged from the discussion. (i) All of these expressions share a common denominator: they create confusion, which people exploit in order to commit race, sex, etc. discrimination. (ii) The confusions run throughout the legal literature. And (iii), discriminatory affirmative action is one of the biggest challenges to the children's rights movement. It challenges us adults to bear greater sacrifices in order to ensure that young people enjoy, without discrimination, their right to education and other resource-intensive rights; it challenges us to take the right of non-discrimination seriously as a human right under international law; and it challenges us to demand greater transparency from commentators.[128]

---

[127] First preambular paragraph of the UDHR.

[128] There is a vast and growing literature on discrimination. In addition to the other works cited, see B. Hepple and E. Szyszczak (eds.), *Discrimination: The Limits of Law* (London/ New York, Mansell Publ., 1993); T. Loenen and P. Rodrigues (eds.), *Non-Discrimination Law: Comparative Perspectives* (The Hague/London/Boston, Kluwer Law Int'l., 1999); E. Appelt and M. Jarosch (eds.), *Combating Racial Discrimination: Affirmative Action as a Model for Europe* (Oxford/ New York, Berg, 2000); A. Numhauser-Henning (ed.), *Legal Perspectives on Equal Treatment and Non-Discrimination* (The Hague, Kluwer Law Int'l., 2001); J. Niessen and I. Chopin (eds.), *The Development of Legal Instruments to Combat Racism in a Diverse Europe* (Leiden/Boston, Martinus

9. The Four Ways That a State Can Be out of Compliance with Article 2(1)

179. The elements-approach makes it relatively easy to determine if State laws are in compliance with the right of non-discrimination in Common Articles 2. By lining up the elements of Article 2(1) to the elements of a national law, one can see immediately if there is a mismatch. There are four kinds of discrepancies to look for.

9.1. The State's Anti-Discrimination Law Has Gaps

180. There can be discrepancies if the State's anti-discrimination laws do not track the language of Article 2(1). The law might not cover all the named grounds of taboo differentiation; for instance, 'disability' may have been omitted.[129] (The law's (a)-variables are 'under inclusive'.) Or the law might not cover all the relevant spheres of life. (The (b)-variables do not correspond to all of the CRC's sectoral rights.) Or the law might not protect all children and adolescents; for instance, the law is framed in terms of 'citizens'.[130] (The law's definition of the right-holders does not correspond to Article 1.)

181. These mismatches do not automatically mean that the State is violating Article 2(1) since the right is a 'negative' obligation not to discriminate, rather than a 'positive' one to enact legislation. But the failure to track the language of the Convention is a warning sign that some state actors might not be living up to the CRC's requirements. Moreover, the duty to take 'appropriate legislative' measures for the realization of CRC rights (Article 4) strongly implies an obligation to pass an anti-discrimination law with enforceable remedies.[131]

Nijhoff Publ., 2004). Except for the Committee's 'four general principles', commentators typically use the confusions in section 8 as the building blocks for their discussions.

On the other hand, some authors have strived to build on conceptual clarity: *e.g.*, R. K. Fullinwider, *The Reverse Discrimination Controversy: A Moral and Legal Analysis* (Totowa, New Jersey, Rowman and Littlefield, 1981); A. Peters, *Women, Quotas and Constitutions* (The Hague/London/Boston, Kluwer Law Int'l., 1999); E. Ellis, *EC Sex Equality Law* (2nd ed., Oxford, Clarendon Press, 1998).

[129] *E.g.*, CRC Comm., *Concl. Obser.: Angola* (UN Doc. CRC/C/143, 2004), para. 399 (disability discrimination omitted); *Singapore* (UN Doc. CRC/C/51/Add.8, 2003), paras. 107–108 (sex discrimination omitted).

[130] CRC Comm., *Concl. Obser.: Lebanon* (UN Doc. CRC/C/42/3, 2006), para. 408.

[131] CRC Comm., *Concl. Obser.: Uzbekistan* (UN Doc. CRC/C/42/3, 2006), para. 636 ('concerned at the lack of specific anti-discrimination legislation').

9.2. *The State Does Not Have an Anti-Discrimination Law*

182. A more fundamental problem occurs when the national law is framed in terms of 'equality', rather than a right of non-discrimination. Laws based on 'equality' usually permit the State to discriminate pursuant to some kind of a balancing test, so they do not serve the three functions of Common Articles 2. Most common are 'equality before the law',[132] 'equal protection of the law',[133] and 'proportionality'.[134]

---

[132] *E.g., Switzerland* (UN Doc. CRC/C/78/Add.3, 2001), para. 61 (equality before the law allows discrimination subject to the proportionality principle), and para. 62 (adding safeguards).

[133] When Article 26 of the CCPR was being created, States stressed the need for the anti-discrimination sub-clause because equality before the law and equal protection of the law can permit race, etc. discrimination. *E.g., Travaux Préparatoires*, GA, 3rd Comm. (UN Doc. A/C.3/SR.1098, 1961), para. 25 (Philippines) (pointing out that 'separate but equal facilities' in the United States and apartheid in South Africa can flourish under 'equality' guarantees); see also (UN Doc. A/C.3/SR.1099, 1961), para. 27 (Cameroon), and para. 45 (Poland). For instance: United States Supreme Court, *Plessy* v. *Ferguson*, 163 U.S. 537 (1896) (race discrimination in admission to public transportation does not violate equal protection of the law), and *Grutter* v. *Bollinger*, 539 U.S. 306 (2003) (race discrimination in admittance to profession education does not violate equal protection of the law). Accord, *Analysis of Article 2 of the [CEDAW]* (UN Doc. CEDAW/C/1995/4, 1994), para. 26 (constitutional guarantees of equality are 'too vague or general to provide substantive protection for women').

[134] *E.g., Norway* (UN Doc. CERD/C/497/Add.1, 2005), paras. 10 & 12 (Under the Anti-Discrimination Act, 'Differential treatment [on the ground of ethnicity, national origin, descent, skin colour, language, religion or belief] that is necessary in order to achieve a legitimate objective [and] that does not constitute a disproportionate intervention for the person or persons affected, is not considered to be discrimination under the Act.').

There is a gargantuan literature on 'equality', which expands by 'rethinking', or redefining, the term. Confusions between the right of non-discrimination and 'equality' can be avoided by making some basic distinctions, starting with the difference between the ordinary meaning of *equal*, and the term-of-art meaning:

(1) 'Equal' means 'same'. Using the ordinary meaning, commentators talk about three kinds of *equality*: (a) same treatment (which is another way to speak about non-discrimination); (b) same results, from a particular act (or set of acts); and (a) same statistical probabilities, resulting from numerous causes working together. In any discussion about 'sameness', clear thinking requires specifying the two variables in the case: the particular ground(s) of potential differentiation, and the interest(s) at stake.

(2) 'Equal' means 'reasonable'. In the term-of-art usage, there is 'equality' between *A* and *B* when the actor treats them 'reasonably'. See, *e.g.,* C. McCrudden, *Buying Social Justice* (Oxford, Oxford Univ. Press, 2007), p. 513 ('*Equality as "rationality"*'). This meaning is useful for legalizing unequal treatment on account of race, sex, etc. (*i.e.,* discrimination); N. Bamforth, 'Limits of Anti-Discrimination Law: Legal and Social Concepts of Equality', in: J. Dine & B. Watt, *Discrimination Law: Concepts, Limitations and Justifications* (London/New York, Longman, 1996), p. 62 ('reinterpreting the legal concepts of discrimination...acts to justify discrimination'). In this usage, people are confusing the word 'equality' with a 'principle of equality', by which they really mean the 'principle of reasonableness'; see note 74.

9.3. *The State's Anti-Discrimination Law Allows Exceptions, but There Is No Corresponding Reservation*

183. National laws sometimes authorize discrimination, but the State has not made the necessary reservation that would allow it to deviate from Common Articles 2. The domestic exception might be contained in the anti-discrimination law,[135] or in the sectoral legislation,[136] or in the constitution, but the international human rights problem is the same.

184. An example of this is found in India's CRC report. The Constitution of India says:

> (1) The State shall not discriminate against any citizen on grounds only of religion, race, caste, sex, place of birth or any of them....
> (3) Nothing in this article shall prevent the State from making any special provision for women and children.[137]

Clause (1) gives citizens a right of non-discrimination analogous to the ones in Common Articles 2, and India treats clause (3) as an exception to the right's categorical prohibition, in accordance with the natural sense of the language, 'Nothing...shall prevent....' And pursuant to this exception, the State practices sex discrimination in primary and secondary education. For instance, it has 'incentive schemes, like free noon meals, free books, free uniforms and attendance scholarships for girls and children from disadvantaged groups', which is discriminatory affirmative action against disadvantaged boys.[138]

185. At the domestic level, India has been faithful to the rule of law: the categorical prohibition of sex discrimination in clause (1) would preclude discriminating against male school children if the constitution did not contain the exception in clause (3). Whether or not one agrees with the political decision to use sex discrimination against children as a means to an end (and against disadvantaged children at that), the constitution provides

---

[135] *E.g.*, the United Kingdom's Sex Discrimination Act 1975, sec. 47(1) (authorizing discrimination in certain training situations); Equality Act 2006, sec. 83 (amending SDA, sec. 21A, Table of Exceptions, item 13) (authorizing sex-based discriminatory affirmative action in all fields covered by the Act, without safeguards or limits). However, there are no corresponding reservations to the CRC or the CESCR.

[136] *E.g.*, the United Kingdom also allows sex discrimination against older men under a number of laws, such as the Social Security Act 1975, Transportation Act 1985, and National Health Service (Charges for Drugs and Appliances) Regulations 1980.

[137] Article 15 of the Constitution of India; cited in *India* (UN Doc. CRC/C/93/Add.5, 2003), para. 219.

[138] *Id.* para. 821.

a loophole, so the political actors who made the trade-off decisions have respected the rule of law. However, knowing that it needed an exception to the ban on sex discrimination in the constitution, India ratified the CRC without making a corresponding reservation to Article 2(1). As a result, its discriminatory affirmative action against boys does not ensure the right of non-discrimination that the injured boys hold under the CRC, when read in conjunction with their right to education.

And since sex discrimination against children and adolescents is not in harmony with Article 2(1), the CRC Committee disapproved of the Government's policies. In a diplomatically worded concluding observation, the Committee said that, while welcoming the increased attention to girls and other needy groups, it was concerned that 'children in situations similar to that of those groups are not receiving the same benefits', and it recommended that the State change to 'special programmes' that are 'based on the child's needs and rights', rather than the child's sex.[139]

186. International human rights law is extremely generous in allowing reservations, so much so that the abuse of the reservation clauses has been a major theme in the human rights literature. There are three things in particular that work together to give States their enormous latitude. (i) The general test for the validity of a reservation is vague (it must not be 'incompatible with the object and purpose of the treaty', Article 19(c) of the VCLT). (ii) The general test is not well suited for human rights treaties (Article 51 of the CRC replicates the general test). And (iii), there is no authority figure in the UN system of state accountability that is entitled to override the State's decision. In the light of the freedom that States enjoy in making reservations, and given the amount of time that they had to think about the CRC before ratifying it (it was ten years in the making), and the even longer period to think about the right of non-discrimination (work on the UDHR began in 1947), only the most extraordinary circumstances should be allowed to excuse a State Party from respecting the rule of law in regard to Article 2(1). As for India's report, it would seem that the Committee held the State Party to the same rule-of-law standard that the country has held itself to in its domestic legal system.

---

[139] CRC Comm., *Concl. Obser.: India* (UN Doc. CRC/C/15/Add.228, 2004), paras. 31–32.

9.4. *The State Made a Ratification Statement That Does Not Constitute a Valid Reservation*

187. While the right of non-discrimination is an absolute right, 'absolute' is a term-of-art that leaves open the possibility that a State could make a valid reservation. A reservation has the legal effect of releasing a Party from the duty to comply with the obligations being reserved to; in a sense, it removes the provision in question from the treaty in regard to that particular State.

Governments make a variety of statements when they file their notices of ratification, and not all of them are reservations. For instance, a statement might be just a declaration or interpretive comment indicating how the Party understands a particular provision,[140] or it might be a hortatory remark; but only a reservation can alter the terms of the treaty (for that Party). So the first question is whether a particular statement is a reservation, an interpretive comment, or just a rhetorical flourish. The matter is not always easy to decide since States don't always label their statements (and a State might later disavow its official characterization).

If a particular statement is interpreted to be a reservation, then the second question is its validity under the 'incompatibility' test. This question is often complicated by the vagueness of the reservations. For one thing, the statement might be so lacking in specificity that one does not know what the State is trying to accomplish. And for another, the statement might be excessively broad. If the State had carefully tailored the reservation to meet a specific need, then its departure from international standards could be tolerated, while an over-broad reservation might destroy the entire right if it were to be accepted as valid.

---

[140] *E.g.*, the United States filed an 'understanding' that the right of non-discrimination in the CCPR is nothing but the reasonableness principle; 31 *International Legal Materials* 645–661 (1992), p. 655.

188. A State's ratification statement could refer to Article 2 specifically.[141] Or it could refer to a sectoral article,[142] or it could be a 'free floating' statement,[143] so that it might have a backdoor effect on the right of non-discrimination. Whether a particular statement relieves a Party from Article 2(1) obligations depends on how the two questions are answered: Is it a reservation? Is it a valid reservation? And since there is no definitive authority to settle the legal disputes, opinions can vary.[144]

---

[141] *E.g.*, Belgium made an 'Interpretative declaration' to Article 2(1); *Reservations [etc.] to the [CRC]* (UN Doc. CRC/C/2/Rev.8, 1999), pp. 14–15. Although ambiguous, the statement indicates that the Government is reading Article 2(1) through the lens of *Belgium Languages*.

[142] France made a 'declaration' about Article 6 (concerning 'the voluntary interrupting of pregnancy') (UN Doc. CRC/C/2/Rev.8, 1999), p. 21; Luxembourg made a 'reservation' to Article 6 (concerning 'the regulation of pregnancy termination'), *id.* p. 28; and the United Kingdom said that it 'interprets the Convention as applicable only following a live birth', *id.* p. 42.

There are two kinds of discrimination that are important to children in the pre-natal period of life with respect to their enjoyment of Articles 6 (right to life) and 24(2)(d) (the child's right to pre-natal care): decisions to terminate the life of the child because of the child's sex, and because the child has a disability. (See further at notes 154 and 173.) A valid reservation to either Article 1 or Article 6 could have the backdoor effect of permitting discrimination on these two (a)-variables.

[143] For instance, numerous States have made ratification statements framed in terms of 'Islamic' laws or values, or 'Shariah'. Some of these might allow three kinds of discrimination. First, a valid reservation could allow a system of 'personal laws' for family matters. Children of the Islamic faith are dealt with under one body of law, and children of another faith under a different body of law, so that one could argue that the State gives different levels of protection or autonomy to children based on their religion. Second, the rules for custody and other issues might hinge on the sex of the child, or the sex of the parent. Third, it might be lawful to forbid youngsters of the Islamic faith from changing their religion. For a useful overview, see K. Hashemi, 'Religious Legal Traditions, Muslim States and the Convention on the Rights of the Child: An Essay on the Relevant UN Documentation', *Human Rights Quarterly* 29 (2007), 194–227. Hashemi's assumptions about the Article 2 are not always supported by the analysis in the present commentary, however; *e.g., id.* p. 208 (out-of-wedlock/inheritance), p. 212 (different ages for marriage); compare to Nos. 194–197, 237, and Nos. 256–257, below.

While Malaysia's reservation was (unartfully) framed in terms of national laws, its report gives a detailed presentation of how personal laws accommodate the Islamic segment of society; see *Malaysia* (UN Doc. CRC/C/MYS/1, 2006). For a vigorous criticism of personal laws, see S. Goonesekere, *Children, Law and Justice: A South Asia Perspective* (New Delhi/London/ Thousand Oaks, Sage Public., 1998).

For a legal discussion of the 'Islamic law and values' ratifying statements, see B. Abramson, 'Reservations to the Convention on the Rights of the Child: A Look at the Reservations of Asian States Parties', in: International Commission of Jurists, *Rights of the Child: Report of a Training Programme in Asia* (Geneva, ICJ, 1994), pp. 314–360 (although not artfully drafted and overbroad, such statements can perform the legitimate function of announcing the value orientation that will govern balancing decisions).

[144] See generally, L. Lijnzaad, *Reservations to UN-Human Rights Treaties: Ratify and Ruin?* (Dordrecht/Boston/London, Martinus Nijhoff Publ., 1995); to appreciate how controversial the disputes can be, see R. Cook, 'Reservations to the Convention on the Elimination of All

10. *Private Actors*

189. As the previous discussions have been about state-imposed discrimination, we need to ask whether the Convention covers discrimination committed by private actors. The State, and only the State, is the duty-bearer of the CRC rights, which means that private actors cannot violate CRC rights.[145] So the question should be: 'Do the State's CRC obligations include the duty to stop private actors from discriminating against young people?' The answer is yes and no. Article 2(1) is an umbrella right that adds extra protection to the sectoral rights, and the answer will depend upon which we look at.

190. Article 2(1) says that the State shall '*ensure* the [sectoral] rights...without [race, etc.] discrimination' (emphasis added). The State can only 'ensure' the conduct of state actors; it cannot 'ensure' the behaviour of civil society actors because they are outside the State's immediate and direct control. The State can 'promote' specified conduct by private actors (*e.g.*, Article 21(e), on adoptions), but it cannot 'ensure' their actions. So the most natural way to read the umbrella right is that the State is promising that its officers and agents will not engage in race, etc. discrimination as they work to fulfil the State's sectoral right obligations: private actor discrimination is not in the claws of Article 2(1).[146]

191. The situation is different when it comes to the sectoral rights. The change is due to what is usually called the horizontal effects of treaty obligations. 'Horizontal effects' refers to the inherent need for the State Party to pass laws regulating private actors if it is to fully realize the interests protected by the rights in the treaty.

One type of horizontal effect is when the sectoral right pertains to private behaviour, either expressly or by implication. For instance, freedom from violence 'while in the care of parent(s)' (Article 19), and the right to 'compulsory' primary education (Article 28), will both require the State to pass laws regulating parental conduct. Another type of horizontal effect is

---

Forms of Discrimination Against Women', *Virginia Journal of International Law* 30, No. 3 (1990), pp. 643–716.

[145] However, private actors can aid and abet state-actor violations (as when a business owner bribes an inspector to overlook child-labour crimes), and private actors become state actors when they act on delegated authority (as in the case of privately owned prisons).

[146] *E.g.*, S. Joseph, et al., *o.c.* (note 56), p. 36 ('A State's horizontal obligations cannot be as strict as its vertical obligations; a State cannot be expected to exercise the same degree of control over private persons as it does over its own servants, lest it encroach the rights of the former persons.').

when rights are framed as end-goals, like the right to an education aimed at developing the youngster's 'fullest potential' (Articles 28 and 29). In order to achieve the prescribed results of these articles, the State will have to address all barriers that stand in the way. This would include societal discrimination, just as it would include poverty and rural isolation. If parents are keeping a child out of school because of their shame over the youngster's disability, or if they send a child of one sex to school because another private actor has given them a subsidy restricted to that sex, while not sending a child of the other sex to school, then the parents' discrimination will prevent their child from getting an education. So either type of horizontal effect will require the State to tackle the private discrimination as an inherent part of what it must do to ensure that right-holders are enjoying their right to an education. (And the societal discrimination would not have to be limited to the grounds named in Article 2(1), since *all* obstacles have to be addressed.)

On the other hand, since the duty to address private actor discrimination comes from the duty to fulfil the sectoral right, the State can make balancing judgments (when the right is context-dependent). This would mean that there is no absolute duty to end all societal discrimination that affects a young person's enjoyment of the sectoral rights. The State has wide latitude of discretion, and its decisions are subject to international accountability under some type of a reasonableness standard under the framework of the CRC, as well as being subject to other accountability mechanisms (such as CERD and CEDAW).[147]

192. So we can say, yes, in these roundabout ways through the horizontal effects, the CRC can cover private actor discrimination. But societal discrimination is a matter to be handled under the sectoral rights, not Article 2(1) – which is the youngster's right to be free from the *State's* race, sex, etc. discrimination.

11. *Applying Article 2(1): The Taboo Grounds of Differentiation*

193. This commentary has concentrated on the structure or elements of the right of non-discrimination since that is where the most serious confusions

---

[147] All words have multiple meanings, and some commentators use 'horizontal effects' in far more expansive ways. S. Joseph, et al., *o.c.* (note 56), p. 36 ('horizontality is a relatively new and consequently underdeveloped area of international human rights law'). Usually, the greater the expansion of the term, the less clarity in the conceptual and theoretical underpinnings; *e.g.,* S. Besson, *l.c.* (note 21), pp. 449–450.

arise. But there are also misunderstandings about the meanings and applications of the various forbidden grounds of differentiation. This section will discuss some of the (a)-variables.

11.1. 'Birth'

194. For instance, what does 'birth' refer to? Is it intended to prevent legal differentiations between children born in and out of wedlock, with respect to inheritance and other matters, as is often believed? Does it preclude adverse differentiations between 'born' and 'unborn' children, with respect to the right to life or the right to health care? Is it referring to place of birth? Does it include the order of birth between siblings? Unfortunately, 'birth' in Common Articles 2 is too ambiguous for the ordinary meaning rule to resolve these questions.

195. In the creation of international agreements, the tendency is to copy the language of previous declarations and treaties without a fresh discussion of the meanings of the terms, and this happened in the formulation of Article 2(1).[148] To understand the intentions behind some of the grounds of distinction, we have to go back to the original sources, which are the legislative records of either the Universal Declaration or the Covenants.

196. In the creation of the Universal Delcaration, the Union of Soviet Socialist Republics proposed the addition of *soslovie*, which roughly means *estate* in English and *état* in French, and which was meant to refer to the 'legally sanctioned inequality such as had existed in feudal Europe when different groups of people had, by reason of their birth, different rights and privileges'.[149] The other delegates picked up on the general idea, but, over the objections of the Soviet delegation, altered the concept by changing the word to 'birth', and by changing its place in the text. One reason was because 'estates' no longer has the same meaning, and another was to broaden the prohibition by using 'birth' to cover class or caste, 'in the sense of inherited privileges for the sons of noblemen, capitalists, party leaders,

---

[148] For the framers' aim for consistency with the other treaties, see note 63.
[149] *Travaux Préparatoires* for the UDHR: *Official Records of the Third Session of the General Assembly*, o.c. (note 113), 101st mtg., p. 137 (Mr. Pavlov, USSR); see also, *id.* p. 135 (Mr. Cassin, France, for the drafting group), and 175th mtg., pp. 851–852 (Mr. Bogomolov, USSR, and Mr. Cassin, France).

and so on', as one delegate put it.[150] There was considerable dissatisfaction with the term 'birth', but the changes were adopted anyway.[151]

197. Given the fuzziness of both the term 'birth' and the delegates' explanations of their intentions, it is not surprising that the treaty monitoring bodies have not been concentrating on this taboo ground of differentiation. But based on the records, one thing can be said with certainty: 'birth' does not pertain to distinctions based on the marital status of the parents, birth order, or the other things mentioned in the introduction.[152]

11.2. 'National Origin'

198. The term 'national origin' is sometimes misunderstood as referring to nationality, in the sense of distinctions between citizens and non-citizens, or to affiliation with a national minority. The records, however, indicate that 'national origin' means the country of one's birth.[153]

---

[150] *Travaux Préparatoires* for the UDHR: *Official Records of the Third Session of the General Assembly, o.c.* (note 113), 101st mtg., p. 137 (Mr. Mayhew, United Kingdom). The words 'class' and 'caste' were mentioned frequently throughout the negotiations of the 100th and 101st meetings. *The Main Types and Causes of Discrimination* interprets 'birth' similarly, *o.c.* (note 23), para. 79 ('classification into noble or plebeian strata').

[151] The Soviet Union insisted that the Russian translation of the UDHR contain *soslovie*, despite its inaccuracy, but there is a proper Russian equivalent of 'birth' in Article 2(1) of the CRC.

[152] Discrimination on the basis of the parents' marital status falls under Article 2(2), not Article 2(1) of the CRC, as discussed in Chapter Five.

Compare to M. Nowak, *o.c.* (note 8), p. 56 ('there can be no doubt that the criterion of birth [in Article 2(1) of the CCPR] relates to the issue of birth in and out of wedlock'). Nowak based that assertion on the summary records pertaining to Article 24 of the CCPR, which, by his own summarizing, do not substantiate his claim, and he does not deal with the summary records for the CRC. His main argument is a hypothetical case: he says that a law that sets different ages for voting according to whether the person was born in or out of wedlock 'clearly constitutes discrimination on the basis of birth and is a violation of Art. 2(1) in conjunction with Art. 25(b)'. First, that is a red herring. The issue is the word 'birth' in Article 2, not the scope of Article 25. Moreover, Article 25 contains a 'reasonableness' test, and he devised the imaginary out-of-wedlock voting law to fail the test. Second, Nowak claims that every conceivable distinction is covered by Article 2(1) – and his proof for that is the same red herring, except that he uses shoe size as a condition for voting instead of the parents' marital status; *id.* p. 47; see note 30. So Nowak is not really interpreting 'birth' in Article 2(1); remove that ground from Article 2(1), and he would make the same claim.

[153] *E.g., Travaux Préparatoires* for the CESCR: (UN Doc. A/C.3/SR.657, 1955), para. 16 (El Salvador) (nationality is a legal relationship, while national origin is a 'factual circumstance. Even if a person changed his nationality several times, he always remained a native of a single country.'); see also, United Kingdom, *id.* para. 24. Accord, *The Main Types and Causes of Discrimination* refers to prejudice '[t]owards people of alien origin who are citizens of the country', *o.c.* (note 23), para. 77. Compare to M. Nowak, *o.c.* (note 8), p. 54 (confusing national origin with citizenship (*i.e.*, nationality), as in 'distinctions between nationals and aliens').

Moreover, the ordinary meaning of *origin* encompasses a person's 'ancestry'.[154] People have a strong tendency to identify both themselves and others according to the place of their ancestral origins, and when there is societal discrimination or antagonism against a particular 'immigrant' group, it is against all the members without regard to the fine points of each member's place of birth or current citizenship. So both policy considerations and the dictionary meaning of *origin* support interpreting 'national origin' to include 'ancestral origin'.

11.3. *'Sex'*

199. Common Articles 2 use the term 'sex', which is a biological concept, so the prohibition refers to differential treatment based on male/female classifications. However, there is a tendency for commentators to substitute 'gender' for 'sex', and this creates confusion because people use *gender* in three ways. (i) 'Gender' is a synonym for the biological usage of 'sex'. (ii) 'Gender' refers to socially constructed roles and identities. (In the UN system, there is a standardized practice of using 'gender' exclusively in this second sense.)[155] And (iii), 'gender' is a synonym for 'women' (as when the 'gender analysis' section of a paper speaks only about the problems of women). This commentary sticks to the word in the text – *sex*, a biological concept – in order to avoid these confusions.[156]

---

[154] *Webster's Third New International Dictionary*, *o.c.* (note 17), p. 1591.
The Committee addressed national origin, although not clearly linked to Article 2(1), in CRC Comm., *Concl. Obser.: Dominican Republic* (UN Doc. CRC/C/15/Add.150, 2001), para. 23 (children of 'Haitian origin born in' the Party's territory of migrant parents).

[155] *E.g., Women 2000* March 2002 (UN Division for the Advancement of Women), p. 2.

[156] Since 'sex' in Common Articles 2 refers to male/female classifications, it does not include sexual orientation. (i) In its ordinary meaning, 'sexual orientation' refers to mental-emotional states of being, not behaviour; see, *e.g.*, The Yogyakarta Principles (2006), fourth preambular para. (defining 'sexual orientation' as a 'person's capacity for' sexual feelings or behaviour, rather than the behaviour itself). In political advocacy, however, the term is sometimes used as a euphemism for sexual behaviours. (ii) 'Sexual orientation' includes attractions to children, to animals, between brother-sister, and between parent-child. Thus, a State might create a narrower, term-of-art definition in its anti-discrimination legislation; *e.g.*, United Kingdom, Equality Act 2006, sec. 35 (excluding attraction to animals). (iii) The HRC said that 'sex' includes 'sexual orientation' in Article 2(1) of the CCPR; *Toonen v. Australia*, No. 488/1992, para. 8.7. While space limits preclude an analysis, note: (a) The HRC held that criminalizing 'indecent practice between male persons' violated Article 17(1) [arbitrary interference with privacy] (paras. 2.3, and 8.6, respectively). Given that ruling, its comment about the meaning of 'sex' in Article 2(1) is dictum. (b) When Australia asked for 'guidance' as to whether *or other status* in Article 26 includes 'sexual orientation', the HRC said it comes under *sex* in Article *2(1)* (para. 8.7). But the HRC gave no reasons; indeed, the meanings of 'sex' and 'sexual orientation' were not discussed, or even raised, in the decision, and the communication was accepted under Articles 17 and 26, not Article 2(1) (para.

200. The UNESCO Convention Against Discrimination in Education provides for sex-segregated public schools (Article 2(a) of the CADE; there are similar provisions for separate schools based on religion and language). Does this conflict with Article 2(1) of the CRC? The answer is the same as the answer to questions about sex-segregated toilets and shower rooms, and, in fact, the same as the answer to any Common Articles 2 question: Does the law fulfil the three elements? In the case of separate schools, the question becomes: 'Is the State using male/female classifications to give different levels of satisfaction to the educational interests of boys and girls (as in Figure 2)?'

As we have seen, Article 2(1) of the CRC does not forbid differential treatment on the ground of sex *per se*; the state-imposed differentiation must impair the protected interests. The right to education encompasses an enormous set of interests, so we need a practical way to combine them into a unit of comparison when applying Element (2), the impairment component, to something as complex as an educational system. The UNESCO Convention provides such a test: sex-segregated schools are not sex discrimination if they give boys and girls 'equivalent access to education', as judged by comparing broad indicators like course content, equipment, and teacher qualifications. So the provision on single-sex schools in the UNESCO treaty is consistent with the CRC because it is framed in terms of equivalent satisfaction of interests.[157]

11.4. 'Race'

201. Commentators often assert that there is no such thing as 'race', that 'race' is an invalid concept. This leads to an apparent paradox: if race does not exist, then how can there be any racial discrimination?

5.2). (c) Commentators sharply criticize the dictum; *e.g.*, M. Nowak, *o.c.* (note 8), pp. 48–49, 623–624. (d) *Toonen* was not a bona fide legal case: Australia and Toonen were in collusion with each other; there was no genuine legal dispute.

Also of interest, the CRC Committee has condemned the intentional termination of the lives of female children during the pre-natal period as a violation of the Convention; *e.g.*, CRC Comm., *Concl. Obser.: India* (UN Doc. CRC/C/15/Add.115, 2000), para. 32 (criticizing 'selective abortions' of girls, under Article 2); see also Fourth United Nations Conference of Women at Beijing, Declaration and Plan of Action, para. 277(c) (calling for laws 'protecting girls from all forms of violence, including pre-natal sex selection'); discussed further at note 173.

[157] Note the wording of Article 2(a) of the CADE: sex-segregated schools 'shall not be deemed' to be 'discrimination' as defined in Article 1 when they 'offer equivalent access to education'. Article 2(a) is not technically necessary in order to allow sex-segregated schools because anything that meets that condition will not be 'discrimination' under the definition in Article 1. *Shall not be deemed* are not words of exception; it is a clarification clause (as explained at Nos. 166–169).

The short answer is that all of our words and concepts are social constructs, and what is important for the purposes of applying anti-discrimination laws is not nature's ultimate reality, but whether the actor perceives
the person to be a member of the group or category in question, and, on
the basis of that perception, treats the person differently in the allocations
of social goods (as illustrated in Figure 2).

202. As to the meaning of *race*, several points are worth mentioning. First,
while all words have multiple meanings, race is a biological notion in the
context of international human rights law. In the early days of the creation
of the Covenants, UNESCO submitted a paper on the meaning of 'race' pre-
pared by a committee of experts. It said that race is a biological concept,
and that there is a consensus among anthropologists that humanity can be
divided into three races, although a variety of terms are used for the three
groupings.[158] (Regardless of the terminology, no one has difficulty placing
the Dalai Lama, Nelson Mandela, and Queen Elizabeth into the three races.)
Scientists also divide the races into subdivisions, and there is considerable
intermixing.[159] Legal prohibitions of race discrimination are workable even
when 'race' is interpreted to include multiple levels of sub-divisions, as long
as the term remains rooted in biology.[160]

203. Second, as the UNESCO experts observed, people often make the 'serious error [...]' of expanding 'race' to include social, cultural, psychological,
and political considerations.[161] Unfortunately, expanding the word creates
arbitrariness, and this undermines the integrity of anti-discrimination laws:

---

[158] *Travaux Préparatoires* for the Covenants: 'Activities of [UNESCO] in the Field of Prevention
of Discrimination and Protection of Minorities' (UN Doc. E/CN.4/Sub.2/121, 1950, incorporating UNESCO/SS/1, 1950), paras. 3, 4, and 7. That and other UNESCO statements are produced
in E. Lawson, *Encyclopedia of Human Rights* (2nd ed., Washington, DC, Taylor & Francis, 1996),
pp. 1215–1223.

[159] *E.g.*, L. L. Cavalli-Sforza, *Genes, Peoples and Languages* (London, Penguin, 2001) (M.
Seielstad, transl.).

[160] Contrary to popular impression, the CERD does not define 'race'. Article 1(1) of the CERD
says: 'In this Convention, the term "*racial* discrimination" shall mean any distinction [etc.]
based on *race*, colour, descent, or national or ethnic origin which…impair[s] the…enjoy-
ment…of human rights…' (emphasis added). The term *racial* is part of 'racial discrimination', which is a legal fiction – *e.g.*, 'national or ethnic origin' are not exclusively biological
concepts –, but *race* is not defined. The CERD leaves us to interpret 'race' in accordance with
the ordinary meaning rule. Compare to M. Nowak, *o.c.* (note 8), p. 49 (saying that Article 1(1)
of the CERD 'offers a broad definition of race' and that it can be used to interpret 'race' in
the CCPR, but failing to note the fiction, and that 'race' is left undefined).

[161] *Travaux Préparatoires*, 'Activities of [UNESCO] in the Field of Prevention of Discrimination
and Protection of Minorities', *o.c.* (note 158), para. 6.

judicial interpretations of national laws that extend 'race' beyond biology result in arbitrary punishment of defendants; this encourages further expansionist claims by plaintiffs and their lawyers; and the continuing expansions erode the healthy stigma normally associated with legal determinations that a person has committed 'racial discrimination'.[162]

11.5. 'Religion'

204. While 'race' and 'sex' refer to demographic groups rooted in biology, 'religion' is a high order abstraction that refers to certain types of beliefs. Moreover, 'religion' can refer just to beliefs, or jointly to the beliefs and the practices that the beliefs give rise to, or collectively to the beliefs, the practices, and all of the people who have those beliefs and engage in those practices. Despite these nuances, the underlying requirement is that the beliefs are 'religious' beliefs. Since a belief is fundamentally different from physical appearances rooted in biology, discrimination on the basis of religion requires a more refined analysis than race and sex discrimination.

205. The objective of international human rights law is to promote respect for the human dignity of each and every person. 'Human dignity' is a holistic notion that includes the material, 'objective', and 'scientific' aspects of a person's being, as well as the intangible and subjective aspects, like thoughts, feelings, understandings, meanings, and values. Within this non-material dimension of human dignity is the spiritual (or religious or metaphysical) dimension. History has seen so many conflicts pertaining to the spiritual dimension of life that the UN lawmakers considered it necessary to formally recognize the existence and importance of this aspect of human dignity. For instance, the General Assembly has proclaimed that 'religion or belief, for anyone who professes either, is one of the fundamental elements in his conception of life and [...] freedom of religion or belief should be fully respected and guaranteed'.[163]

---

[162] The HRC has never found a case of racial discrimination under Article 2(1) of the CCPR in the individual communications, and this is due in part to frivolous extensions of 'race' by the claimants; see case summaries in M. Nowak, *o.c.* (note 8), pp. 49–51. As an example of an expansion, Nowak says that 'race' entails 'congenital' qualities, and then implies that 'Muslims' constitute a race under Article 2(1) of the CCPR; *id.* The arbitrariness in expanding 'race' beyond biology is well illustrated in I. F. H. Lopez , *White By Law: The Legal Construction of Race* (New York, New York Univ. Press, 1996).

[163] Declaration on the Elimination of All Forms of Intolerance and of Discrimination Based on Religion or Belief, *o.c.* (note 40), fourth preambular para. 'Belief' was added because of the impossibility of getting people to agree on what 'religion' means. The principal dispute is whether a belief in a being-like God is a necessary part of the definition of 'religion', or

The General Assembly has also recognized the importance of the spiritual dimension of life by protecting it through a number of human rights. One of the main protections is the 'right to freedom of thought, conscience and religion' (Article 18 of the CCPR; Article 14 of the CRC). There are two aspects of this freedom. There is the right *to think* as one chooses to think – the right to hold an opinion or have a belief, including beliefs classified as 'religious' –, which is an absolute right (Article 18(1) of the CCPR; Article 14(1) of the CRC).[164] And there is the right *to express* or manifest 'one's religion or beliefs', which is context-dependent (Article 18(3) of the CCPR; Article 14(3) of the CRC). (The right to manifest one's beliefs is a subset of, or particularized application of, the 'right to freedom of expression' in Article 19(2) of the CCPR, and Article 13(1) of the CRC.)

206. Another main way that the General Assembly has protected the spiritual dimension of human dignity is through the right of non-discrimination. As we have seen, context-dependent rights require balancing decisions to translate the abstract level of the right into concrete entitlements. Throughout history, conflicts pertaining to the spiritual dimension of life have resulted in many abuses of power when authorities allocate social goods.

Sometimes the abuses stem from the intolerance that the members of one religion have towards another; for example, members of religion *A* think that the beliefs of religion *B* are so seriously wrong that they persecute and oppress members of *B*. In other cases, abuses occur because the people in power do not value the spiritual dimension of human dignity. For the right-holder, the religious beliefs and practices can be profoundly important, giving meaning, purpose, direction, fulfilment, comfort, security, discipline, and so on to that person's life. But for the state actors making the trade-off decisions, the spiritual dimension may be seen as a delusion, and a harmful one at that; such actors may consider religion to be nothing more than superstition, emotionalism, prejudices, and other bad things that humanity needs to eliminate or curtail.[165] When state actors devalue the spiritual

---

whether it can also include beliefs in a god-like force. Because there is no settled definition, this commentary speaks of 'beliefs classified as "religious"'. For thoughtful attempts at definitions, see R. Ahdar and I. Leigh, *Religious Freedom in the Liberal State* (Oxford, Oxford Univ. Press, 2005), pp. 110–126; T. J. Gunn, 'The Complexity of Religion and the Definition of "Religion" in International Law', *Harvard Human Rights Journal* 16 (Spring) (2003), pp. 189–215.

[164] The right to freedom of religious belief in Article 18(1) of the CCPR is an absolute right when read in conjunction with paragraphs (2) and (3) of that Article, and with the prohibition of derogations in Article 4 of the CCPR.

[165] See, *e.g.*, R. Dawkins, *The God Delusion* (London, Bantam, 2006); C. Hitchens, *God Is Not Great* (London, Atlantic Books, 2007), p. 13 ('*Religion poisons everything.*'), p. 15 ('Religion Kills').

dimension, they may give right-holders a lesser scope of liberty in expressing their beliefs simply because their beliefs are classified as 'religious'.

As a consequence of these two kinds of attitudes, authorities might use 'religion' as a ground of differential treatment that impairs the well-being of members of religious groups. This is where the absolute right of non-discrimination serves its second function: it puts a trump on decision-making processes that could end up treating right-holders adversely on the basis of membership in a group defined in terms of religion. (In Figure 2, the allocate-branch A could be defined as 'non-Muslim', or 'Catholic', or 'atheist', for instance, with the deny-branch B defined as everyone outside of A).[166]

207. There are two basic ways that States engage in religious discrimination: (i) differential treatment in the allocation of liberty or finite resources, and (ii) differential respect of human dignity when making balancing judgments about freedom of expression.

208. *Differential treatment.* Because 'religion' can refer to beliefs, practices or people, laws that discriminate on the ground of religion can frame the criterion of differentiation – the (a)-variable in Element (1) – in a variety of ways. For instance, the waiver rule for school fees in Ahmed's case was framed in terms of 'Muslims', which calls for classifying *people* according to their beliefs. The criterion for differential treatment can also require that *objects or behaviours* be classified in terms of 'religion'. Regardless of the particular wording of these laws, the reference is ultimately to beliefs that are considered to be 'religious' beliefs.

For example, let us say that a school has a rule against displaying religious symbols on campus. Five girls go to school wearing necklaces: Anne's neck-lace has a heart symbol, Betty's has the national flag, Carol's has a circle with a small cross extending from the bottom (the medical notation for 'female' that has been adopted as a feminist symbol), Dina's has a flame symbolizing human rights, and Ellen's shows a Hindu symbol, the word 'Om', written in an Indian script. Each girl is wearing her necklace in order to express her beliefs. Someone reports Ellen to the headmaster, and she is sent home for violating the rule against religious symbols. The school has (1) treated Ellen differently from the other girls on the ground of religion in respect to the

---

[166] Other recognitions of the spiritual dimension in the CRC include Articles 17 ('spiritual [...] well-being'), 20(3) ('religious [...] background'), 27(1) ('spiritual [...] development'), 29(1)(d) ('religious groups'), 30 (religious minorities), 32(1) ('spiritual...development'), and, indirectly, all of the references to 'morals', given the role of religion in shaping people's understandings of morality: Articles 10(2), 13(2), 15(2), 17, and 27(1).

interest in expressing one's beliefs, (2) the treatment impairs that interest, and (3) the interest is protected by a sectoral right.

In some sense, the school has treated all of the students in the same way: no one can display the word 'Om'. But the interest at stake needs to be defined at the highest degree of particularity. What is at stake here is the interest in 'expressing one's opinions or beliefs by displaying a symbol of those beliefs'. It is with respect to this interest that the school treats Ellen differently. The other girls are free to express their beliefs symbolically, but Ellen cannot, and the reason is that her necklace is an expression of 'religion'.[167]

What is important to note is that the school authorities have not directed the no-religious-symbols rule at the designs themselves, since a design has no intrinsic meaning. Nor is it directed at a specific symbol because of something tangibly harmful about that symbol, as determined by a close examination of the facts (as might happen when a Nazi swastika is suppressed, not because it is a 'political' symbol, but because of the particular message that it communicates, and the harm that that does to other people). Rather, the rule is aimed at suppressing symbolic expressions of 'religious' beliefs. The school's criterion for adverse differentiation requires the headmaster to classify beliefs under one of the categories named in Article 2(1) – *this* design is a symbol of a 'religion' (and thus forbidden by the policy); *that* design is not a symbol of a 'religion' (and therefore allowed). This means that the rule is ultimately aimed at suppressing manifestations of the beliefs of members of religious groups, since it is they who have turned arbitrary

---

[167] Since wearing a religious symbol means exclusion from school, the policy can be treated as a condition for enjoying the right to education (Article 28), which gives us a second interest at stake. Article 29 of the CRC defines the aims of education to include: developing 'the child's personality...to the [...] fullest potential'; developing the child's respect 'for human rights', 'for the child's...values', and for different 'civilizations'; and preparing the youngster to live a life of 'understanding, peace, [and] tolerance...among all...religious groups'. Given that human dignity includes a spiritual dimension, those aims of education cannot be achieved if the State suppresses all religious expressions in public schools. Moreover, if we read these aims as statements about the content of the right to education, then Ellen has a context-dependent right to have the school, through its dress codes and other conduct, teach tolerance for her religious beliefs and practices, and respect for her human right to express those beliefs, symbolically and otherwise. Apparent accord, E. Brems, *Article 14: The Right to Freedom of Thought, Conscience and Religion*, in: A. Alen, J. Vande Lanotte, E. Verhellen, F. Ang, E. Berghmans and M. Verheyde (eds.), *A Commentary on the UN Convention on the Rights of the Child* (Leiden/Boston, Martinus Nijhoff Publ., 2006), p. 9 (citing CRC Comm., *Concl. Obser.: Germany* (UN Doc. CRC/C/15/Add.226, 2004), paras. 30–31 (teachers' headscarves)); see also, *id.* pp. 21, 37.

designs into 'religious symbols', and it is they who display these symbols for the purpose of expressing their 'religious' beliefs.[168]

209. *Differential respect of human dignity.* The second type of religious discrimination occurs when state actors devalue the spiritual dimension of human dignity. When authorities make the trade-off decisions that translate the abstract right of religious expression into concrete entitlements, they will be making subjective judgments. If the actor does not value the spiritual dimension of human dignity, then the right-holder will not get a fair balancing decision.

210. To illustrate the problem, let's say that Alex wants to wear a head covering as a manifestation of his religion, but the covering is in conflict with the school's policy on uniforms. Alex asks for an exception so that he can enjoy his human right to manifest his religious beliefs, and the headmaster says 'No.' Has the school violated Alex's CRC rights?

There are two human rights at issue here, Alex's context-dependent right to express his religious beliefs, and his absolute right of non-discrimination on the ground of religion when exercising freedom of expression. Before starting the analysis, we should note that the school's uniform rule does not, on its face, discriminate against Alex on the ground of religion, and

---

[168] France has a law that excludes young people from school if they 'wear [...] symbols or dress by which the students ostensibly manifest religious membership', quoted in full in E. Brems, 'Above Children's Heads: The Headscarf Controversy in European Schools From the Perspective of Children's Rights', *International Journal of Children's Rights* 14, No. 2 (2006), pp. 119–120 (Brems' translation). Five points are worth noting. (i) The law, on its face, treats CRC right-holders adversely on the basis of membership in a religious group, in regard to the interest in expressing one's beliefs, and the interest in receiving an education. (ii) The law is not framed in terms of the symbol or clothing injuring others, but in terms of 'membership' in a religiously-defined group. (iii) In many if not most cases, it is probably not accurate to say that the *right-holder* is *manifesting membership* in a religious group by wearing the symbol or dress, but is *manifesting* a variety of *beliefs*, attitudes, and so forth; see, *e.g.*, *id.* p. 124, n. 11 (summarizing a sociological study). More accurately, it is the *observer* who *assigns* 'membership' in a religious group by treating the things the right-holder is wearing as a marker for classification. In other words, despite the wording of the law, the social problem that the State is aiming to prevent, to the extent that there is a problem, lies in the conduct of people other than the right-holder, and in the stereotyped thinking that gives rise to their conduct. (iv) Given the public debates that surrounded passage of this law, it is quite possible that the lawmakers' intention was to suppress freedom of expression of Muslims, and they hid this intention by writing the law so as to include all religions; in other words, covert religious discrimination against Muslims. The Special Rapporteur on freedom of religion appears to believe that this is the case; *id.* pp. 127–128, quoting (UN Doc. E/CN.4/2006/5/Add.4), para. 101 ('target girls from a Muslim background'). (v) Regulations make an exception for Christian crosses if they are not 'of manifestly exaggerated dimensions', but a similar exception is not granted for the symbols of other religions; *id.* p. 120.

we will also assume that it was not written in a facially-neutral manner as a subterfuge for censoring religious expression.

The freedom of expression issue is typically handled under the notion of 'reasonable accommodation': the right to manifest one's religious beliefs entails an obligation of the State to make 'reasonable' exceptions to rules so as to permit the right-holders to practice their religions. The resolution of disputes pertaining to this (and all other) context-dependent rights is determined by what is usually spoken of as 'balancing': officials must 'weigh' the importance of the interest at stake to the right-holders' sense of well-being, 'weigh' the impact of the suppression on the right-holders, 'weigh' the competing social interests, and then 'strike a balance' that is reasonable (proportionate, fair, etc.).

211. This commentary has frequently spoken of 'balancing', but, unfortunately, the metaphor utterly fails to convey what the authorities are really doing. The metaphor comes from the balance scale traditionally used by shopkeepers. A standardized weight is placed on one pan, a piece of cheese (let us say) on the other pan, and a neutral force – gravity – acts upon the two objects, showing their relative masses. So the balance scale compares two things of the same underlying nature (the cheese and the weight are both composed of atoms); it is objective; and it settles the question of price with precision and fairness (in the absence of fraud).

But when it comes to translating abstract rights into concrete entitlements, what determines the 'balance' is not a neutral force acting upon identical interests; the concrete right is determined by value judgments. Rather than *balancing*, the judges (or other designated officials) make a *trade-off* between competing interests that are usually fundamentally different in nature. They sacrifice (aspects of) the well-being of one set of people in order to promote (aspects of) the well-being of another set of people. The trade-off is a value judgment: the officials believe that what they are sacrificing is less important than what they are seeking to gain: the sacrifice is a means to an end, and the end is worth the price that the 'victims' will have to pay. The so-called 'balancing decisions' are really subjective opinions based on value judgments.[169]

---

[169] For an example of the balancing metaphor in action, see D. J. Harris, et al., *o.c.* (note 28), pp. 296–301. Note the conceptual confusions as the language shifts between a balancing of 'interests', a balancing of 'rights' against 'interests', *id.* p. 299, a 'balance of factors', *id.* p. 300, a 'resolution of forces', *id.* p. 299, and the incoherent, 'reasons are proportionate to the limitation', *id.* p. 301; and note the silence about the role of values in the trade-off decisions. Taking the balance-scale metaphor literally is a sure way to miss the role of values, as

212. When the right at stake is the freedom to manifest one's religious beliefs, then the actor's negative value judgement about the spiritual dimension of human dignity can be the deciding factor.

If Alex's headmaster does not recognize or value the spiritual dimension of human dignity, it will be very difficult if not impossible for him to make a fair trade-off judgment when deciding what is a 'reasonable accommodation'. In the language of the balancing metaphor, the decision-maker must first 'weigh' the interest at stake, and 'weigh' the impact of the interference on the individual; that is to say, the actor has to evaluate the significance of the matter to the religiously-grounded right-holder. But if the headmaster does not value the spiritual dimension of human dignity, it will be very hard to 'weigh' those interests fairly. It would be like someone who is deaf trying to judge a singing competition. Next, the decision-maker has to 'strike a fair balance' between the competing interests or competing sets of people. But a decision-maker who devalues the spiritual dimension of human dignity will have prejudged the trade-off; the actor will have already determined that the aspects of well-being that are at stake for the right-holder are of little or no value. (Indeed, some decision-makers may believe that the more that religious practices are suppressed the better it will be for the right-holders because, the actor believes, all religions are harmful self-delusions.) The actor's negative value judgment about religion is like the shopkeeper putting his thumb on the scale.[170]

213. As discussed earlier, 'an act of discrimination' is a shorthand way to speak about a series of acts. The initial act of discrimination is always a mental act, entailing a perception and a valuation: the actor mentally categorizes people (or beliefs or practices) in terms of religion, race, sex, or another named ground in Common Articles 2 (*this* person is a member of A, and *that* person is a member of B; or *this* behaviour is not religious, *that* behaviour is), and those classifications determine how the actor assigns

---

happens in B. Çali, 'Balancing Human Rights? Methodological Problems with Weights, Scales and Proportions', *Human Rights Quarterly* 29 (2007), 251–270. Compare to O. M. Arnardóttir, *o.c.* (note 73), p. 13 ('inevitably based on certain underlying values').

[170] Negative value judgements can enter into decision-making in other ways as well. For instance, the actors might value the spiritual dimension of human dignity, but have negative attitudes towards a particular religion, and this causes them to be insensitive to the human dignity of the particular right-holders in the case. Or the actors might truly value the spiritual dimension, but believe that, as public officials, they are under a duty to adopt a particular attitude towards religious matters, and this attitude causes them to undervalue or ignore the impact of the suppression on the right-holders.

value. The initial mental act of discrimination is then manifested in various behavioural acts that eventually impair the enjoyment of a human right. For Ellen and Alex, what is at stake is being allowed to express themselves in ways that give meaning to their lives, but the state actors who make the decisions do not respect this interest simply because of the actors' negative attitudes towards 'religion'. In Ellen's case, the mental act of religious intolerance produces a rule, so the Common Articles 2 analysis is the same here as in cases involving race, sex, etc. discrimination. But in Alex's case, the intolerance affects another mental act – it influences the actor's discretionary judgment about granting a request for a 'reasonable accommodation' so that Alex can manifest his religion. This requires us to fine tune the legal analysis.

The refinement in the legal analysis is simple: in Element (1), 'different treatment' includes not only physical acts but mental acts. To be more specific, the mental act is the devaluing of the right-holder's interest in expressing beliefs, when the actor has classified the beliefs as 'religious'. In other words, the right of non-discrimination protects individuals from state actors who are intolerant of religion, when the actors are making discretionary decisions about manifestations of religion (*i.e.*, when translating the abstract right into concrete entitlements). Common Articles 2 do not guarantee that the individual will be allowed the accommodation; what the right-holder is entitled to is a decision-maker who is not prejudiced against religious beliefs.

214. The challenge in 'reasonable accommodation' cases is not conceptual, but practical: the decision-makers' negative attitudes about religion are often hidden from view. Alex's lawyer might get a chance to cross-examine the headmaster on the witness stand, but it could still be hard to bring the headmaster's intolerance out into the light. People can easily lie about their lack of respect for religion; people can lie to themselves by not admitting their prejudices; and even the most honest people can have trouble articulating their values and beliefs, and the role that these played in their decisions.

These kinds of proof problems are not unique to freedom of religion cases. There are countless civil and criminal laws that require judges and juries to determine what is in the hearts and minds of people, and covert discrimination cases have always faced these evidentiary challenges. What is new is getting the problem out into the open: freedom to manifest one's religion does not really involve 'balancing', it involves subjective value judgments; all of the problems of religious intolerance that have plagued humanity throughout the ages, and which motivated the General Assembly to create the right not to be discriminated against on the ground of religion, are still with us today; and this intolerance is the central problem in 'reasonable accommodation' cases involving freedom of religion.

215. And finally, while we often think of the courts as the ultimate vindicators of rights, it is, ironically, the judiciary that poses the greatest challenge to the ban on religious discrimination. As a civil-and-political right, the right to freedom of expression under national and regional law is usually considered justiciable, so it will be the judges who make the final trade-off decisions, and it will be their opinions about the spiritual dimension of human dignity that will determine the outcomes. However, Alex's lawyer will not be allowed to question *these* state actors about their possible negative attitudes towards the spiritual dimension of human dignity. And without full transparency and accountability in regard to the judges' negative value judgments about religion, the right to be free from religious discrimination can be a right without an effective remedy.[171]

216. Since mental acts cannot be observed directly, the problem of hidden religious discrimination in the trade-off decisions will never go away. In the light of this, the actual ability of children and their parents to enjoy their rights of non-discrimination and to freedom of religion can depend more on the prevailing attitudes in society than on the enforcement of national and regional laws. This is why 'it is essential to promote understanding, tolerance and respect in matters relating to freedom of religion', in the words of the General Assembly.[172]

---

[171] See, *e.g.*, N. Lerner, *Religion, Secular Beliefs and Human Rights* (Leiden/Boston, Martinus Nijhoff Publ., 2006), pp. 199–200) (In the head scarf case, the European Court 'did not attempt' [to give its reasons]. . . . Secularism cannot [read, 'must not'] be intolerant.'); the same criticism, in sharper tones, E. Brems, *l.c.* (note 168), p. 124 (raising the question of the 'orientalism and islamophobia' of the judges of the European Court).

[172] Declaration on the Elimination of All Forms of Intolerance and of Discrimination Based on Religion or Belief, *o.c.* (note 40), fifth preambular para.

For a detailed examination of a single controversy, see D. McGoldrick, *Human Rights and Religion - The Islamic Headscarf Debate in Europe* (Oxford/Portland, Hart Publ., 2006). For illuminating discussions of many issues, see R. Ahdar and I. Leigh, *Religious Freedom in the Liberal State*, *o.c.* (note 163). At the opposite end of the spectrum is C. D. de Jong, *The Freedom of Thought, Conscience and Religion or Belief in the United Nations (1946-1992)* (Antwerpen/Groningen/Oxford, Intersentia-Hart, 2000); *e.g.*, pp. 213–215, 222–224 (asserting, without explanation, that the impairment component of 'discrimination' - our Element (2) - is the 'arbitrary element', so States can practice religious discrimination - as long as they are being 'reasonable').

11.6. 'Disability'

217. The General Assembly expanded the right of non-discrimination by adding 'disability' to Article 2(1), and this new ground requires us to refine our analysis. For instance, does a State have to give a driver's licence to a minor even though the youngster is blind? Denying a license to a blind person is differential treatment on the ground of a disability, but it would be absurd to interpret the CRC as forbidding all adverse distinctions based on physical and mental impairments. We cannot solve this problem by reading a 'reasonableness' test into Article 2(1), however, because adding a new Element would destroy the three functions of the right, and open the door to race, sex, etc. discrimination. Moreover, the Convention does not say 'a disability' – a person's specific impairment; the prohibition is framed in terms of an abstraction – 'disability'. So the task before us is to assimilate 'disability discrimination' into our understanding of race, sex, etc. discrimination: we need to interpret the new ground of 'disability' in a way that is faithful to the text, gives meaningful protection, and does not lead to absurd results or the weakening of the absolute right of non-discrimination.[173]

218. This commentary reaches the conclusion that 'disability' refers to an abstract labelling of individuals, rather than to a right-holder's specific type and degree of impairment in functioning. There are three main considerations behind this interpretation.

219. The first consideration is the word *discrimination*: 'to make a difference in treatment or favor on a class or categorical basis in disregard of individual merit.'[174] A disability is an impairment or deficiency in the functioning of an organ or other part of the body. A 'disability' is, by definition, a merit-based notion: we have to treat an individual with an impaired ability to function differently from the way that we treat individuals who do not have that limitation. (We help a blind person to cross the street; we don't allow a blind person to drive a car.) That practical necessity of life is why we have the notion of disability. So differential treatment on the basis of 'a disability' – the right-holder's specific type and degree of impairment – is not 'discrimination', in the ordinary sense of the word. By contrast, differential treatment on the basis of an abstract label, like 'handicapped',

---

[173] The Russian version of the CRC mistranslates *disability* as 'state of health'; A. Ovsiouk, 'A Need For Combating and Overcoming Discrimination Against Persons With Disabilities', *Moscow Journal of International Law* No. 3 (2003), pp. 64, 66 (titles translated).
[174] *Webster's Third New International Dictionary, o.c.* (note 17).

'crippled', 'visually impaired', or 'disabled', is 'discrimination'. These broad classifications treat a person as a member of a class or category, rather than according to merit. These labels are so abstract that they tell us nothing about the person's actual needs, limitations, or capabilities that we would need to know in order to response to the person in a proper way when it comes to limiting the enjoyment of a sectoral right.

Making the distinction between 'disability' and 'a disability' harmonises the new taboo ground with the older ones. For instance, 'race', 'sex' and 'disability' are labels based on physical characteristics; 'African', 'Asian', 'man', 'woman', 'handicapped', 'hearing impaired', and so forth, lump together an extraordinary diversity of individuals; broad labelling not only leads to stereotypes, but the stereotypes are often infested by myths about inferiority; and using these broad labels as the criteria for allocating social goods has caused an enormous amount of suffering and injustice throughout history. So in Figure 2, the 'deny' and 'allocate' branches of the decision-tree need to be defined in relatively abstract terms, like 'handicapped' and 'not handicapped', or 'mobility impaired' and 'not mobility impaired'. This makes 'disability discrimination' a similar concept to discrimination based on the other grounds, like the religious discrimination in Ahmed's case where the branches are 'Muslim' and 'non-Muslim'.

Moreover, we need to relate this to the first function of the right of non-discrimination: to protect people from assaults on their human dignity. Depriving people of important things in life on the basis of abstract labels, like 'handicapped' and 'crippled', is an assault on human dignity, particularly when the label invokes stereotypes and stigma. But differential treatment on the basis of the person's specific impairment is not an assault on human dignity. In individual cases, the person might not welcome the treatment in question, or the treatment might be misguided, but these kinds of problems are not assaults on human dignity like the injuries caused by limiting human rights on the basis of abstract labelling.

220. The second consideration is that the right of non-discrimination is an absolute right, so we have to be able to apply our interpretation of 'disability' to real-life cases without any intermediate balancing decisions. Interpreting 'disability' to refer to a person's specific type and degree of visual impairment – to 'a disability' – would not make practical sense; it would prohibit vision tests for a driver's license, for example, and that is absurd. But interpreting 'disability' as referring to abstract labels like 'visually impaired' can function as an absolute prohibition: it forces States to redefine the Element (1a) ground of distinction, replacing abstractions (like

'visually impaired') with a specific criterion that has a merit-based relevance to the limitation on the sectoral right in question (like passing a vision test to get a driver's license).

We can also relate this to the third function of the right of non-discrimination – the right reflects, vindicates, and transmits a moral value. There is no doubt that is morally wrong to deprive people of important things based on abstract labels like 'handicapped', and that moral value needs to be embodied in the law. But it is not morally wrong to deny a social good on the basis of an impairment when proficiency in functioning is a meritorious criterion for the enjoyment of that social good.

221. The third consideration is that the right of non-discrimination is an umbrella right, so we need an interpretation of 'disability' that assigns the correct roles to the absolute umbrella right, and to the sectoral rights which require balancing. We achieve this when we read Article 2(1) as allowing limitations on sectoral rights based on the right-holder's specific type and degree of disability. Sectoral rights require line-drawing, which is based on trade-off decisions, and there will be constant disputes about where to draw the lines and how to strike the balances. (Is Billy's learning disability so serious that he should be placed in the 'special needs' class, contrary to his parents' wishes? The school says that Susan's disability is not serious enough to justify putting her in 'special education', but her parents disagree. Who is right?) Disputes about line-drawing and trade-off decisions pertaining to specific types and degrees of disability are disputes about differential treatment, but these kinds of controversies have to be handled directly under the sectoral rights, in accordance with the nation's political processes. The second function of the right of non-discrimination – trumping the political processes – is served only when 'disability' is interpreted as referring to abstracting labelling.

222. In short, we need to read 'disability' – the Element (1a) variable in Article 2(1) – as referring to an abstract classification. Under this reading, the absolute right of non-discrimination on the ground of disability will not categorically prohibit adverse distinctions based on a right-holder's specific type and degree of impairment.

223. One of the themes in this commentary is how making too much of the right of non-discrimination ends up diminishing the right. Since this is also happening in the discourse over 'Disability discrimination!', we need to clarify the relation of the rights in Article 2(1) to the overall situation of injustices to persons with disabilities. As we will see in the discussion below,

the right of non-discrimination on the ground of disability in international law plays a limited role as a *legal right*; however, including 'disability' within the rhetoric of the 'right of non-discrimination' has powerful consequences in the *social-political* arena.

224. First of all, not many state laws discriminate on the ground of 'disability', as this commentary has interpreted that word in the context of Article 2(1). However, disability discrimination can also occur when state actors make discretionary judgments that affect the enjoyment of sectoral rights. The essence of the problem is that the state actor responds to an impairment in such a way that the actor loses sight of the full humanity of the individual – the capabilities, needs, rights, feelings and potentials of the person who has the disability. This failure to respect human dignity has many sources, such as superstitions, stereotypes, ignorance, unfamiliarity with persons who have disabilities, and business-as-usual habits. The State is always responsible for these abuses of discretion, because it is responsible for the actions of everyone who exercises governmental authority, and it must take action on many fronts to end these problems. For example, the State will need to have clear rules about when impairments can and cannot be the criteria of differentiation, the rules must be carefully written to match the impairment to the limitation, there will need to be complaint procedures and monitoring by specialized bodies, and, above all, education and peer pressure to overcome each source of abuse of discretion. The obligation to take these steps comes from two places in the CRC; it comes from the sectoral rights, since failure to act reasonably in the realization of a context-dependent right violates the right, and it comes from Article 2(1).[175]

---

[175] For basic prevention measures, see Articles 4 and 8 of the Convention on the Rights of Persons With Disabilities (CRPWD), *o.c.* (note 11).

The *Implementation Handbook* gives no information on disability discrimination in the chapter on Article 2, and in the chapter on Article 23, in a section titled 'Non-discrimination legislation', it gives only four concrete examples of state discrimination: forced sterilization, compulsory segregation, intentional termination of the lives of neo-natal children, and intentional termination of the lives of pre-natal children; R. Hodgkin and P. Newell, *o.c.* (note 103), pp. 331–332. Curiously, none of these are mentioned in the Article 2 sections of CRC Comm., *Gen. Com. No. 9: The Rights of Children With Disabilities* (2006) (UN Doc. CRC/C/GC/9), and only two are clearly mentioned elsewhere; paras. 31 (disability-based infanticide), 60 (forced sterilization).

But is the Committee correct when it says that (state-sanctioned) pre-natal violence against children with disabilities is a CRC violation (*e.g.*, UN Doc. CRC/C/69 [Day of Discussion], para. 338), as is pre-natal violence against female children (note 156)? When creating the CRC, draft Article 1 contained a 'from the moment of [...] birth' limitation, which the framers removed in order to ensure that CRC rights 'include the entire period from the moment of conception', *Travaux Préparatoires* (UN Doc. E/CN.4/1349, 1979), and (UN Doc. E/CN.4/L.1542,

225. Secondly, the greatest source of injustice to people with disabilities is not state-imposed discrimination. The greatest amount of suffering comes from societal discrimination. Children with disabilities are often neglected, rejected, isolated, degraded, and even intentionally killed because of social norms that devalue human beings on account of 'abnormalities'. Parents and family members are often the main perpetrators, but social norms are the root of the problem.[176] The State's obligation to change these norms comes from the 'horizontal effects' of the sectoral rights, not from Article 2(1).[177]

226. Thirdly, a major source of hardship to people with disabilities comes from the fact that enjoyment of sectoral rights depends upon resource allocations. Impairments in functioning will cause people to have lower levels of well-being in various areas of life, so society will have to give them a greater share of resources in order for their well-being to be as close as possible to that of people who do not have disabilities: greater needs require greater allocations, to produce equivalent outcomes in well-being. (For instance, it costs more to educate students with learning disabilities, and the costs increase with the severity of the impairment.) However, allocation decisions entail political competition between different sets of citizens, and, historically, people with disabilities have not had the power to command more favourable allocations. A major objective of the disability-rights movement is to change the social, political and legal environments so that people with disabilities will get more resources.[178]

227. One way to increase allocations is by adopting 'reasonable accommodation' laws and policies: if an impairment is the reason that a person cannot meet a legal requirement for enjoying a social good, then the person is entitled to a 'reasonable' exemption; and if the arrangement of the

---

1980), paras. 29–31, respectively, reproduced in *Legislative History of the Convention on the Rights of the Child*, *o.c.* (note 63), p. 305. They also made Article 24's right to 'pre-natal care for the mother' *the child's* right, according to the text, and, since 'pre-natal' is unrestricted, the child holds the right from the start of the pre-natal period; this makes the right to pre-natal care consistent with Article 1, and with preambular para. 9 ('legal protection, before...hirth'). So the Committee is correct, since CRC rights run from conception to 18 years.

[176] *E.g.*, in the United Kingdom, parents are terminating the lives of babies for having a cleft palate, a club foot, webbed fingers, or an extra digit; *Daily Mail* (London), 28 May 2006. To the extent that such private acts are permitted by state law, they are Article 2(1) problems (in conjunction with Article 6).

[177] 'Horizontal effects' is discussed in section 9 ('Private Actors'); see Article 8 of the CRPWD for obligations to change harmful social norms.

[178] Article 4(2) of the CRPWD ('maximum' resources) is patterned after Article 4 of the CRC; see also Article 23 of the CRC.

physical environment makes it difficult to enjoy a social good, a disabled person is entitled to have 'reasonable' modifications (like adding ramps for wheelchairs). 'Reasonable accommodation' requires the State to give more social goods to disabled persons, but it is not 'disability discrimination' since these measures do not conform to Figure 2: the actor does not deprive an individual member of Group B – 'persons without a disability' – of a social good in order to give the good to an individual member of Group A – 'persons with a disability', wherein 'disability' is the criterion of allocation. 'Reasonable accommodation' entailing material resources is a type of *non-discriminatory* affirmative action. Moreover, the demand is that 'reasonable accommodation' laws be extended to include private actors, where the requirement will function as a kind of tax.[179]

Complaints about failures to make reasonable accommodations, and about unfairness in allocating extra resources, are not disability discrimination questions under Article 2(1); they are balancing disputes to be handled under the sectoral rights, in accordance with the State's legal and political processes.[180]

---

[179] Many articles in the CRPWD pertain to reasonable accommodation.

[180] Article 2 (second para.) of the CRPWD says that a decision not to make a reasonable accommodation is a 'form [...] of' discrimination. This conflicts with its definition of 'discrimination on the basis of disability' in Article 1 (second para.): (i) a decision denying a reasonable accommodation is not a 'distinction on the basis of disability', it is a decision based on an erroneous balancing of interests (with 'erroneous' being a subjective judgement), and (ii) 'reasonable accommodation' entails balancing, while CRPWD's definition of discrimination does not. A refusal to accommodate would be disability discrimination only if the decision-maker is biased against persons with disabilities. CRPWD's legal error is replicated in CRC Comm., *Gen. Com. No. 9*, *o.c.* (note 175), para. 8.

Both the CRC and the CRPWD prohibit the use of 'disability' as the criterion of differentiation without expressly limiting the protection to people with disabilities. This allows non-disabled persons to also claim protection from adverse distinctions based on that ground, as might happen when a *discriminatory* affirmative action measure sets a quota for allocating scholarships or jobs to persons with disabilities. (In applying Figure 2: (i) The allocate-branch A can be defined as 'persons without a disability' and the deny-branch B as 'persons with a disability'. Or (ii), the definitions can be reversed: A is 'persons with a disability' and B is 'persons without a disability'. In both situations, 'disability' is the criterion for granting and denying the social good.)

The CRPWD is a support treaty devoted to the interests of disabled persons, so one can find some textual support for reading it as protecting only members of that group, but this is not so for the CRC, and it is the CRC that is the human rights treaty that creates the right of non-discrimination. In Article 2(1), 'each child' has a right to be free from discrimination on the ground of 'disability' – an abstract, non-meritorious, criterion of differential treatment. Trying to limit the right only to youngsters with a disability is as contrary to the text as saying that only boys have the right to freedom from sex discrimination, and it is contrary to the premise that all children and adolescents have the same human rights.

228. The critical reader will have wondered about the legal significance of adding 'disability' to Article 2(1), given the way that the commentary has interpreted that ground of distinction. Since the Article cannot be read as absolutely forbidding a person's disability to be used as a criterion for impairing protected interests, what does it add to the CRC? Surely disputes about balancing and abstract labelling can be handled under the sectoral rights?

In theory, that is correct. Translating context-dependent rights into concrete entitlements is subject to some sort of a reasonableness test, and using a person's disability as a ground of adverse distinction *sometimes* is the right thing to do. When the youngster's impairment in functioning is a merit-based consideration for limiting the enjoyment of a right, then disputes about the reasonableness of the definition of the criterion being used, and conflicts over the reasonableness of the limitation, are sectoral right issues. The Article 2(1) cases arise when the definition of the criterion is too abstract. But it is unreasonable to use an abstract criterion to limit sectoral rights, because it loses its merit-based connection to the need for a limitation, so the issue of abstractness could just as well be handled under the sectoral right. From a strict legal perspective, there is no logical need to add 'disability' to Article 2(1).

229. But that does not mean that there is no value in adding disability to Article 2(1). The rhetoric of 'Disability discrimination!' is a powerful political tool for raising awareness, changing attitudes, and generating changes in laws and institutions. And the CRC Committee has made good use of 'disability discrimination' to address societal discrimination and institutional barriers, which would have been more difficult to do under the rather weak Article 23 (on disabilities). Moreover, 'reasonable accommodation' and other efforts to increase the realization of sectoral rights require balancing decisions, and these judgments depend upon perceptions and values. The rhetoric of 'Disability discrimination!' and 'the rights of persons with disabilities' is being successfully used to transform the socio-political environment in which the balancing takes place. So there is great value in adding disability to Article 2(1), but the value lies in the socio-political dimension, not the legal dimension.

230. These gains are not without their costs, however. As this commentary has repeatedly noted, making too much of the rhetoric of non-discrimination can make too little of the right. 'Disability discrimination' can be handled under Article 2(1) without any problems, provided that a simple distinction

is made between *a disability* – a specific type and degree of impairment –, and *disability* – a generalized description, with only the latter coming under the Article. This will allow the right of discrimination on the ground of disability to remain an absolute right, and that, in turn, will preserve the absoluteness of the ban on discrimination on race, sex, and the other named grounds. But people are not making that conceptual distinction, and that poses a risk to perceptions about the right in Article 2(1).[181]

231. In this section, we have looked at the forbidden grounds of distinction as a matter of legal interpretation under the Vienna Convention on the Law of Treaties. We will return to the matter of 'grounds' in the last chapter, on the Committee's application of the CRC.

---

[181] The definitions in Articles 1 and 2 of the CRPWD, together with the unqualified obligations in Article 5(2), require a State to prohibit *any* adverse distinction on the basis of a (long-term) impairment, under *any* circumstance. (No matter how severe the loss, impaired vision cannot be used as a criterion for preventing a person from driving a school bus, for instance. Compare to real-life: 'Blind man arrested for driving a car', Reuters, 6 August 2007.) Only radical surgery can make the CRPWD workable, like a 'reasonableness clause' transplant, by way of 'interpretation'. But that transplant will endanger perceptions about the absolute nature of the right of non-discrimination in Common Articles 2 of the CRC and the Covenants.

Note also 'specific measures' in Article 5(4) of the CRPWD: Is it an exception that allows here-and-now discrimination against individual disabled persons as a means for promoting the future well-being of people with disabilities as a whole (*e.g.*, forced sterilization)? Or is it a clarification clause?

CHAPTER FOUR

SCOPE OF ARTICLE 2(1): THE JURISDICTIONAL CLAUSE

232. Part of Article 2(1) is not an element of the right of non-discrimination, but a part of the treaty's jurisdictional statement: the State must realize the CRC rights of each child *within [its] jurisdiction* without race, etc. discrimination. A jurisdictional statement defines who the right-holders are, and Article 1 is the main provision: the CRC covers 'every human being under the age of 18 unless...'. But that is qualified by 'within [its] jurisdiction', so the complete jurisdictional statement is spread over two provisions, Articles 1 and 2(1).

233. There are two points here worth commenting on. The first is that the scope of the CRC is broader than that of the CCPR, which has an additional qualification: all individuals '*within its territory* and subject to its jurisdiction' (Article 2(1) of the CCPR, emphasis added). Sometimes States exercise governmental powers over land and water that is not recognized by all of the international community as being within the State's legal borders, so a territorial clause can give rise to serious legal and political disputes. The CRC's lawmakers brushed these problems aside by omitting the territorial qualification from Article 2(1). If the State Party is exercising state-like powers over an area, then it must treat the children and adolescents in that area as CRC right-holders: the State is accountable, under the framework of the CRC, for how its actions and inactions impact on the lives and well-being of those young people.[182]

---

[182] During Indonesia's first review, tensions arose when the discussion turned to East Timor, with one Committee member indirectly invoking Article 2(1)'s jurisdictional clause; *Summary Records* (UN Doc. CRC/C/SR.162, 1994), paras. 32, 38 (Santos Pais). However, Indonesia did not dispute the CRC's application to the disputed territory. Rather, the tensions related to perceptions that several members had gone beyond the dialogue role of the Committee. *Summary Records* (UN Doc. CRC/C/SR.79, 1993; CRC/C/SR.80, 1993; CRC/C/SR.81, 1993; CRC/C/SR.161, 1994; CRC/C/SR.162, 1994).

To be entirely precise about the scope of right-holders under the CRC, parents have the right to supervise or direct their children's exercise of CRC rights under Article 5, and Article 37's right not to be subject to capital punishment is held throughout adulthood if the crime was committed while under 18 years of age.

234. The second point relates to the interpretation of Article 4: a State is to realize economic and social rights 'to the maximum extent of its available resources within the framework of *international cooperation*' (emphasis added). Does 'international cooperation' obligate the State to use its resources to fulfil the CRC rights of young people who live in other countries? Does it mean that the Party has to give foreign aid to other Parties that are lacking in resources?

The jurisdictional clause in Article 2(1) defines the right-holders as the under-18 year-olds 'within [its] jurisdiction', so a State does not have a legal duty to finance the CRC rights of youngsters in other countries under Article 4. The legal and other duties to provide assistance come from being a Member State of the United Nations, and other specific sources, not the CRC. The 'international cooperation' clause is there to close a loophole. A Government that has not actively sought assistance, or that has alienated donor countries and intergovernmental institutions by failure to practice good governance, cannot be allowed to plead poverty as the reason for the suffering of the nation's children. So there is an Article 4 duty to seek outside assistance, but not a duty to give assistance.[183]

---

[183] Apparent accord, M. Rishmawi, *o.c.* (note 8), para. 92 (linking duty to give to the Charter).

The legislative records confirm the conclusion in the main text: *Travaux Préparatoires* (UN Doc. E/CN.4/1989/48, 1989), para. 64 (proposed amendment of preamble contained 'cooperation and assistance'); para. 68 (United States) (objecting to 'assistance' to other countries since the CRC is about States' duties to 'respect the rights of, and render assistance to, their own citizens'); para. 71 ('assistance' deleted), paras. 170–177 (discussions of a Party's duty to implement rights are framed in reference to that Party's own resources, under Article 4); reproduced in *Legislative History*, *o.c.* (note 63), pp. 298, 355–356.

CHAPTER FIVE

SCOPE OF ARTICLE 2(2): NO DISCRIMINATION OR PUNISHMENT ON ACCOUNT OF PARENTAL ACTIONS

235. While the right of non-discrimination in Article 2(1) is nearly identical to its counterparts in Common Articles 2, the rights in Article 2(2) are unique: the State should not discriminate against or punish the right-holder on account of a parent's (or relative's) actions, beliefs, or status. The thrust of the paragraph is clear enough: the State should not deliberately make children suffer because of the behaviour of the parents.

The well-being of adolescents and children is heavily dependent upon their parents and other family members, but while this dependency-defined relationship is usually a source of positive things that promote healthy development, it sometimes is just the opposite. Sometimes a government makes youngsters suffer on account of the things that their parents or relatives have done. There are two problems that stand out. First, sometimes the law makes children suffer because their parents are not married; children 'born out of wedlock' (that awkward phrase having replaced the stigmatising 'illegitimate') are discriminated against because of their parents' actions. And second, when parents or relatives are members of 'subversive' political parties, social movements, religious sects, or illegal organizations, the repressive measures that the authorities take against the group and its members are sometimes also directed at their innocent offspring: the children are punished because of the beliefs and actions of the adults. In both situations, the government is making children suffer because of their parents or relatives – in the first case, as a consequence of pursuing other objectives, and in the second, making them suffer on purpose.

But while the general point is easy to discern, it is difficult to specify the elements of Article 2(2). This is partly because the paragraph is not drafted in precise legal language, but also because there are no counterparts in other treaties to draw upon, and because the legislative records are not very informative. The best that this commentary can do is to offer a suggestion for how the elements should be framed.

236. Discrimination and punishment are two different things, so there are two rights in Article 2(2), and each right has four parts. The State Party is forbidden:

1. To (a) unreasonably (b) treat the right-holder differently on the basis of (c) the parents' (or guardians' or family members') (d) actions, beliefs, or status; or
2. To (a) purposely (b) make the right-holder suffer for (c) the actions, beliefs, or status (d) of the parents (or guardians or family members).

Component (1) is the non-discrimination right, and component (2) is the no-punishment right. The discussion below will outline the reasons for choosing these components and subcomponents.

237. As for the non-discrimination right, components (1b) to (1d) capture the idea that the State must not discriminate against young people on the grounds named in Article 2(2). The 'unreasonably' qualification in component (1a) makes it clear that the right is context-dependent. The phrase 'take appropriate measures' indicates that the framers did not intend that all such differential treatment be eliminated; the State Party can exercise discretion as it translates the abstract right of non-discrimination into concrete entitlements. Another reason for the qualification is that an absolute prohibition would be unworkable given the vast scope of things that can come under the notion of 'actions'. (For instance, adoption depends upon the actions of two sets of adults, the birth parents and the adoptive parents, and the adoption will alter the legal relations of the child to both sets. Once the child's legal status changes, the State will treat the youngster differently; the child will not be allowed to inherit from the birth parents, whereas the non-adopted birth-siblings can, for example.) Absolute rights can be hard to live with, and it is not reasonable to believe that the General Assembly would have created an absolute right that is so novel and so sweeping without having taken care to define the obligations so as to avoid unexpected or unwanted consequences.

Finally, the legislative records support treating 'appropriate' as a balancing device. For many years, the UN system of lawmaking has been concerned about the discriminatory treatment of non-marital children.[184] This kind of discrimination does not come under Article 2(1) since 'being born out of wedlock' is not a characteristic of the child, like race, sex, religion, etc., which are attributes of the person; it is a label for a status that derives

---

[184] Article 25(2) of the UDHR.

from the *actions of the parents*: it is an Article 2(2) matter. There are two things in the legislative records that bear upon our reading 'appropriate' as a balancing device. First, there were proposals for adding to Article 2(1) a prohibition of discrimination against children born out of wedlock, but no consensus could be reached because too many States were concerned that that would undermine families, and upset inheritance laws.[185] And second, some States that objected to the proposal said that the matter was already covered in Article 2.[186] These two positions are harmonised if we read 'appropriate' as a balancing device. Discrimination between children born in and out of wedlock is in fact covered – it comes under Article 2(2); and since Article 2(2) allows balancing, States Parties have discretion, subject to international accountability, to allow discrimination in certain situations, such as inheritance.[187]

In short, the 'reasonableness' test in component (1a) has textual support in the word 'appropriate', it makes practical sense, and it is consistent with the legislative records.

238. As for the no-punishment right, components (2a) and (2b) capture the idea of 'punishment': acting with the purpose or aim of making a person suffer (as happens in retribution, or just deserts). The 'purposely' test is important because children often suffer as a result of state action that responds to a parent's behaviour (as when the State takes family property to pay a fine imposed on the adult, or a parent is fired from a job, goes into

---

[185] *Travaux Préparatoires* (UN Doc. E/CN.4/1349, 1980), p. 3 ('basic working text' prohibited in-/out-of-wedlock discrimination in forerunner of Article 2(1)); (UN Doc. E/CN.4/1986/39, 1986), para. 13 (two proposals for protecting out-of-wedlock children), para. 16 (four States objecting to adding an in-/out-of-wedlock provision due to conflicts with domestic laws), and paras. 18 and 21 (proposals withdrawn or deadlocked).

[186] *Travaux Préparatoires* (UN Doc. E/CN.4/1986/39, 1986), para. 14 ('already covered under Article 4 [final Article 2]').

[187] One State said that the 1986 session had made it 'very clear' that out-of-wedlock protection is 'covered by Article 4 [final Article 2] which established the principle of non-discrimination on the basis of birth'. *Travaux Préparatoires* (UN Doc. E/CN.4/1988/28), para. 228. But that comment seems an error since the records only show a reference to 'Article 4', not to 'birth'. The records in this and the two preceding notes are reproduced in *Legislative History, o.c.* (note 63), pp. 319, 325–326, and 328.

If Article 2(1) were read as prohibiting distinctions based on whether or not the parents were married at the child's conception or birth, it would still not cover discrimination pertaining to inheritance. The interest at stake in inheritance is a type of property interest, but there is neither a general right to property, nor a specific right to inherit, in the CRC and the two Covenants.

The question of inheritance also arises in cases of 'assisted reproduction' where a third party is the biological father or mother. These are also Article 2(2) matters, and the State can make balancing judgements about inheritance, disclosure of the biological parent's identity, and other sensitive matters.

bankruptcy, or is sent to jail for committing a crime). But while the State cannot prevent suffering as a result of all parental actions, it can promise that it will never act *with the aim* of hurting a child *on account of* the parent's conduct. In addition, the word 'appropriate' is not being applied as a balancing element in the no-punishment right for a simple reason: it is preposterous to think that the General Assembly intended that States have the right to act with the aim of making an innocent child suffer as a response to the wrongdoing of a parent or relative.[188]

239. The rights of non-discrimination and no-punishment are framed as prohibitions only against state action, thus excluding private behaviour. This is because Article 2(2) concerns state actors only, as represented in the chapeau of the elements: 'The State Party is forbidden...'. On the one hand, the language of Article 2(2) – 'the child is protected against' – suggests that it could also apply to the conduct of private actors. But on the other, extending it to cover civil society would be an unreasonable burden on the government, and would entail unreasonable intrusions into private life. Moreover, the State cannot 'ensure' that private actors will not do the proscribed things; it can only 'promote' civil society behaviours. (In guiding the development of their children, parents take into account the actions of the parents of their children's peers, for instance. Mom does not allow Kim to play at Chris's house because Chris's parents are neo-Nazis, with prior convictions for paedophilia. So Chris is 'being discriminated against' on the grounds of the 'activities', 'statuses', and 'beliefs' of the parents. Surely the General Assembly did not intend for the CRC to prevent parents from exercising normal discretion in child-rearing.) In addition, since paragraph (2) is poorly written as a legal text, we have to give more weight to commonsense than to the literal reading of the words.

240. Finally, Article 2(2) is not framed as an umbrella right because there is no textual support for that reading, and because there is no practical need to limit the scope of the two rights by tying them to the sectoral rights.

241. In conclusion, Article 2(2) is not well drafted, so we have to do the best we can to make sense of it. This section has made suggestions for how the elements can be framed, and has outlined its reasons.

---

[188] For an unusually direct report on the no-punishment right, see *Mali* (UN Doc. CRC/C/MLI/2, 2006), para. 146. See also, CRC Comm., *Concl. Obser.: Turkmenistan* (UN Doc. CRC/C/42/3, 2006), para. 712.

CHAPTER SIX

THE COMMITTEE ON THE RIGHTS OF THE CHILD

1. *Confusions about the Nature and Status of the Committee's Statements*

242. The Committee on the Rights of the Child speaks as a collective body in its reporting guidelines, concluding observations, and general comments, while members speak as individuals in the dialogues with States. Unfortunately, there is confusion in the literature as to how these various statements should be viewed; there are confusions about the *nature* of the statements, and about the *status* of the statements.

243. A good example comes from UNICEF's *Implementation Handbook for the Convention on the Rights of the Child*, written by Peter Newell and Rachael Hodgkin.[189] In the chapter on Article 2, there is a box labelled 'Grounds for discrimination against children.' It contains a list of seventy things, including 'social disparities', 'rural exodus', and 'children born on unlucky days', to give a few examples.[190] The box, when read in the context of the entire chapter, gives readers the impression that the Committee has determined that these seventy criteria fall under the prohibitions of the right of non-discrimination in Article 2(1) and 2(2). The perception that the Committee has interpreted the article to include these grounds is a confusion pertaining to the *nature* of the statements contained in the concluding observations.

244. A statement made, let us say, under the *heading* 'definition of the child' is not the same thing as an *interpretation* of Article 1; a statement under the *heading* 'non-discrimination' is not the same as an *interpretation* of Article 2(1). Failure to distinguish the two things confuses the nature (or content) of the utterances.

For instance, Article 1, the main jurisdictional clause, defines the CRC right-holders as 'every human being under the age of 18 years *unless, under the law applicable to the child, majority is attained earlier*' (emphasis added). In monitoring implementation, there are two questions that are relevant to the 'unless...' qualification. First, does the State have a general law that defines majority below eighteen, pursuant to which the Party does not consider the

---

[189] R. Hodgkin and P. Newell, *o.c.* (note 103).
[190] *Id.* p. 28. Oddly, only half of the grounds named in Article 2(1) are in the list.

person a CRC right-holder? The General Guidelines asks this question under the heading 'Definition of the child' (although it is not asked with legal precision).[191] Second, is there any special law that causes an under-18 year old to cease to be a right-holder? For instance, if a minor marries, or goes into the military, or goes through a legal emancipation procedure, does the State consider that that act triggers the 'unless...' clause? The Committee does not ask the second question in either the guidelines or its dialogues. Instead, the guidelines ask about the minimum legal ages for things like sexual consent and the consumption of alcohol.[192] If the Convention did not exist, these questions could be appropriate when inquiring about the well-being of young people under a thematic heading 'minimum age laws', but none of those things are rational questions with respect to Article 1. Unfortunately, in its haste to produce the initial guidelines for reporting, the original Committee made a mistake when it came to questions about Article 1.

Subsequent members have come to realize that error, and few if any of them try to defend the mistake, but they have not changed the Committee's practices. So, under the heading of 'Definition of the Child,' States still report on the lower and upper ages of compulsory education, the age for testifying in court, and all their other minimum age laws in response to the guidelines.[193] And under that same heading in the concluding observations, the Committee will express its concerns about those ages, as well as about things somehow related to them. For instance, the Committee is concerned about 'the young age at which girls can marry according to traditional customs and about the high number of girls who do marry early'.[194] How shall we describe that statement? Is it an *interpretation* of Article 1? No it's not; it is a *statement about problems* stemming from early marriage *made under the heading* 'Definition of the Child,' a statement that has been placed under that heading because the original Committee made a mistake, and because the subsequent members have failed to correct the error.

245. The conceptual confusions are deeper when it comes to Article 2(1) and 2(2), and the errors more serious because of how they affect perceptions of the three rights in that article.

---

[191] CRC Comm., *General Guidelines Regarding the Form and Content of Initial Reports* (UN Doc. CRC/C/5, 1991), para. 12.
[192] *Id.*
[193] *E.g., Chile* (UN Doc. CRC/C/CHL/3, 2005), para. 35.
[194] CRC Comm., *Concl. Obser.: Equatorial Guinea* (UN Doc. CRC/C/143, 2004), para. 332.

To give one example, under the heading of 'Non-discrimination,' a concluding observation to one Party says that the 'Committee is [...] concerned at [sic] the prevailing disparities in the enjoyment of rights of children, in particular...in regions with socio-economic development problems';[195] and to another Party, the 'Committee is concerned that societal discrimination and cultural practices persist against vulnerable groups of children, in particular...children from poor and rural families....'[196] If those were statements about Article 2, they would be seriously in error because the right of non-discrimination is *not* about *disparities* in well-being in general, and because it *forbids state*-imposed discrimination, rather than private actor discrimination, which includes 'cultural practices' that negatively affect young people. But read those statements carefully: they do not actually say that these things are violations of Article 2, or even Article 2 matters. Rather, they are statements about the Committee's *concerns* that are *placed under the heading* 'Non-discrimination,' under the broader heading 'General principles.' Nevertheless, it is with statements like these that Newell and Hodgkin have built their 'Grounds of discrimination' box.

246. There are two problems that lie behind the long list of things included under the heading 'Non-discrimination,' and they both pertain to misuse of language, and to the failure to take Article 2 seriously as human rights law. The first is the tendency to use the label 'discrimination' for *any difference in treatment* that the person does not like. The second is the tendency to use 'discrimination' for *any disparity in well-being* that the person disapproves of. When Committee members expand 'discrimination' in these two ways, then they can monitor all of the sectoral rights under the heading of 'non-discrimination', since all laws and policies entail differential treatment of some kind, and every matter of concern is about some type of difference in well-being. And various Committee members have in fact been 'frontloading' the implementation reviews in this way. If readers think that a seventy-item list is long, it is only the tip of the iceberg. The box only pertains to the first nine years of implementation reviews, and the list comes only from the concluding observations, which contain just a fraction of the things that Committee members have labelled 'discrimination' in their individual questions during the dialogues with States. Some members have been attentive to language and to Article 2 as a human right, while some have shown little self-discipline in applying the label 'discrimination' to anything that

---

[195] CRC Comm., *Concl. Obser.: Uzbekistan* (UN Doc. CRC/C/42/3, 2006), p. 138, para. 637.
[196] CRC Comm., *Concl. Obser.: Equatorial Guinea* (UN Doc. CRC/C/143, 2004), para. 334.

catches their eye; but when any member misuses the language, or fails to take Article 2 seriously as a legal provision, frontloading is pushed further in the direction represented by the box.[197]

Let us now return to the box and see how the authors of the *Implementation Handbook* have presented their list to their readers: 'The following grounds for discrimination and groups affected by discrimination have been identified by the Committee in its examination of Initial Reports....' Read the sentence again. Notice that they do not claim that the Committee has said that those seventy things are forbidden grounds under Article 2; and 'groups affected by discrimination' is not even a ground of differentiation. But given the title of the box, 'Grounds for discrimination against children,' and given the title of the chapter, 'Non-discrimination Article 2,' and considering the presentation of the chapter as a whole, readers come away with false perceptions about the nature and content of the Committee's statements. And these mistakes lead to erroneous understandings of the three rights in Article 2(1) and 2(2).[198]

---

[197] Under the heading 'Non-discrimination,' the guidelines ask about 'economic, social and geographic disparities', for example. CRC Comm., *General Guidelines Regarding the Form and Contents of Periodic Reports* (UN Doc. CRC/C/58, 1996), para. 27. In response to this question, one Party spent five pages of the non-discrimination section reporting on such projects as National Disaster Mitigation, Rural Land Management, Sustainable Coastal Development, and Health Sector Reform; *Honduras* (UN Doc. CRC/C/HND/3, 2006), paras. 125–141.

[198] On occasion, the Committee has made the conceptual distinction in the main text; CRC Comm., *Report*, o.c. (note 89), para. 41 ('In addition to the prohibited grounds of discrimination in article 2, the Committee has identified groups who may be especially vulnerable to experiencing disparities in the enjoyment of their rights.')

The common practice in the literature is to use the named grounds as subject headings under which to catalogue what the treaty bodies have said in their concluding observations, and, usually, without the commentator subjecting them to legal analysis. *E.g.*, W. Vandenhole, o.c. (note 73) (using the grounds as headings for hundreds of concluding observations).

On the positive side, the CRC Committee has vigorously addressed caste discrimination as an Article 2(1) issue. The Committee criticised India's first report for ignoring caste discrimination, and in doing so, it seems to have been the first treaty-body to cross-reference the concluding observations of another committee. CRC Comm., *Concl. Obser.: India* (CRC/C/15/Add.115, 2000), para. 31. In its second report, India forthrightly discussed the situation of Dalit and Tribal children. Unfortunately, India did not discuss caste discrimination or caste disparities under the sectoral rights, but in a separate section, which tends to marginalize these youngsters, their problems, and their rights.

Earlier, India objected to the CERD Committee's interpreting Article 1(1) of the CERD to cover Dalits, and it strenuously, and successfully, opposed inclusion of caste in the Declaration and Programme of Action, of the World Conference Against Racial Discrimination, Xenophobia and Related Intolerances (August to September, 2001). And yet India had proposed adding 'caste' as a named ground in the creation of Article 2 of the UDHR, and withdrew its proposal only after other delegations said that caste was inherently covered by the existing named grounds, an important historical and legal point that previous commentators have not been mentioning. *Travaux Préparatoires* for the UDHR: *Official Records of the Third Session of the General*

247. Another example comes from Cynthia Price Cohen's *Jurisprudence on the Rights of the Child*, which is a four volume, 4170 page compilation of extracts of statements in the concluding observation, organized by article.[199] The word 'jurisprudence' is normally used in domestic legal systems to refer to the case law, or the decisions of courts, and, in international human rights law, the traditional meaning has been extended to refer to the decisions of the Human Rights Committee when it handles individual 'communications' under the Optional Protocol, and of the other treaty monitoring bodies that have a similar 'quasi-judicial'[200] authority. When Cohen calls the concluding observations 'jurisprudence', she is implying that those statements are entitled to a degree of deference, respect, or 'reverence' similar to what is accorded to judicial rulings. In particular, labelling them as 'jurisprudence' gives readers the impression that the concluding observations are *legal interpretations* issued by a *court-like* body. The use of 'jurisprudence' to induce these perceptions is subtle because she does not actually claim that the concluding observations are legal interpretations of the CRC, or that the Committee has court-like authority; in fact, she makes no concrete statements at all about the legal significance of the Committee's observations.

248. The label 'jurisprudence' causes confusion about both the nature and the status of the observations. A statement cannot be a 'legal interpretation' of a CRC article if it is not an *interpretation*, and we have sufficiently examined this problem in the discussion of the UNICEF *Handbook*. In addition, a statement cannot be a *legal* interpretation if it is not the product of legal reasoning. And if a statement is not a legal interpretation given by a *court* or court-like body, then it is not entitled to the status – to the deference or awe – that we give to judicial rulings on the meanings of legal texts.

249. There is an increasing tendency of people to give the treaty-monitoring bodies the status of courts, to speak of the bodies as if they have the 'normative and institutional legitimacy' of courts of law.[201] There is also the question of using the interpretations and other statements of one treaty body to understand the provisions in another treaty, such as using the decisions of

---

Assembly, o.c. (note 113), 101st mtg. (13 Oct. 1948), p. 138 (Mr. Habib, India), and p. 139 (Mr. Chang, China; and Mr. Appadorai, India).

[199] C. P. Cohen, *Jurisprudence on the Rights of the Child* (Ardsley, N.Y., Transnational Publ., 2005).

[200] T. Buergenthal, 'The U.N. Human Rights Committee', *Max Planck UNYB* 5 (2001), pp. 341, 390.

[201] *Id.* pp. 397–398.

the Human Rights Committee in its 'individual communications' to interpret the CRC. We therefore need to give some additional attention to the nature and the status of the pronouncements of monitoring committees.

People usually accord judges a high degree of deference or respect, and there are three attributes in particular that lie behind their special social-political status: (i) the court has been authorized, pursuant to some higher authority, to make binding legal decisions in designated controversies; (ii) the judges have an impartiality, or separateness from political actors, that allows them to be accepted as the final decision-makers in those disputes; and, (iii) the judges make their decisions based upon the rule of law, rather than their personal opinions about the controversies. The degree to which any given entity will enjoy the social-political status normally given to courts will depend heavily on the degree to which it is perceived as having these three attributes. Because of space limitations, we will look at Cohen's 'jurisprudence' only in regard to the last attribute.

250. If a decision of a court is to be a bona fide legal ruling, the judicial officers must respect the rule of law. Basically, the rule of law means that judges decide the dispute by applying the law to the facts, and to resolve controversies over the meaning of a legal text, they follow the rules of legal interpretation. In the Vienna Convention on the Law of Treaties, one of the elements of the ordinary meaning rule is that the authorities doing the interpretation must act in 'good faith'.[202] This is an important requirement, and since it receives virtually no attention in the literature, we need to elaborate on it.

Interpreting a legal text in 'good faith' means, at a minimum: (i) that the judges actually use the established rules of legal interpretation to produce their ruling on the meaning of the text in question. This is to be contrasted with 'result-oriented' decision-making, where a person first makes the policy or political decision of what the law should be, or which side should win the case, and then manufactures an 'interpretation' of the law that produces that result. (ii) That the judges show how they arrived at their decision, that they give an adequate oral or written explanation of their lines of reasoning. In human rights circles, this is being called the '"right to a reasoned judgment"'.[203] It is part of the 'good governance' notion that power must always be exercised with 'transparency and accountability'. And (iii), the

---

[202] Article 31(1) of the VCLT, quoted at No. 31.
[203] Office of the United Nations High Commissioner for Human Rights, *Human Rights in the Administration of Justice* (Geneva, United Nations, 2002) (UN Doc. HR/P/PT/9), p. 293.

judges' explanations must be an honest account of their actual reasoning processes. This is a corollary to the requirement that judges not engage in resulted-oriented decision-making, where the explanations end up being constructed to fit the desired result.

The CRC Committee and the Human Rights Committee are poles apart in applying legal methodologies to their respective treaties. With handling over eight hundred individual complaints in thirty years, the HRC has been under much more pressure to respect the rule of law than the CRC Committee. But the HRC has always had serious difficulties in meeting the three components of the good faith rule, and this is probably more true of its discrimination cases than most of its other cases. While this commentary has used the HRC's definition of 'discrimination' as a helpful introduction to the three elements of the right of non-discrimination, none of the committee's so-called jurisprudence has been considered useful for interpreting Article 2(1) of the CRC. (The reasons are outlined in the margin.)[204]

---

[204] The first reason for not using the HRC's decisions is lack of relevancy: (i) the HRC handles 'discrimination' cases under Article 26 of the CCPR, with, at most, only token reference to Article 2(1); (ii) the HRC treats the two equality clauses in Article 26 of the CCPR as the principle of proportionality (or reasonableness); and (iii), it ignores the built-in anti-discrimination clause in Article 26, for reasons that it has not disclosed.

The second reason is their lack of usefulness as legal opinions. In using a decision from one jurisdiction or UN body in the interpretation of a legal provision in the law of another jurisdiction or treaty, what is transferable are the lines of reasoning, rather than the legal conclusion itself: if the decision gives reasons, then one must evaluate their cogency, and then incorporate them within the analysis, giving each reason its appropriate weight. Two problems stand out: (i) The HRC's decisions are impaired by the confusions discussed in Chapter 3.8. And (ii), the HRC has serious difficulties complying with the three components of the good faith rule: e.g., it gives 'few clues as to how the decision was reached', in the words of S. Joseph, et al., o.c. (note 56), p. 50, and it needs to work harder to ensure that its interpretations and applications are perceived as 'objective and legally sound', in particular, it must 'spell out in greater detail [its] legal reasons' and it must not engage in selectivity, according to Thomas Buergenthal, 'The U.N. Human Rights Committee', l.c. (note 200), p. 395. Those are polite ways to say that the HRC is not respecting the rule of law.

These problems are well illustrated by comparing Broeks v. The Netherlands, No. 172/1984, to Vos v. The Netherlands, No. 218/1986. Broeks said that sex discrimination against women in a social security law violates Article 26 of the CCPR because it denied women entitlements 'on an equal footing with men' (at para. 15). Two years later, Vos said that a similar law did not violate Article 26. But instead of applying the 'equal footing' test of Broeks, the HRC said that 'differences in result of the uniform application of laws [i.e., hurting women by overt sex discrimination in a comprehensive social security act] do not per se constitute prohibited discrimination' (para. 11.3). In plain English: depriving a disabled woman of a disability pension, on the sole ground that the claimant is a woman, is not sex discrimination! The HRC made no effort to square the second case with the first; in fact, it never even mentioned Broeks in connection with the discrimination issue. These cases demonstrate the arbitrariness of the reasonableness principle, and are 'textbook illustrations' of violating the right to a reasoned judgment.

2. Too Much, and Too Little

251. In the light of the sheer number of things that are included under the 'Non-discrimination' heading, a quick read through the concluding observations can give the impression that the Committee is vigilant in its efforts to protect young people from being discriminated against. And the Committee's frontloading seems to be popular with many consumers of the concluding observations. 'Discrimination!' has a militant bite, and no doubt it is gratifying to see one's key concerns included under the heading 'Non-discrimination' even if the matter is not really an Article 2 issue. But expanding 'discrimination' to cover anything that Committee members do not like comes at a cost, and the price is paid by the adolescents and children who need CRC rights the most.

252. When 'discrimination' is anything that a person does not like, then the word loses its meaning, and the CRC's right of non-discrimination contracts and expands according to the feelings of adults, rather than being respected as a matter of international law. The two main problems are 'selectivity', or double standards, and superficiality.

2.1. Boys and Selectivity

253. Concerning selectivity, the Committee is not equally vigilant towards all groups of youngsters; in particular, there has been systemic marginalization of boys.

With regard to Article 2(1), State-imposed sex discrimination against boys has been overlooked; for example, when the law allows courts to punish boys with whipping, the Committee will criticize the corporal punishment as a violation of the Convention, but turn a blind eye to the sex discrimination.[205] This never happens when laws discriminate against girls.

While there are not many laws that commit sex discrimination against boys, apart from discriminatory affirmative action, boys are the 'victims' of numerous types of disparities. Unfortunately, the Committee has routinely ignored differences in well-being when boys are on the losing end, and, when it does notice a disparity, it avoids labelling it 'discrimination'. This is just the opposite of how the Committee responds to disparities when girls

---

[205] Compare *Sudan* (UN Doc. CRC/C/3/Add.3, 1992), para. 163 (only boys are whipped), to the silence about the sex discrimination in CRC Comm., *Concl. Obser.: Sudan* (UN Doc. CRC/C/15/Add.10, 1993), and *Sudan* (UN Doc. CRC/C/15/Add.190, 2002).

are faring worse. The increasing under-representation of boys in school has already been mentioned; in addition, boys are seriously over-represented in detention facilities and prisons, as 'street children', in armed groups, as victims of street violence, in fatal car accidents, in drowning, and so forth, but the gender dimension has been routinely ignored. When boys have a suicide rate three times higher than girls, the Committee expresses its concern about the 'incidence of suicide among *young people'*, leaving out the gender dimension, for instance.[206] And ways are found for the girls to upstage the boys when boys are doing worse; when a State reports that cigarette smoking is predominately a boys' problem, the concluding observation will express concern 'at the high and increasing' prevalence of tobacco use 'notably among girls'.[207]

254. On the positive side, there has been significant improvement in the past few years in acknowledging the gender dimension when boys are being adversely affected. But institutional marginalization is not easy to overcome in any situation, and there is room for improvement in the Committee's attention to the right of boys to be free from sex discrimination, and to disparities in boys' enjoyment of their sectoral rights.[208]

---

[206] Emphasis added, CRC Comm., *Concl. Obser.: Australia* (UN Doc. CRC/C/15/Add.79, 1997), para. 18.

[207] CRC Comm., *Concl. Obser.: Switzerland* (UN Doc. CRC/C/15/Add.182, 2002), para. 40.

[208] The turning point for boys may have been when the Committee confronted discriminatory affirmative action against boys in India's report; Nos. 184–185. Some positive examples include: CRC Comm., *Report, o.c.* (note 89), para. 42 ('[I]n some States gender bias is seen when boys underperform or underachieve in school in comparison to girls.'); CRC Comm., *Concl. Obser.: Singapore* (UN Doc. CRC/C/15/Add.220, 2003), paras. 32–33 (whipping of boys); CRC Comm., *Concl. Obser.: Antigua and Barbuda* (UN Doc. CRC/C/143, 2004), paras. 509 and 511 (boys' drop out rates); CRC Comm., *Concl. Obser.: Latvia* (UN Doc. CRC/C/42/3, 2006), paras. 223–224 (suicide of boys); and CRC Comm., *Concl. Obser.: Lebanon* (UN Doc. CRC/C/42/3, 2006), paras. 428–429 (rape of boys). But while the sex discrimination and disparities are mentioned as observations, they are not addressed in the recommendations section; by contrast, there are recommendations when disparities hurt girls.
Compare to W. Vandenhole, *o.c.* (note 73), p. 164 (the CRC Committee has 'systematically' paid attention to 'gender bias faced by boys'). Perhaps that assessment is based only on reading the concluding observations, and therefore has missed the marginalization of boys that one sees by comparing the observations to the sex discrimination against boys, and to the disparities affecting boys, that are revealed in the state reports, the dialogues, and the NGO materials submitted to the Committee. Or perhaps the assessment is itself an example of the marginalization of boys.

2.2. Girls and Superficiality

Early Marriage

255. The refrain 'particularly girls' appears frequently in the Committee's statements, so does this mean that girls are getting the attention that they need? Superficiality is the other problem when the accusation of 'Discrimination!' hinges on feelings rather than human rights. This problem is well illustrated by how the Committee addresses the problems that girls experience when they get married during adolescence. Early marriage leads to early pregnancies, and this leads to devastating impacts on the ability of girls to enjoy three sectoral rights – the rights to life, health, and education.

First, while girls can conceive in early adolescence, their bodies are not sufficiently mature to support a safe delivery without good medical intervention; in countries where there are high rates of teenage marriages, there are higher rates of maternal mortality and medical complications. The most dramatic complication is fistula. An obstetric fistula is a hole in the birth canal caused by prolonged labour without medical assistance, and it can result in the death of the baby, and a lifetime of incontinence for the mother, along with the emotional trauma, stigma, and health care problems that come with the inability to control one's bowels and bladder. At conservative estimates, this is happening to an additional 100,000 girls and women each year. And second, early pregnancy leads to girls dropping out of school without having acquired a basic education.

The historical pattern throughout the world has been for the minimum age for marriage to be lower for females than for males. The respective ages are even lower in developing countries, and the customary-law ages for marriage in traditional societies are lower still. So in a number of regions in the world, the widespread practice of early marriage combines with weak health and educational systems to have profound consequences on girls' enjoyment of three sectoral rights.

The Committee on the Rights of the Child does not address these human rights problems through the sectoral rights, however. Based on what has been said about frontloading, readers may have anticipated the Committee's approach: it treats the problem as sex discrimination against girls in the marriage laws, which it handles, irrationally, as a 'Definition of the Child' issue under Article 1, or under the 'Non-discrimination' heading (or sometimes as a 'traditional practice' harmful to the health of girls under Article 24).

Different Minimum Ages for Marriage

256. The legal mistake regarding Article 1 is self-evident, but the discrimination mistake needs elaborating. Different minimum ages for marriage is not an Article 2(1) matter, and this becomes clear when one applies the three elements: marriage is not a sectoral right in the CRC, so Element (3) is not satisfied. Marriage is a right in the CCPR (Article 23), however, and the Committee could use Article 41 of the CRC to address the discrimination. But when there is a lower age of marriage for girls, the victims of the discrimination are *boys*. Again the elements-approach makes this clear. The sex-based differentiation in Element (1a) pertains to the exercise of personal autonomy: the interest at stake in Element (1b) is the freedom to enter into marriage; when a girl of sixteen has this freedom but a boy must wait until eighteen or twenty-one, then it is the males who suffer the impairment in Element (2).

257. Some sceptics might argue that a lower age of marriage for girls is 'sex discrimination' against them because it deprives them of the protection that the higher age law is giving to boys. There is some merit in looking at the matter as a failure of 'protection', but it still leads to legal misunderstandings of Article 2(1). It loses sight of three things. In the first place, discrimination is a here-and-now event: the differential treatment in Element (1) impairs the protected interest in Element (2) right now, not months or years later. But the harms to girls' health and education are things that happen down the road, after the interplay of other causal events: laws that allow early marriage lead to more girls getting married at an early age, which leads to more early pregnancies, which leads to the health and education problems – and 'leads to' not 'causes', because other causal factors must be involved, and because the tragedy happens to only a portion of the group. (Likewise, the failure to protect boys from growing up in families without their fathers eventually 'leads to' their overrepresentation in prison, but 'the cause' of them being in jail is not sex discrimination or the absence of fathers – other factors must also come into play to produce their over-representation.) In the second place, equalizing the ages will not necessarily solve the problem: dropping the age for boys to that of girls removes the sex discrimination but does not help the girls. And in the third place, girls face the problems of early pregnancies for unique biological reasons, so there is no valid comparator for the purposes of the right of non-discrimination. In short, to protect girls against all of the problems that stem from early pregnancy throughout their lifecycle, we must focus directly on their sectoral rights – life, health, and education.

The discrimination against males in the marriage laws is not a burning human rights issue, needless to say, simply because few young men under 18 years of age are ready, willing and able to take on the roles of husband and father that society assigns to them. But still, one cannot take CRC rights seriously if one cannot accept the fact that it is the *boys'* right of non-discrimination that is being violated, and the fact that what is violated is their *CCPR* right of non-discrimination (in conjunction with the sectoral right to marry), not their Article 2(1) right in the CRC.

Marginalizing Girls' Sectoral Rights
258. But while the Committee has (once again) been blind to sex discrimination against boys, and (once again) has turned the tables on the boys by incorrectly making girls the victims of 'discrimination', we must not lose sight of our concern: girls are suffering enormous injustices in regards to three sectoral rights, and early marriages are a key part of the problem, with the weak health care and education systems being major contributing causes. The Committee has not completely ignored the effects of early marriages on health and education, but it has marginalized them by defining the problem as 'a discriminatory definition of the child'. Simply put, the Committee has not been using its advocacy platforms – the dialogues with States, the concluding observations, and the general comments – to mobilize action to protect the interests of girls where they need protecting. The United Nations launched an End Fistula Campaign in 2003,[209] and the General Assembly has even passed a resolution on the problem,[210] but the Committee on the Rights of the Child is not on the bandwagon. For instance, the General Comment on Adolescent Health clearly states the link between early marriage and dropping out of school, but the vague reference to 'maternal morbidity and mortality', without mention of fistula or other problems, deprives girls of the concrete advocacy that they need, and deserve.[211]

It has been 'too much, and too little': by making too much of the *rhetoric* of 'Discrimination against girls!', the Committee has made too little of the girls' sectoral *rights* – their rights to life, health and education.

---

[209] See, www.endfistula.org, from which the information in the main text was drawn.
[210] GA, *Resolution* (UN Doc. A/RES/60/141, 2005), penultimate preambular para.
[211] CRC Comm., *Gen. Com. No. 4: Adolescent Health and Development* (2003) (UN Doc. HRI/GEN/1/Rev.8, 2006), paras. 5, 6, 16, 27. Compare to the excellent advocacy in UNICEF, *Excluded and Invisible, o.c.* (note 97), p. 47.

259. The remedy for these problems is to respect the relation between Article 2(1) and the sectoral rights: one must take the right of non-discrimination seriously as an umbrella right that plays specific roles in protecting sectoral rights, and take the sectoral rights seriously by using them to address disparities in well-being, whenever state-imposed sex (race, etc.) discrimination is not the principal cause.

CONCLUSION

260. The Introduction promised to give a legal interpretation of Article 2, in strict conformity with the Vienna Convention on the Laws of Treaties, and to give its lines of reasoning with as much transparency and accountability as the space limitations allow.

261. The main focus has been the umbrella right of non-discrimination in Article 2(1). The analysis shows that it is made up of three simple elements; that it serves three related functions; and that it can be applied to real-life situations without any intermediate balancing decisions – it is an absolute right. We have also seen the extraordinary amount of confusion that surrounds the right of non-discrimination, as people make too much of the right, while at the same time making too little of it.

The analysis also shows that Article 2(2) contains two separate rights, a non-discrimination right that is context-dependent, and a no-punishment right that is absolute. Very little attention has been given to these two rights by the Committee and others, in part because paragraph (2) is not well written, and thus is difficult to understand, and in part because of the general failure to take CRC 'rights' seriously as *legal* rights.

And the analysis has shown that Article 2(1) contains a jurisdictional clause that works together with the jurisdictional clause of Article 1 to define the right-holders. Article 2(1)'s jurisdictional clause is legally significant, but has had very little practice importance in the monitoring of the Convention.

262. The commentary has also validated the conclusions of *Children's Rights: Reality or Rhetoric?* that were quoted in the Introduction: 'There is an alarming ignorance of what the Convention is and what it means.' This is nowhere truer than with the right of non-discrimination. But the problem is more than just a failure to take adolescents and children seriously as right-holders, and more than just a failure to take CRC rights seriously as legal rights. There are active efforts to create confusion about the right of non-discrimination, a problem that runs throughout the entire legal literature.

263. The situation is like an irresistible force meeting an immovable object. The immovable object is the individually-held human right that absolutely forbids race, etc. discrimination in the enjoyment of other human rights, backed up by the Charter's requirement that States promote the realization

of human rights 'without distinction as to race, sex, language, or religion'. The irresistible force is the human urge to discriminate.

All of the confusions we have looked at – 'indirect discrimination', 'discriminatory effects', 'the principle of non-discrimination', 'the principle of proportionality', reading the right of non-discrimination in Common Articles 2 through the prism of the case law of the European Court of Human Rights, the multiple meanings of 'affirmative action', and so forth – foster State-imposed discrimination based on race, sex, and the other forbidden grounds. People exploit these confusions to satisfy their desire to discriminate.

264. The right of non-discrimination in Article 2(1) is a challenge to all of us. It challenges us to be faithful to the rule of law; to take international human rights law seriously as law; to take adolescents and children seriously as right-holders; to fight our way through an 'army' of confusions; to critically assess what other commentators have said, including judges and treaty-monitoring committees; to set aside preconceptions; and to re-examine personal views about using race, sex, religious, etc. discrimination as a means to an end, especially when the targets are children and adolescents.

The aim of this commentary is to provide a resource to readers as they come to their own conclusions about Article 2(1) and 2(2). And to do so grounded in legal interpretation, and in respect for the human dignity of adolescents and children – the 'real parties in interest' in our, the adults', discussions, debates, and disputes.

BOOKS AND ARTICLES CITED

Abramson, B., 'Reservations to the Convention on the Rights of the Child: A Look at the Reservations of Asian States Parties', in: International Commission of Jurists, *Rights of the Child: Report of a Training Programme in Asia*, Geneva: ICJ, 1994.

Ahdar, R. and Leigh, I., *Religious Freedom in the Liberal State*, Oxford: Oxford Univ. Press, 2005.

Appelt, A., and Jarosch, M. (eds.), *Combating Racial Discrimination: Affirmative Action as a Model for Europe*, Oxford/New York: Berg, 2000.

Arnardóttir, O. M., *Equality and Non-Discrimination Under the European Convention on Human Rights*, The Hague/London/New York: Martinus Nijhoff Publ., 2003.

Bamforth, N., 'Limits of Anti-Discrimination Law: Legal and Social Concepts of Equality', in: J. Dine & B. Watt, *Discrimination Law: Concepts, Limitations and Justifications*, London/New York: Longman, 1996.

Banton, M., *Discrimination*, Buckingham/Philadelphia: Open Univ. Press, 1994.

——, *International Action Against Racial Discrimination*, Oxford: Clarendon Press, 1996.

Bayefsky, A., 'The Principle of Equality or Non-Discrimination in International Law', Human Rights Journal 11 (1990), 1–34.

Besson, S., 'The Principle of Non-Discrimination in the Convention on the Rights of the Child', *International Journal of Children's Rights* 13, No. 4 (2005), 433–461.

Boerefijn, I., Coomans, F., Goldschmidt, J., Holtmaat, R., and Wolleswinkel, R. (eds.), *Temporary Special Measures*, Antwerpen/Oxford/New York: Intersentia, 2003.

Bossuyt, M., *L'interdiction de la discrimination dans le droit international des droits de l'homme*, Brussels: Emile Bruylant, 1976.

——, 'The Concept and Practice of Affirmative Action' (UN Doc. E/CN.4/Sub.2/2000/11, 2000).

Brems, E., 'Above Children's Heads: The Headscarf Controversy in European Schools from the Perspective of Children's Rights', *International Journal of Children's Rights* 14, No. 2 (2006), 119–136.

——, *Article 14: The Right to Freedom of Thought, Conscience and Religion*, in: A. Alen, J. Vande Lanotte, E. Verhellen, F. Ang, E. Berghmans and M. Verheyde (eds.), *A Commentary on the UN Convention on the Rights of the Child*, Leiden/Boston: Martinus Nijhoff Publ., 2006.

Buergenthal, T., 'To Respect and to Ensure: State Obligations and Permissible Derogations', in: L. Henkin (ed.), *The International Bill of Rights: The Covenant on Civil and Political Rights*, New York: Columbia Univ. Press, 1981.

——, 'The U.N. Human Rights Committee', *Max Planck UNYB* 5 (2001), 341–398.

Buhman, K., 'Administrative Law Reform in the PRC', in: H.-O. Sano and G. Alfredsson, *Human Rights and Good Governance*, The Hague/London/New York: Martinus Nijhoff Publ., 2002.

Bunn-Livingstone, S., *Juricultural Pluralism vis-à-vis Treaty Law*, The Hague/Boston: Martinus Nijhoff Publ., 2002.

Çali, B., 'Balancing Human Rights? Methodological Problems with Weights, Scales and Proportions', *Human Rights Quarterly* 29 (2007), 251–270.

Cavalli-Sforza, L. L., *Genes, Peoples and Languages* (M. Seielstad, transl.), London: Penguin, 2001.

Chutikul, S., 'Helping the Girl Child', *Global Futures*, 2nd Quarter, 2003.

Cohen, C. P., *Jurisprudence on the Rights of the Child*, Ardsley, N.Y.: Transnational Publ., 2005.

Committee on Economic, Social and Cultural Rights, *General Comment No. 5: Persons With Disabilities* (1994) (UN Doc. HRI/GEN/Rev.8, 2006).

——, *General Comment No. 13: The Right to Education* (1999) (UN Doc. HRI/GEN/1/Rev.8, 2006).

Committee on the Elimination of Discrimination Against Women, *General Recommendation No. 25: Article 4, paragraph 1* (2004) (UN Doc. HRI/GEN/1/Rev.8, 2006).

Committee on the Elimination of Racial Discrimination, *General Recommendation No. 30: Discrimination against non-citizens* (2005) (UN Doc. HRI/GEN/1/Rev.8, 2006).

Committee on the Rights of the Child, *General Comment No. 4: Adolescent Health and Development* (2003) (UN Doc. HRI/GEN/1/Rev.8, 2006).

——, *General Comment No. 5: General Measures* (2003) (UN Doc. HRI/GEN/Rev.8, 2006).

——, *General Comment No. 9: The Rights of Children With Disabilities* (2006) (UN Doc. CRC/C/GC/9).

——, *General Guidelines Regarding the Form and Content of Initial Reports* (UN Doc. CRC/C/5, 1991).

——, *General Guidelines Regarding the Form and Contents of Periodic Reports* (UN Doc. CRC/C/58, 1996).

——, *Matters Relating to the Committee's Methods of Work* (UN Doc. CRC/C/L.2, 1991).

The Concise Oxford Dictionary of Current English (8th ed.), Oxford: Clarendon Press, 1990.

Conte, A., Davidson, S., and Burchill, R., *Defining Civil and Political Rights: The Jurisprudence of the United Nations Human Rights Committee*, Hants, UK: Ashgate, 2004.

Cook, R., 'Obligations to Adopt Temporary Special Measures [Under CEDAW]', in: I. Boerefijn, F. Coomans, J. Goldschmidt, R. Holtmaat, and R. Wolleswinkel (eds.), *Temporary Special Measures*, Antwerpen/Oxford/New York: Intersentia, 2003.

——, 'Reservations to the Convention on the Elimination of All Forms of Discrimination Against Women', *Virginia Journal of International Law* 30, No. 3 (1990), 643–716.

Craven, M., *The International Covenant on Economic, Social, and Cultural Rights*, Oxford: Clarendon Press, 1995.

Dawkins, R., *The God Delusion*, London: Bantam, 2006.

Detrick, S. (ed.), *The United Nations Convention on the Rights of the Child: A Guide to the "Travaux Préparatoires"*, Dordrecht/Boston/London: Martinus Nijhoff Publ., 1992.

van Dijk, P., and van Hoof, F., *Theory and Practice of the European Convention on Human Rights* (3rd ed.), The Hague/London/Boston: Kluwer, 1998.

Doebbler, C., *Introduction to International Human Rights Law*, Washington, DC: CD Publ., 2006.

Dworkin, R., *Taking Rights Seriously*, London: Duckworth, 1977.

Eide, A., 'Possible ways and means of facilitating the peaceful and constructive solution of problems involving minorities' (UN Doc. E/CN.4/Sub.2/1993/34).

Ellis, E., *EC Sex Equality Law* (2nd ed.), Oxford: Clarendon Press, 1998.

Evatt, E., 'The Practical Relevance of Article 4 CEDAW', in: I. Boerefijn, F. Coomans, J. Goldschmidt, R. Holtmaat, and R. Wolleswinkel (eds.), *Temporary Special Measures*, Antwerpen/Oxford/New York: Intersentia, 2003.

Foighel, I., 'Reflections of a Former Judge of the European Court of Human Rights', in: S. Lagoutte, H.-O. Sano, P. S. Smith, *Human Rights in Turmoil*, Leiden/Boston: Martinus Nijhoff Publ., 2007.

Freeman, M., 'Temporary Special Measures', in: I. Boerefijn, F. Coomans, J. Goldschmidt, R. Holtmaat, and R. Wolleswinkel (eds.), *Temporary Special Measures*, Antwerpen/Oxford/New York: Intersentia, 2003.

Fullinwider, R. K., *The Reverse Discrimination Controversy: A Moral and Legal Analysis*, Totowa, New Jersey: Rowman and Littlefield, 1981.

Goonesekere, S., *Children, Law and Justice: A South Asia Perspective*, New Delhi/London/Thousand Oaks: Sage Public., 1998.

Gunn, T. J., 'The Complexity of Religion and the Definition of "Religion" in International Law', *Harvard Human Rights Journal* 16 (Spring) (2003), 189–215.

Hammarberg, T., and Belembaogo, A., 'Proactive Measures Against Discrimination', in *Children's Rights: Turning Principles Into Practice*, Stockholm: Save the Children Sweden, 2000.

Harris, D. J., O'Boyle. M., and Warbrick, C., *Law of the European Convention on Human Rights*, London/Dublin/Edinburgh: Butterworths, 1995.

Hashemi, K., 'Religious Legal Traditions, Muslim States and the Convention on the Rights of the Child: An Essay on the Relevant UN Documentation', *Human Rights Quarterly* 29 (2007), 194–227.

Henkin, L., 'Introduction', in: L. Henkin (ed.), *The International Bill of Rights: The Covenant on Civil and Political Rights*, New York: Columbia Univ. Press, 1981.

Hepple, B., and Szyszczak, E. (eds.), *Discrimination: The Limits of Law*, London/New York: Mansell Publ., 1993.

Heringa, A. W., 'Comments on the Contribution by Professor Cook', in: I. Boerefijn, F. Coomans, J. Goldschmidt, R. Holtmaat, and R. Wolleswinkel (eds.), *Temporary Special Measures*, Antwerpen/Oxford/New York: Intersentia, 2003.

Hillgruber, C., and Jestaedt, M., *The European Convention on Human Rights and the Protection of National Minorities* (S. Less & N. Solomon, transl.), Köln, Germany: Verlag Wissenschaft und Politik, 1994.

Hitchens, C., *God Is Not Great*, London: Atlantic Books, 2007.

Hodgkin, R., and Newell, P., *Implementation Handbook for the Convention on the Rights of the Child* (2nd ed.), New York/Geneva: UNICEF, 2002.

Holtmatt, R., 'Building Blocks for a General Recommendation on Article 4(1)', in: I. Boerefijn, F. Coomans, J. Goldschmidt, R. Holtmaat, and R. Wolleswinkel (eds.), *Temporary Special Measures*, Antwerpen/Oxford/New York: Intersentia, 2003.

Human Rights Committee, *General Comment No. 18* (1989) (UN Doc. HRI/GEN/1/Rev.8, 2006).

——, *General Comment No. 29: Article 4: Derogations* (2001) (UN Doc. HRI/GEN/1/Rev.8, 2006).

International Labour Office, *Equality at Work: Tackling the Challenges*, Geneva: ILO, 2007.

International Law Commission, *Report of the International Law Commission: Fifty-third session* (UN Doc. A/56/10, Supp. 10, 2001).

International Save the Children Alliance, *Children's Rights: Equal Rights?*, London: International Save the Children Alliance, 2000.

——, *Children's Rights: Reality or Rhetoric?*, London: International Save the Children Alliance, 2000.

de Jong, C. D., *The Freedom of Thought, Conscience and Religion or Belief in the United Nations (1946–1992)*, Antwerpen/Groningen/Oxford: Intersentia-Hart, 2000.

Joseph, S., Schultz, J., and Castan, M., *The International Covenant on Civil and Political Rights: Cases, Materials, and Commentary* (2nd ed.), Oxford: Oxford Univ. Press, 2004.

Lawson, E., *Encyclopedia of Human Rights* (2nd ed.), Washington, DC: Taylor & Francis, 1996.

Lerner, N., *Religion, Secular Beliefs and Human Rights*, Leiden/Boston: Martinus Nijhoff Publ., 2006.

Lijnzaad, L., *Reservations to UN-Human Rights Treaties: Ratify and Ruin?*, Dordrecht/Boston/London: Martinus Nijhoff Publ., 1995.

Loenen T., and Rodrigues, P. (eds.), *Non-Discrimination Law: Comparative Perspectives*, The Hague/London/Boston: Kluwer Law Int'l., 1999.

Lopez, I. F. H., *White by Law: The Legal Construction of Race*, New York: New York Univ. Press, 1996.

McCrudden, C., *Buying Social Justice*, Oxford: Oxford Univ. Press, 2007.

McGoldrick, D., *Human Rights and Religion – The Islamic Headscarf Debate in Europe*, Oxford/Portland: Hart Publ., 2006.

McKean, W., *Equality and Discrimination Under International Law*, Oxford: Clarendon Press, 1983.

——, W. A., 'The Meaning of Discrimination in International and Municipal Law', *British Yearbook of Int'l. Law* 44 (1970), 177–192.

Meron, T., *Human Rights Law-Making in the United Nations*, Oxford: Clarendon Press, 1986.

A New English Dictionary on Historical Principles (vol. 3), Oxford: Clarendon Press, 1897.

Niessen, J., and Chopin, I. (eds.), *The Development of Legal Instruments to Combat Racism in a Diverse Europe*, Leiden/Boston: Martinus Nijhoff Publ., 2004.

Nowak, M., *Article 6: The Right to Life, Survival and Development*, in: A. Alen, J. Vande Lanotte, E. Verhellen, F. Ang, E. Berghmans and M. Verheyde (eds.), *A Commentary on the UN Convention on the Rights of the Child*, Leiden/Boston: Martinus Nijhoff, 2005.
——, *U.N. Covenant on Civil and Political Rights: CCPR Commentary* (2nd ed.), Kehl/Strasbourg/Arlington: N. P. Engel Publ., 2005.
Numhauser-Henning, A. (ed.), *Legal Perspectives on Equal Treatment and Non-Discrimination*, The Hague: Kluwer Law Int'l., 2001.
Office of the United Nations High Commissioner for Human Rights, *Legislative History of the Convention on the Rights of the Child*, New York/Geneva: United Nations, 2007.
——, *Human Rights in the Administration of Justice*, Geneva: United Nations, 2002. (UN Doc. HR/P/PT/9).
Örücü, E., *The Enigma of Comparative Law*, Leiden/Boston: Martinus Nijhoff Publ., 2004.
Orwell, G., *Nineteen Eighty-Four*, Harmondsworth: Penguin Books, 1975.
Ovsiouk, A., 'A Need for Combating and Overcoming Discrimination Against Persons with Disabilities', *Moscow Journal of International Law* No. 3 (2003) [titles translated].
The Oxford English Dictionary (vol. 4) (2nd ed.), Oxford: Clarendon Press, 1989.
Peters, A., *Women, Quotas and Constitutions*, The Hague/London/Boston: Kluwer Law Int'l., 1999.
Ramcharan, B. G., 'Equality and Nondiscrimination', in: L. Henkin (ed.), *The International Bill of Rights: The Covenant on Civil and Political Rights*, New York: Columbia Univ. Press, 1981.
Rishmawi, M., *Article 4: The Nature of States Parties' Obligations*, in: A. Alen, J. Vande Lanotte, E. Verhellen, F. Ang, E. Berghmans and M. Verheyde (eds.), *A Commentary on the UN Convention on the Rights of the Child*, Leiden/Boston: Martinus Nijhoff Publ., 2006.
Schabas, W. A., 'Public Opinion and the Death Penalty', in: P. Hodgkinson & W. A. Schabas (eds.), *Capital Punishment*, Cambridge: Cambridge Univ. Press, 2004.
Schwarzenberger, G., *International Law*, London: Stevens & Sons, 1957.
Sicilianos, L.-A., 'L'actualité et les potentialités de la Convention sur l'élimination de la discrimination raciale', *Revue Trimestrielle des Droits de L'Homme* 64 (2005), 869–921.
de S.-O.-L'E. Lasser, M., *Judicial Deliberations: A Comparative Analysis of Judicial Transparency and Legitimacy*, Oxford: Oxford Univ. Press, 1999.
Sowell, T., *Affirmative Action Around the World: An Empirical Study*, New Haven/London: Yale Univ. Press, 2004.
Stromquist, N., *Increasing Girls' and Women's Participation in Basic Education*, Paris: UNESCO, 1997.
Sweet, A. S., *The Judicial Construction of Europe*, Oxford: Oxford Univ. Press, 2004.
Thornberry, P., 'The Committee on the Elimination of Racial Discrimination – Questions of concept and practice', in: R. F. Jørgensen & K. Slavensky (eds.), *Implementing Human Rights: Essays in Honour of Morten Kjærum*, Copenhagen: Danish Institute for Human Rights, 2007.
——, *International Law and the Rights of Minorities*, Oxford: Clarendon Press, 1991.
Tomuschat, C., *Human Rights: Between Idealism and Realism*, Oxford: Oxford Univ. Press, 2003.
UN Division for the Advancement of Women, *Women2000*, March 2002.
UNESCO, 'Activities of [UNESCO] in the Field of Prevention of Discrimination and Protection of Minorities' (UN Doc. E/CN.4/Sub.2/121, 1959, incorporating UNESCO/SS/1, 1950).
UNICEF, *The Convention on the Rights of the Child: Human Rights Begin With Children's Rights*, New York: UNICEF, undated [circa 2002].
——, *Educating Girls and Women: A Moral Imperative*, New York: UNICEF, 1992.
——, *Educational For All?* (Regional Monitoring Report No. 5), Florence: UNICEF, International Child Development Centre, 1998.
——, *State of the World's Children 2006: Excluded and Invisible*, New York: UNICEF, 2005.
United Nations, Secretary-General, *The Main Types and Causes of Discrimination: Memorandum submitted by the Secretary General* (UN Doc. E/CN.4/Sub.2/40/Rev.1, 1949) (Sales No. 1949. XIV.3).
Vandenhole, W., *Non-Discrimination and Equality in the View of the UN Human Rights Treaty Bodies*, Antwerpen/Oxford: Intersentia, 2005.

Vierdag, E. W., *The Concept of Discrimination in International Law*, The Hague: Martinus Nijhoff, 1973.

Webster's New Collegiate Dictionary, Springfield, Mass.: G. & C. Merriam, 1980.

Webster's Third New International Dictionary, London: Bell & Sons/Springfield, Mass.: G. & C. Merriam, 1961.

The World Conference to Combat Racism and Racial Discrimination, *Declaration* (UN Publ. Sales No. E.79.XIV.2,chap.II), *reprinted in* (UN Doc. E/CN.4/1999/WG.1/BP.1).

Zemanek, K., 'Basic Principles of UN Charter Law', in: R. St. John Macdonald & D. M. Johnston (eds.), *Towards World Constitutionalism*, Leiden/Boston: Martinus Nijhoff Publ., 2005.